AF555913

# LIFE INSURANCE IN INDIA
Principles and Practices

# LIFE INSURANCE IN INDIA

## Principles and Practices

**DR. K.C. SHARMA**

*Foreword by*

**DR. A.K. VASHISHT**
Professor and Dean (Commerce Faculty),
University Business School, Panjab University,
Chandigarh-160014

**REGAL PUBLICATIONS**
New Delhi-110027

LIFE INSURANCE IN INDIA
Principles and Practices

ISBN 978-81-8484-226-5



*Typeset by*
S.S. COMPOSERS
3190, Mohindra Park, Shakur Basti, Delhi-110034.

*Printed in India at*
MAYUR ENTERPRISES
WZ Plot No. 3, Gujjar Market, Tihar Village, New Delhi-110018.

*Published by*
REGAL PUBLICATIONS
F-159, Rajouri Garden, New Delhi-110027.
Phone: +91-11-45546396
E-mail: regalbookspub@yahoo.com

*Dedicated to*
*Professor P. Parkash Arya,*
*my Mentor and Guide*

# Contents

Foreword xiii

Preface xv

1. **Introduction** 1
Evolution of Insurance; Indian Insurance Scenario; Evolution of Indian Insurance Market; Indian Insurance Act; 1938.

2. **Kinds of Risk and Risk Management** 13
Meaning of Risk; Definition of Risk; Characteristics of Insurable Risks; Insurable Interest; Pure and Major Risk; Quantifiable Risks; Risks in Money Terms; Risks that are Common; Risk must be Causal; Risks with Legal Objective; Risk must be Real; Catastrophic Risks; Risk having Reasonable Insurance Cost; Causes of Risks; Natural Causes; Unnatural Causes; Other Causes; Type of Risks; Financial and Non-financial Risks; Pure and Speculative Risks; Dynamic and Static Risks; Fundamental and Particular Risks; Risk Management or Control over Risk; Control of Speculative Risks; 22Control of Pure Risk; Risk Handling Techniques; Avoiding Risk; 24 Risk Reduction; Assumption of Risk; Transfer of Risks; Insurance; Reasons for Rise of Risk Management Practices;

3. **Insurance: Meaning, Definition and its Nature** 27
Background; Meaning of Insurance; Definition of Insurance; Functional Definitions; Legal/Contractual Definition; Important Terms Used in Insurance, Insured, Insurer, Premium, Compensation, Insurance Policy, Insured Amount, Risk, Contingency, Peril; Characteristics of Insurance, Contract, Consideration, Sharing of Financial Risk, Co-operative Device, Risk Evaluation in Advance, Good Faith, Contract of Indemnity, Amount of Payment, Insurance is not a Gambling; , Large Number of Insured Persons, Insurance is not Charity, Insurable Interest, Compensation at the Occurrence of Contingency; Functions

of Insurance; ,Primary Function, Secondary Functions, Other Functions; Uses/Role and Importance of Insurance or relevance of Insurance in developing country like India, Relevance of Insurance to an Individual, Relevance to Business, Relevance to Society

4. **Scope and Dimensions of Insurance** 45

Introduction; Classification of Insurance; Classification on the Basis of Nature of Insurance; Life Insurance and Non-life Insurance (General Insurance); Life Insurance; Definition of Life Insurance; Characteristics of Life Insurance; Procedure for Taking a Life Insurance Policy; General Insurance; Definition of Fire Insurance; Characteristics of Fire Insurance; Scope of Fire Insurance; Procedure for Taking a Fire Insurance Policy; Marine Insurance; Definition of Marine Insurance; Characteristics of Marine Insurance; Scope or Subject Matter of Marine Insurance; Procedure for Taking Marine Insurance Policy; Marine Insurance from an Insurance Company; Marine insurance by Lloyd's Association; Social Insurance; Forms of Social Insurance; Miscellaneous Insurance Schemes; Motor Insurance; Export/Import Duty Insurance; Erection All Risks Insurance (EAR); Contractor's All Risk Insurance (CAR); Machinery Breakdown Insurance; Product Liability Insurance; Cash Insurance; Business premises' Burglary Insurance; Shopkeepers' Insurance Policy; Rural Insurance (Agricultural/Allied Activities); Milch cattle and/or Draught Animal Insurance; Sheep and Goat Insurance; Plantation/Horticulture Insurance; Householder's Insurance Policy (HHI); Rajeswari Mahilla Kalyan Bima Yojna; Sports Insurance; Classification of Insurance from the Business Point of View; Classification of Insurance from Risk Point of View; Distinction between Life Insurance; Fire Insurance and Marine Insurance;

5. **Principles of Insurance** 69

Introduction; Priciples of Insurance; General Principles (or Essentials of Insurance Contract); Specific or Fundamental Principles of Insurance Contracts; Main Features of Indemnity; Conditions for Indemnity; Liability of Insurer to Pay Compensation; Methods of Indemnifying; Principle of Subrogation; Definition of Subrogation; Essentials of Subrogation; Need of Subrogation; Features of Subrogation; How Right of Subrogation Arises?; Principle of Causa Proxima (Immediate and the Nearest Cause); Meaning and Definition of the Doctrine of Causa Proxima; Practical Aspects of Doctrine of Causa Proxima; Principle of Mitigation of Loss; Principle of Contribution; Definition of Contribution; Miscellaneous Principles; Principle of Return of Premium; New for Old Part(s) Principle; Reinstatement;

Agreed Value; Material Fact; Reciprocal Duty; Condition of Average; General Average; Particular Average; Sue and Labour/Particular Charges; Excess and Deductibles; Co-insurance or Co-pay; Performance Ratios; Net Earned Premium; Solvency Margin; IAIS Core Principles; Insurance Core Principles and Methodology; Summary.

6. **Life Insurance: Nature and Uses of Life Insurance** 125
History; Life Insurance in India; Meaning of Life Insurance; Definitions; Characteristics of Life Insurance; Procedure for Taking a Life Insurance Policy; Nature of Life Insurance; Economic Nature of Life Insurance; Legal nature of Life Insurance.

7. **Nature of Life Insurance Contract** 137
Introduction; Nature of General Contract; There must be an Agreement; Competency of the Parties to Contract; Free Consent of the Parties Essential for a Valid Contract; Lawful Consideration is Necessary Element in Contract; Legal Object is the Foundation of a Valid Contract; Insurable Interest; Insurable Interest in Policyholder's Own Life; Insurable Interest in the Life of Others; General Rule Relating to Insurable interest Applicable in Life Insurance; Life Insurance is Based on Utmost Good Faith; Which are the Material Facts?; Warranties; Proximate Cause; Assignment and Nomination; Return of Premium; By Agreement in the Policy; For Reason of Equity; Other Features of Life Insurance; Alcatory Contract; Unilateral Contract; Conditional Contract; Contract of Adhesion; Indemnity Contract is not Applied.

8. **Life Insurance Corporation of India: Organisational Set-up** 152
Introduction; Objectives of Life Insurance Corporation of India; To Widen the Scope of Insurance; To Provide Protection; Mobilizing the Savings for Development; To Act as Trustees; To Meet Insurance Needs; To Provide Services to the Public; Organizational Set-up of LIC; The Set-up of LIC Involves; Functions of Central Office; Different Departments of LIC; Organizational Structure of the Life Insurance Corporation of India; Functions of a Zonal Office; Departments of a Divisional Office of LIC; Functions of a Branch Office.

9. **Insurance Legislation in India** 164
The Insurance Act; 1938; The Insurance Amendment Act, 1950; The Insurance Amendment Act, 1968; The General

Insurance Business (Nationalization) Act, 1972 (GIBNA); Machinery of the Insurance System; How is Insurance Regulated?; Watch on Funds; Ensuring Long-term Financial Solvency; Standardizing Insurance Products; Preventing Fraud and Speculation by Insurers; Creating a Level Playing Ground; Monitoring Re-insurance; Pricing of Insurance Products; Data Repository and Risk Evaluation; Theory of Large Numbers; Reserving; Present Day Trends in Insurance; Summary of the Above Discussion; Defects in the Acts; Reasons for Replacement of Act of 1912; Demand for Another Act,Insurance Act of 1938; Important Provisions of Insurance Act, 1938; Wide Scope; Requirement as to Capital; Deposits; Registration; Submission of Returns; Restriction of Commission and Prohibition of Rebating; Limitations of Expenditure on Commission; Licensing of Insurance Agents (Section 42) of the Insurance Act, Investments; Prohibition of Loan [(U/S 29(1)] of the Insurance Act, Investigation (Under Section 33) of the Insurance Act, Duties and Power of Controller of Insurance.

**10. Insurance Regulatory and Development Authority (IRDA)** 206

Introduction; Preamble of IRDA Act; Contents of the Act; Short title; extent and commencement; Definitions of various Terms used in the Act; Brief Profile of IRDA Act and its Functioning; Summary of the above Discussions.

**11. Privatization of Insurance Sector** 222

Introduction; Privatization of Insurance Industry in India—Steps Taken by the Government to Privatize the Insurance Sector; Purposes of Malhotra Committee; Malhotra Committee's Recommendations; Impact of Privatization and Liberalization on Insurance Industry; Scenario of Insurance Industry in India as it obtains today.

**12. Asset-Liability Management (ALM)** 238

Introduction; Meaning of ALM; Objectives of Asset-liability Management (ALM); Balance Sheet Structure: Implications for Asset-Liability Management (ALM); Balance Sheet Structure; Liabilities Side; Assets Side; Scope of Asset-Liability Management; Liquidity Risk; Measurement of Liquidity Risk; Interest Rate Risk (IRR); Measurement of Interest Rate Risk; Market Risk.

**13. Premiums and Bonuses** 252

What is Premium?; Risk; Net and Pure Premium; Loadings; Level Premiums; Office Premium; Extra Premiums;

Calculation of Age; Premium Calculation; Life Fund; Actuarial Valuation; Bonus;

**14. Underwriting** **263**
Introduction; Financial Underwriting; Data for Underwriting; Assessing the Risk; Non-Medical Underwriting; Female Lives; Underwriting by Agents; Recent Trends.

**15. Group Insurance** **271**
Introduction; Essential Features of Group Insurance Schemes; Special Schemes; Group Leave Encashment Scheme (GLES); Retrenchment Schemes; Health Insurance; Agent's Role.

**16. Insurance for Rural and Social Sectors** **278**
Legal Provisions; Rural Sector; Social Sector.

**17. Life Insurance Marketing** **285**
Introduction; The Distribution Channel; Sold Not Bought; The Customer; Strengthening Relationships; Functions of an Agent; Advantages; Keeping Customers Happy.

**18. Role of an Insurance Agent** **294**
Introduction; Prerequisties for Success; Selling Insurance; Pre-Approach; Approach; Interview; Objections; Closing Service; Ethical Behaviour.

**19. Personal Development through Insurance Business** **303**
Scope; Product Knowledge; Customer Orientation; Business Target; Personal Growth; Records and Review; Time Management; Target Market; Trustworthiness; Long-term Relationships; Motivation; Morale; Communication Skills; Persuassive Skills; Analytical Ability; Behaviour with Others.

**20. Consumer Protection Act, 1986 (COPRA)** **316**
Ombusman; Other Acts; Income Tax Act, Married Women's Property Act, 1874; Financial Planning and Taxation; Savings and Investment Schemes; Liquidity; Unit Trust and Mutual Funds; Shares; Comparisons between Insurance Plans.

**21. Information Technology** **324**
Introduction; Intranet and Internet; Benefit to Agents; Benfits to Policy-holders/Prospects; Kiosks; IT in the Rural Areas.

22. **IRDA (Licencing of Corporate Agents) Regulations, 2002** 328

Important Provisions.

23. **Bancassurance** **330**

Introduction; What is Bancassurance?; Bancassurance Abroad; Vale Proposition; The Indian Context; Benefits to the Insurer; Benefits to the Bank; The Legal Requirements; The Problems; Concept of Universal Banking; Rider—Descriptions and Premium Rates; Accidental Death Benefits; Accidental Death and Dismemberment; Benefits; Accidental Burns; Double Indemnity; Waiver of Premiom; Waiver of Premium; Payer Benefit; Term Riders; Critical Illness Rider (Accelerated Benefit); Critical Illness Rider (Accelerated Benefit); Premium Collection Process and Bank Details; Premium Collection; Renewal Payments; Third Party Cheques; Resignation or Termination of an Agent; Form IRDA/RI–Request for Registration Application; Form IRDA/R2–Application for Registration; For Irda/R3–Certificate of Registration; Form IRDA/R4 Issue of Duplicate Certificate of Registration; Form IRDA/R5–Application for Renewal; Form IRDA/R6 Certificate of Renewal of Registration;

Annexures 352

Bibliography 360

Index 361

# Foreword

Risk management is the need of the present era. Insurance is a cover for risk. The concept of insurance originated as a formal business in the late 17th Century. This business became sophisticated in post-Renaissance Europe. In the seventeenth century, coffee houses were opened in Europe and people from all walks of life visited those coffee houses as a routine and ritual and thus such places became meeting venues. People discussed matters of interest to them and exchanged information. Mr. Edward Lloyd also opened a coffee house that became a popular haunt of ship owners, merchants, and ships captains. His coffee house became a reliable source of the latest shipping and trade-related news. Lloyd's became the meeting place for parties wishing to insure cargoes and ships. Lloyd's of London remains the leading market for marine and other specialist types of insurance even today.

It is heartening to note that the Sanskrit term 'yogakshema' or well-being of the society is found in the Rig Veda; it is interpreted as insurance. The 'Joint Family System' practiced in India is a form of 'micro-insurance' to take care of situations as consequence of calamities.

The British Government became interested to streamline the insurance law. Therefore, it appointed S.C. Sen, a well-known solicitor of India in 1934 to study and report on the amendments to insurance legislation. The government set-up an Informal Advisory Committee of leading insurance men, headed by N.N. Sircar who was at the material time Law Member in the British India government. The Committee submitted a bill to the Legislative Assembly in 1937 which resulted in the passage of the Insurance Act, 1938. That Act became the corner-stone and landmark of insurance legislation in India.

A historic moment occurred in India on May 13, 1971 when an ordinance was promulgated by the President of India to take over the ownership and management of 107 general insurance companies which were doing business in India at that time. General Insurance Business (Nationalization) Act, 1972 or GIBNA became the guiding act of General Insurance. IRDA Act was passed in 1999 containing all regulations governing insurance and it also established autonomous regulating authority.

Emerging out of the precarious foreign exchange position in 1991, at the instance of International Monetary Fund (IMF), sweeping economic reforms were initiated by the government to restructure economy and effect enabling changes in legal environment including in socio-economic institutions. In that process, Banking and Insurance sectors have also been affected. These sectors have been opened for private sector and global competition by providing level-playing field to the players in the economy. Foreign companies have started operating in India in collaboration with Indian partners.

The book on life insurance written by Dr. K.C. Sharma, manuscript of which has been studied by me, is a good attempt at codifying the rules, regulations and practices obtaining in the insurance business regime for the benefit of general readers. The book is written in simple language and his own lucid style presenting all the essentials and relevant contents and presents an interesting reading. The book can be of help to the students of management and practitioners of insurance business.

Dr. Sharma is an established writer and I trust he will turn over many more books on management and miscellaneous subjects in due course. I wish him success in his endeavours in general interest.

Professor (Dr.) A.K. Vashisht,
Dean, Faculty of Commerce,
University Business School, Panjab University,
Chandigarh-160014

# Preface

I feel great pleasure in presenting the readers of management and technical courses the first edition of Life Insurance in India: Principles and Practices. It is felt that the understanding of Banking and Insurance is essential for not only all students, teachers and researchers, especially those in commerce and management streams, but also for all citizens. As most Indians are fatalists and do not believe in insurance, life insurance is confined to minuscule educated persons. Of late, with the advent of private companies, the awareness level of benefits and necessity of insurance has been increased.

During the last two decades, there has been a revolutionary development in the fields of banking and insurance. These sectors of the economy have been opened up for foreign players, introducing competition, and thus providing ground for innovative insurance products for wider choice of the insured. A fairly long path has been traversed since the establishment of development banks, social control on banks, and nationalization of major commercial banks and opening of banking and insurance business to private sector, and now steadily the foreign companies have started coming. These developments have resulted in width and depth of service-products apart from growth in these sectors. On account of growing demand and vast opportunities opened for employment in these sectors, many Indian Universities have introduced banking and insurance subject in their curriculum.

This book deals with Life Insurance only. I most gratefully acknowledge the debt due by me to my colleagues and friends for their contribution in the completion of the present work. My special gratitude goes to my wife, Vidya and daughters, Anjana and Anupama and grandchildren (Abhimanyu and Utkarsh).

While my wife encouraged me, the daughters contributed their ideas, Abhimanyu helped with the computer and Utkarsh fiddled with the computer reminding me of the work.

I am particularly thankful to Regal Publications, New Delhi for bringing out this book within a very short time and in a nice get-up.

Omissions may be frankly pointed out. Suggestions, comments and observations are solicited.

DR. K.C. SHARMA

# 1

# Introduction

Insurance in the modern sense originated as a formal business in the late 17th Century. Insurance assumed sophistication in post-Renaissance Europe. In the late 1680s, Mr. Edward Lloyd opened a coffee house that became a popular haunt of ship owners, merchants, and ship-captains. As reliable source of the latest shipping news, Lloyd's became the meeting place for parties wishing to insure cargoes and ships. Lloyd's of London remains the market leader for marine and other specialist types of insurance.

Indian scholars observe that the Sanskrit term 'yogakshema' or well-being of the society (or insurance) is found in the Rig Veda. The 'Joint Family system' practised in India is a form of micro-insurance to take care of calamitous situations. In day-to-day transactions, too, individuals have been standing guarantee for the debts raised from the money-lenders by their friends and relatives. This guarantee was a kind of insurance, though in a crude manner.

In 1934, the Government of India appointed S.C. Sen, a well-known solicitor, to study and report on the amendments to insurance legislation. The government set-up an Informal Advisory Committee of leading insurance men, headed by N.N. Sircar, the then Law Member in the Council of the Governor-General and Viceroy. This committee submitted a Bill to the

Legislative Assembly in 1937. At last, the Insurance Act, 1938 was enacted. The Insurance Act became the corner-stone of Indian insurance legislation.

Life Insurance was Nationalised in India in 1956. On May 13, 1971, an ordinance was promulgated by the President of India to take over the management of 107 general insurance companies by the Government of India. General Insurance Business (Nationalization) Act, 1972 or GIBNA became the guiding Act of General Insurance till the IRDA Act was passed in 1999.

The process or method of evaluating an insurer's promises to perform certain obligations under certain specified future situations is not an easy task for the customers of insurance (the insured). The degree of standardization of general insurance products varies from country to country, from rigidly controlled tariff markets to open markets with minimal controls.

Past observations regarding the working of the insurers brought to sharp focus the intensive and unregulated competition in marketing general insurance products can produce inadequate rates and insolvency. It also breeds sharp loss adjusting practices, abortive policy language and tendencies towards monopolization. These are recognized to be against public interest.

There is no economic activity where profit is given a go-by. All businesses and industries aim at profits for their survival and sustenance. Therefore, the insurers need to enter into different types of reinsurance contracts as part of their business. The regulator has to ensure that foreign exchange is not unduly drained-off through reckless reinsurance programmes of the insurers. Many regulations specify that the insurers shall cede a certain percentage of the sum assured (SA) on each policy for different classes of insurance written in the country to national reinsure(s) registered in the country.

Rates of premium should be such as to ensure the survival of the insurance company, achieving optimum strategy positioning, providing quality and value for the service, contributing to the society's well-being and optimizing the returns for a given type of risk.

Any circumstance of characteristic or factor that is within the knowledge of the insuring person and is likely to influence the insurer in deciding whether he will accept or refuse the risk, or influence him in assessing the premium that he will charge, must be fully disclosed to the insurer before the contract is concluded. The action of the proposer in withholding these vital details from the insurer is not in keeping with the principle of utmost good faith in insurance. Such behaviour smacks of undesirable business ethics.

The common man knows that insurable interest denotes such an interest in the object insured, whereby any loss or damage to the object would seriously prejudice the interests of the insured. Insurance thrives on theory of large numbers; insurance covers only the pure loss not the speculative loss. Only losses covered by insurance are paid as claim by the insurers not all losses; this is the principle of nearest cause in insurance.

Indians have not considered insurance as necessary; they are fatalists and take any loss or damage as the will of God. It is this reason why insurance industry in India is lagging behind its counterparts in the developed countries in the fields like risk management and loss prevention techniques as well as the non-life actuarial studies and arbitration. The industry also lacks credible data for insurance product development by loss modelling.

Business of life and general insurance is still in its movement in rapid growth mode. General and life insurers are contributing to the corporate risk management and protection of underlying assets of financing banks. With litigations and consumer activism, general insurance is also assisting in liability or casualty management of individuals and corporate bodies. Fire, marine and miscellaneous including motor insurance are major lines of general insurance. There are various types of policies offered in life insurance.

## EVOLUTION OF INSURANCE

It is a historical fact that the relatively modern societies that built up economies with money and financial instruments evolved other forms of insurance down the centuries. In the money economy context, Chinese and Babylonian traders evolved some methods of transferring or distributing risk as long ago as the 3rd and 2nd millennia BC, respectively. Chinese merchants travelling treacherous river rapids would redistribute their risks across many vessels to limit the loss due to any single vessel being capsized. As recorded in the famous code of Hammurabi, the Babylonians developed a system around 1750 BC that was practised by early Mediterranean sailing merchants. It meant if a merchant received a loan to fund his shipment, he would pay the lender an additional sum in exchange for the lender's guarantee to cancel the loan should the shipment be stolen. The Code of Hammurabi indicates that ancient Babylon had government insurances for theft and crop as well as for adoption of annuity plan. Personal insurance on contribution principle has been found in the Thiasoi of the ancient Greece.

It is believed that Achaemenian monarchs were the first to insure their people through an official process by registering donations to the monarch in governmental notary offices. Each year, in Norouz (beginning of the Iranian New year), the heads of different ethnic groups as well as others who were willing to take part in the process, presented gifts to the monarch. When a gift was worth more than 10,000 Derrik (Achaemenian gold coin weighing 8.35 – 8.42g), it was registered in a special office so that whenever the person who presented the gift was in trouble, the monarch and the court would help him. As per Jahez, a historian and writer, whenever the donor of the present was in trouble or wanted to construct a building, set-up a fest or have his children married, the court would check the registration and the donor would receive double the amount. The ancient inhabitants of Rhodes invented the concept of the 'general average' whereby merchants whose goods were being shipped together would pay a proportionally divided premium which would be used to reimburse any merchant whose goods were jettisoned (thrown out of a hip to save the ship, lives or other goods) during storm or sinking.

It is believed that the Greeks and the Romans introduced the origins of health and life insurance around 600 AD when they organized guilds called benevolent societies that cared for the families and paid funeral expenses of members upon death. Rome evolved the Fund of Collegia of the soldiery. Funds of the Collegia Tenuiorum were used to meet the unexpected expenses, burial expenses and needs of the soldiers' families; guilds in the middle ages served a similar purpose.

What we now understand about the concept of Insurance, we may like to find how it worked in a different manner before insurance was established in the late 17th century in the modern, systemic and scientific sense. Friendly societies existed in England in which people donated amounts of money to a general pool that could be used for overcoming emergent situations. Stand alone insurance contracts or insurance policies, as we find today, not bundled with loans or other kinds of contracts, are believed to have been invented in Genoa in the 14th century. Insurance pools were formed and backed by pledges of landed estates. These new insurance contracts allowed insurance to be separated from investment. It is interesting to know that Insurance became far more sophisticated in post-renaissance Europe, and its specialized varieties developed.

As England had acquired hegemony over three-fourths of the world countries, either as colonies or under suzerainty, London's growing importance as a centre for trade by the end of the seventeenth century created a sudden spurt in demand for marine insurance. In the late 1680s, Mr. Edward Lloyd opened a coffee house that became a popular haunt of ship owners, merchants, and ship-captains, and thereby the coffee house became a reliable source of the latest shipping news. It became the meeting place for parties wishing to insure cargoes and ships, and also for those willing to underwrite such ventures. Today, Lloyd's of London remains the leading market insurer (note that it is not an insurance company) for marine and other specialized types of insurance, but it works rather differently than the more familiar kinds of insurance that we know.

Regarding regulating Insurance through legal provisions, the earliest version of insurance law relates to marine insurance for which the English are indebted to the Lombards, who, driven away from their native states in Northern and Central Italy about the middle of the 13th century, settled in every maritime country in Europe. It appears that laws issued by the magistrates of Barcelona, laws published in Venice in 1468 and other regulations were familiar to the Lombards. Those laws and regulations formed the basis upon which the Lomnbards effected insurance on English merchandise from their residences in Lombard Street in London. The power of the Lombards was broken by a decree in 1597. Keate and Gurney state that the most important laws came from an unknown French source in a set of regulations published probably at Rouen in the 17th century. In British statute books, we find no mention of Marine insurance untill 1601 when an Act was passed "concerning matters of assurance amongst Merchants". The Act of Parliament promulgated in 1720 vested monopoly rights of marine insurance in the two companies, Royal Exchange and London Assurance, and Lloyds, until the Act was repealed in 1824. However, there was no marked development in the British Laws until 1756, untill Lord Mansfield became Lord Chief Justice and devoted himself earnestly to the study of the principles of marine insurance and their application in other countries. From Lord Mansfield's times, till the Marine Insurance Act of 1906, the law of marine insurance was administered by an appeal to precedent.

One of the most momentous events of the century happened in London in June 1861 having had unfavourable bearing on the insurance front; it triggered deep thinking and wise theorizing by the finance experts. It was the Great Fire (the greatest since 1666 when insurance was born in rudiments) at Tooley Street, Southward. The devastating and menacing fire apparently started in stored hemp, spread furiously all around the store; it could not be fully extinguished for a fortnight. The fire offices sustained an enormous loss estimated between pound sterling 1 and 2 million. The companies noted and learnt a bitter lesson and concluded that the situation had gone out of hand due to the high loss and low premiums due excessive competition among the insurance firms. In the aftermath of this 'Great Fire of London', that destroyed/devoured 13,200 houses, Nicholas Barbon opened an office to insure buildings. In 1680, he established England's fire insurance company, the Fire Office, to insure brick and frame homes. Insurers came together and to ensure that a repeat of this 'Great Fire of London' would not happen in the future, a new institution, the Fire Offices Committee (FOC), a voluntary and autonomous association, was formally created by the various fire insurance offices (called those days as simply Fire Offices) in 1868. Under the broad understanding and comprehensive arrangement that was worked out, the companies transacting fire insurance agreed to adhere to certain minimum rates (cartel of insurers established with unanimity). Thus born, the FOC ushered in a new era of cooperation among British insurers. Taking a cue from this development, such organizational framework was adopted by Accident Offices Association (AOA), Engineering Offices Association (EOA) and Aviation Offices Insurance Association (AOIA). It was through this entire process that insurance evolved and established as an independent subject and profession, distinctly different from other branches of financial transitions.

Learning from the United Kingdom's experience, though indirectly, the concept of insurance was given shape in the United States. The first insurance company that underwrote the fire insurance was formed in Charles Town (modern day Charleston) in South Carolina, in 1732. Benjamin Franklin helped to popularize the concept; he also helped to standardise the practice of insurance, particularly that against fire, in the form of perpetual insurance. In 1752, he founded the 'Philadelphia Contributionship' for the insurance of Houses from Loss by Fire. Franklin's company was the first in the US to make contributions towards fire prevention pool. Besides, his company warned against certain fire hazards. In case of certain buildings where the risk of fire was too great, such as all wooden houses, his company refused insurance.

## INDIAN INSURANCE SCENARIO

The concept of insurance was not absolutely new in India; it was still new in the organized form as witnessed in the West. The fundamental insurance principle of a group sharing the losses of a few had been appreciated in India in some way or other from very ancient times. Hinduism, like other ancient religions, exhorts man to help his fellow men in distress; this attitude was the result of internalization of values and extended from personal life to the field of commerce in some way or the other. Scholars observe that the Sanskrit term 'Yogakshema' (well-being of the society at large) is found in the Rig Veda and that some kind of community insurance was practised by the Aryan tribes of India nearly 3000 years ago. Manu Smriti speaks of a system of 'collective co-operation. Yajnavalkya, an author and theoretician of the ancient times in India, mentions some transactions akin to insurance. In its earliest and crude form, insurance was probably perceived as a function of the State. In the ninth chapter of the magnum opus, Shrimad Bhagavad Gita, Lord Krishna (Lord Vishnu incarnate) promises yogakshema to devotees. The kings were expected to look after their people and praja ranjan (welfare of the subjects) alone could justify their existence according to ancient Sanskrit literature. The 'Joint Family System' practised in India is seen by many as a form of micro insurance to take care of calamitous situations, including death and sickness within the extended family. In course of time, many monarchs turned despotic and the functions of the State in even advanced countries were limited to the protection of subjects against foreign attacks and maintenance of law and order within the country. In the Indian religious and philosophical contexts (economic transactions included), religion and 'other worldliness' dominated the economic institutions. This state continued until the arrival of the Europeans on the Indian soil and organization of economic activity by them in the fashion/ design, as we see it in the modern world that took shape.

We may give credit to the British who started modern life insurance in India through their influence. Many English companies extended their branches to India for underwriting European lives and later Parsee and Indian lives too. Sir John Child, who was the Governor of Bombay Presidency between 1681 and 1690, was instructed by the Court of Directors of East India Company to constitute an insurance office on the Bombay Island. It is not known what came of this organization. The Bombay Insurance Society was set-up in 1793 on Bombay Island by a few well-known European merchants. Life Insurance in its present form came to India from the United Kingdom with the establishment of a British firm, Oriental Life Insurance Company, in Calcutta (now named Kolkata) in 1818 to help the widows of the European community. This was followed by the formation of the Bombay Life Assurance Company in 1829, and the Oriental Government Security Life Insurance Company in 1874. It has been documented that as early as 1822, when Indian social reformers were opposing the prevalent practice of Sati, Raja Ram Mohan Roy appealed through the Calcutta Journal to the good sense of the rich to start a fund for widows and orphans. Round about the decade beginning from 1850, considerable pressure seems to have been brought to bear upon the then British Government of India to operate life insurance business under government control through a department of the State. History tells us that the proposal was turned down as the government did not possess sufficient data on Indian lives and that the insurance consciousness was not present to an adequate degree among the masses. The Princely State of Travancore (part of present Kerala State) was issuing life insurance policies in the late 19th century, and policies of 1896 are still preserved by the Kerala State Insurance Department, Thiruvananthapuram (old name Trivandrum).

There is evidence in India of the earliest known policy in English (dated 1555). It is expressed as on the good ship Santa Cruz 'from any port in the isles of Indea or Calicut unto Lixborne'. It is known that members of the East India Company handled Bottomry Bond transactions as they were allowed to do business or engage in any occupation or pursuit of choice while also being in the service of Company. The first general insurance company, the Triton Insurance company Limited, was established in Calcutta in 1850; it transacted selected business. The Indian Mercantile Insurance Company Limited, which was set-up in Bombay in 1907, was the first Indian company to transact all classes of general insurance business.

We can rely upon the documented information on non-life insurance operations in the country, as available from the early 20th century. The Royal Exchange Assurance opened shop in India in 1900, and by 1907 almost 10 per cent of its accident insurance business came from India and six other foreign agencies. Royal Exchange Assurance's net marine premium from India for the year 1914 is recorded as pound sterling 40,000 as against pound sterling 17,000 from Australia and pound sterling 10,000 from South Africa. Thus Indian businessmen, Europeans included, availed of insurance facility.

Bombay (now Mumbai) emerged from the First World War as the centre of Indian trade. Inspired by the growth of Indian trade and industry, and encouraged by the undercurrent of nationalism, leading businessmen in Mumbai rose to give concrete shape to proposals for meeting the insurance needs of Indian trade. Five Indian owned insurance offices were established in 1919, almost simultaneously, for transacting general insurance business. The newly formed insurance companies received support from the growth of nationalism in India.

Mahatma Gandhi stated, "The keynote of all our Swaraj is in placing all our insurance with our Indian companies". Jawahar Lal Nehru said, "I hope Indians will realize the importance of patronizing only Indian insurance institutions".

A few years after 1922 were critical for Indian insurance when six new Indian offices were pitted against nearly 150 foreign offices, including some of the largest insurance groups in the world. The general economic conditions were against the Indian offices and political agitation was at its zenith. Simultaneously, a powerful combination of American Offices began their operations followed by a number of French companies a year later. To make matters worse for Indian companies, an all round reduction in rates was enforced in 1928, depression set in a year later, volume and value of foreign trade fell immediately, farm prices came down and purchasing power fell, and internal economy collapsed, while serious fire losses in Karachi (now in Pakistan) and heavy riot losses in Mumbai were incurred

However, the Indian industry came to the rescue of Indian insures and hundreds of Indian businessmen signed a pledge to insure only with Indian offices. By this time, Indian industries such as sugar, paper, matches, paint and cement had gradually begun to take root, aided by a protective tariff system. Indian insurers' share of the total business written in India rose from a mere 11 per cent in 1928 to 22 per cent in 1935 and 32 per cent in 1939, largely at the expense of foreign offices, while the total business itself had registered an increase of only 5 per cent during the period. This tells encouraging story of the success of Indian insurance companies/offices.

## EVOLUTION OF INDIAN INSURANCE MARKET

So far, we have discussed the evolution of the market prior to the passing of the Insurance Act, 1938. The second phase of evolution of insurance started from the middle of the 1930s. Here, we should know that physical or service product has a life cycle—introduction, adolescence, adult, maturity, decline and finally extinct (or exit). On this analogy, during this period, the Indian market came out of its adolescence and started addressing problems similar to those faced by the more nature markets. The market and the government were seized by the gravity of the situation, and concerted efforts were made leading to the enactment of the Insurance Act, 1938. The introduction of this Act of 1938 is generally regarded as the turning point for insurance regulation in India and the beginning of the insurance market as it existed in recent times. It would be beneficial at this stage to have a peep into the provisions of this Act.

## INDIAN INSURANCE ACT, 1938

The British government appointed in 1934 S.C. Sen, a well-known solicitor, as Officer on Special Duty in the Department of Commerce to study and report on the amendments to insurance legislation. Insurance legislation by then was based on the decrees of the Governor-General and Viceroy in Council. Sen studied the British model. He propounded the British ideal of minimum statutory control with maximum publicity and put up his proposal. The government set-up an informal Advisory Committee of leading insurance men, headed by N.N. Sircar, the then Law Member in the Viceroy's Executive Council, with some modifications to the proposal put up by Sen. This Committee elicited views and suggestions from many stakeholders and submitted a Bill to the Legislative Assembly in 1937. The Bill stirred up intense public interest in the country, trade associations submitted memoranda, insurance associations pressed for amendments and a Lloyd's representative flew over from London to watch their interest. Over a thousand amendments were suggested from various quarters and at last the Insurance Act, 1938 was enacted.

However, soon the market started criticizing the Act for its drafting mistakes, contradictions and impractical clauses. It may widely be conceded that the Act wrote a fresh chapter into the history of Indian insurance by attempting to prevent the formation and continuation of mushrooming companies and by introducing sound insurance business practices, some authors commented that it became the most controversial law among Indian statutes.

In quick response to the criticism of various provisions of the Act, the government made two amendments to the Act in 1939. Not only these amendments, but also the Act was again amended in 1940 to remove certain difficulties in administration of the Act. The market situation that came up with World War II and the insurers' experience of working with the Act necessitated further changes and so, further amendments were made in 1941, 1942, 1944, 1946 and 1948.

Despite the flaws that were pointed out by the concerned, the 1938 Act gave the Indian market a regulatory foundation and among other things, provided for the establishment/constitution of a Department of Insurance, compulsory registration of insurance companies, provision for mobilizing deposits by the insurance companies, control on investment of funds, filing of returns on investments and financial condition, licensing of agents, control on commission, prohibition of rebates, filing of policy conditions and premium rates duly certified by an actuary (in the case of life business), periodical valuation of liabilities, and provision for policyholders' directors on the Boards of the companies. The Act granted very wide powers to the Controller of Insurance in the matter of insurance regulation. The government visualized that the Controller of Insurance should be a person of extraordinary calibre, be actuarially qualified, having human considerations and broad outlook to administer law tactfully and even-handedly. The Indian insurance legislation turned into a good piece of legislation; it was lauded by contemporary commentators as an excellent attempt to penalize the corrupt directors and executive officers, check wild cat schemes and scandals, and to stop acquisition of insurance companies by designing financiers.

The Insurance Act became the corner-stone of Indian insurance legislation and along with the insurance Rules framed under it, still remains the most comprehensive legislation on the subject.

# 2

# *Kinds of Risk and Risk Management*

Risk is the basis of insurance. Everybody wants to get his activities insured in order to cover the losses arising out of uncertainties. The term 'insurance' is a general term. Everybody is quite familiar and uses the term knowingly or unknowingly. Insurance may be understood as a way of reducing uncertainty of occurrence of an event. The basic purpose of the insurances is to counteract the financial loss due to some unfavourable event. It is the financial mechanism through which the persons who are exposed to a similar risk contribute money to a common pool. A few unfortunate people of this group who face the loss, are compensated out of the pool. Hence, insurance is based on the principle of co-operation. The persons who are fortunate and do not suffer a loss, share the burden of the unfortunate sufferers.

## MEANING OF RISK

By risk we mean 'uncertainty'. In other words, it refers to 'possibility' or 'chance' of meeting a danger or suffering or change of exposure to adversity or danger. The risk due to uncertainty of an event can be positive or negative to human life. It is blessing as it give rise to hope, a curse as it give rise to dispute, fear, defense, tactics, failure and retrogression.

## DEFINITION OF RISK

As the subject of Insurance is still evolving, there is no single universally accepted definition of the word 'Risk'. It is used to describe the different situations. Some of the definitions are on the definition on the 'Risk' given by different authors are as follows:

**According to Frank Knight,** "Risk is a measurable uncertainty".

**According to A.H. Willet,** "Risk is an objectified uncertainty regarding the occurrence of an undesirable event".

**According to Federation Invariance Institute,** "The risk can be thought of as the degree of variation in the possible outcome from an uncertainty event, or as the variation in the possible outcomes".

Considering the above definitions, it may be concluded that 'Risk' may be defined as the phenomenon which is closely associated with uncertain event or peril to which the object is exposed and may cause loss or injury to something of value.

## CHARACTERISTICS OF INSURABLE RISKS

The concept of 'risk' in insurance refers to only those uncertainties which are related to economic matters. Non-

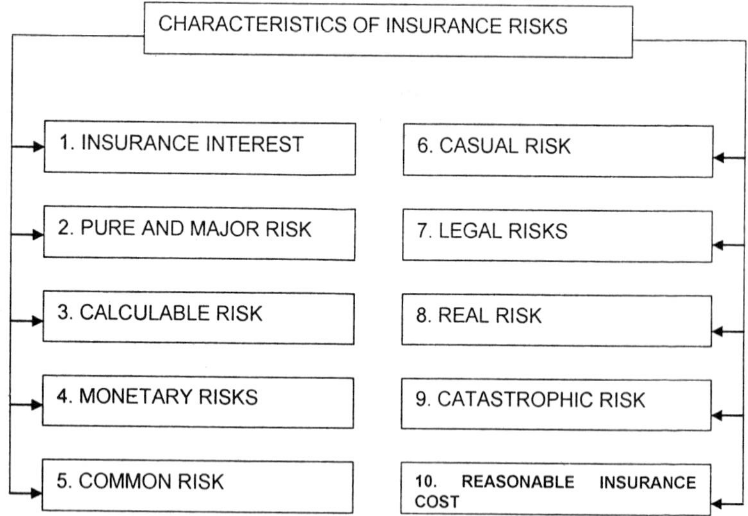

economic risks such as risk of respect, reputation, insult, prestige, or love, are not insurable risks. There is no specific criterion to decide whether any risk is insurable or not. However, the following can be considered as the main features that should be present in any risk to be insurable:

### (1) Insurable Interest

It is a settled fact that no "Risk" can be insured unless one has insurable interest in its object or in a person life. Stated in simple words, insurable interest is understood to exist when one is financially benefited by its existence and is prejudiced by the damage on its non-existence. Essentially, insurable interest is in the nature of pecuniary or financial interest in a life or thing. It follows that one can have an insurable interest only when one would stand to benefit financially by the continuance of the life or object insured, or when, in other words, one would be put to financial loss through the happening of the event against which the thing, or the life of a person has been insured. It is pecuniary interest and it follows that the loss caused by the risk insured against must be capable of estimation in terms of money.

### (2) Pure and Major Risk

One risk is pure (i.e. casual, uncertain and non-speculative) and the other is major (i.e. involving huge amount of loss). Both categories of risks are insurable. Insurance is concerned with only pure risk. Only in case of pure risks, the outcome of the event is uncertain. Speculative risks may produce two outcomes either profit or loss. Pure risk can produce only one outcome, i.e. loss. There is question of loss of profit. In insurance, only those risks need to be insured which cause large amount of loss; small risks do not prove to be advantageous if insured at high costs; cost is called premium.

### (3) Quantifiable Risks

Estimation or approximate assessment of possibility of risk is the basis of insurance. Some risks are capable of being measured quantitatively but some are not. Only those risks which are capable of quantitatively measured are insured.

### (4) Risks in Money Terms

Only those risks that are payable in money are insurable whenever there is occurrence of loss. The losses which cannot be paid in terms of money are not insurable.

### (5) Risks that are Common

Risks must be such by which many persons are affected at the same time. In other words, there must be a large number of persons who are affected at the same time. In other words, there must be a large number of persons who are affected by or rather likely to be affected by the common risk. Risk affecting a minority section of society are not feasible to be insured because spread of risk distribution will be among a fewer persons and in such a case, cost will be more to the insured since the corpus formed out of the accumulated aggregate premia would be small, not enough to pay for the loss or damage to those affected by the uncertainty insured against.

### (6) Risk must be Causal

It is settled principle in insurance that Risk must be uncertain and not expected, certain or capable of being insured. Risks, in which the loss is certain, are not insurable. For example, in life insurance, death is certain but the time of death cannot be predetermined.

### (7) Risks with Legal Objective

Insurable risk must possess a valid object. Any risk whose object is against the public policy or public interest (i.e. acts of smugglers, thieves, dacoits, etc.) is not insurable. In the same way, the act/behaviour of a person while driving a vehicle, not following the traffic rules, resulting in an accident and causing a loss, is not insurable.

### (8) Risk must be Real

It is another principle that Risk being insured need to be real and not imaginary. Therefore, the risks arising on account of theft, death, fire and accident only are insurable. For example, if a person plans to commit a suicide and does it, the loss caused by his death is not a real risk and it cannot be insured.

**(9) Catastrophic Risks**

Risks of catastrophic nature (i.e. affecting a large number of persons), e.g. war, earthquake, floods, storms, typhoon, cyclone, tsunami, etc. are not insurable due to their high cost of insurance. A risk to be insurable must repeat or revisit after a short interval and affect only a small number of persons insured, e.g. accidents, fire, theft, etc. (not all).

**(10) Risk having Reasonable Insurance Cost**

In general, only those risks are insured which carry low premium/insurance cost. In case the premium is high, few persons will purchase the insurance policy and it will not be feasible rather economically viable for the insurance companies to carry such polices. Therefore, the risk must have wide spread effect, and magnitude of risk (loss) and the possibility of occurrence should be less. The premium or insurance cost shall be low on such risks.

## CAUSES OF RISKS

The theory of 'cause' and 'effect' equally applies to risk also. Generally, all risks are caused by certain factors or forces, and concentration of these factors causes a loss. The major causes of risk are shown in the following figure:

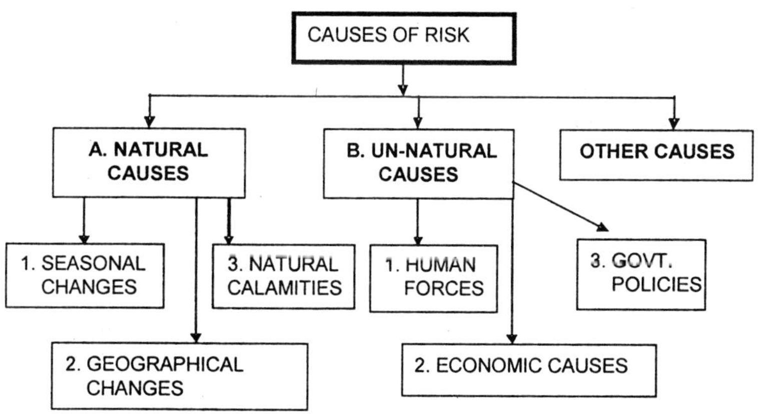

As depicted in the above figure, the risks are caused by certain factors. These factors are explained in brief below:

### (1) Natural Causes

The risks caused by the natural factors such as floods, earthquake, storms, draughts, etc. are known as natural causes. These causes can be further sub-divided into the following groups:

#### *(a) Seasonal Changes*

These risks are caused by excessive heat in summer, snowfall in winter, heavy rains in the rainy season, etc.

#### *(b) Geographical Changes*

These are the risks that occur due to changes in earth like earthquake, etc.

#### *(c) Natural Calamities*

The risks which occur due to natural calamities like storm, dusty winds, hail stones, snowfall, earthquake, etc. are sub-classified under natural calamities.

### (2) Unnatural Causes

Unnatural causes of risk include the following categories:

#### *(a) Human Forces*

There are risks caused by changes in people's preference, taste of customers, lock-outs by Industrial managements, strikes or pens downs by workers or by the anti-social elements.

#### *(b) Economic Causes*

Such risks are caused by the changes in trade cycle, demand and supply situations, market competition, etc.

#### *(c) Government Policy*

Risks are caused by the changes in Government policy like fiscal policy, monetary policy, credit policy, Export-Import (Exim) policy, industrial policy, etc. and affect the common man and business adversely.

### (3) Other Causes

The above list is illustrative, not exhaustive. Therefore, In addition to the above mentioned natural and unnatural causes, sometime causes like inefficient management, adulteration in food articles, lower quality of product, etc. may cause loss.

## TYPE OF RISKS

Risks can be classified into the following categories:

Financial and Non-financial Risks
Pure and Speculative Risks
Dynamic Risks and Static Risks
Fundamental and Particular Risks

### (1) Financial and Non-financial Risks

Financial risks are those risks outcomes of which can be measured in terms of money. For example, loss of property due to theft, loss of property due to fire, loss of profits in case of consequential loss policy, personal injury to a person in case of accident insurance policy are such risks. In all these situations, the outcome of risky situations can be measured in terms of money.

But in case of non-financial risks, the outcome cannot be measured in terms of money. For example, when one buys a car or a person chooses a career or a person chooses to marry a woman who is having children, risks cannot be measured in monetary terms. These events may or may not involve any financial implications. These are better governed by human criteria. But in the business world, we are primarily concerned with risks having financially measurable outcome only.

### (2) Pure and Speculative Risks

Risks which can produce only loss are known as pure risks. There is no chance of profit in such risks. Pure risks either cause a loss or at the best break-even situation. Therefore, the outcome can only be unfavourable or can leave us in the same position as before the event had taken place. These types of risks can be further classified into the following:

*Personal Risks*

Personal risks are those risks which are related to persons. Human life is surrounded by a number of uncertainties, such as illness, unemployment, death, old age, bodily injury, etc. Such risks cause a financial loss either to the concerned human or his dependent.

*Property Risks*

Outcome of the risks which cause a loss to the property, are classified as property risks. For example, fire may destroy houses, godown, factory, or a ship may sink on high seas or loss to the property may be caused by earthquake, floods, war, riots, etc.

*Liability Risks*

The risks which create a financial liability on a person on the occurrence of some uncertain event are known as liability risks. For example, when a person is injured in a accident, the owner of the vehicle may be held liable to compensate the injured person for the damage or loss.

When there is a possibility of loss or break even or gain as an outcome of an event, such risks are known as speculative risks. For example, investment of money in shares of certain companies may result into a profit or loss or break-even (no profit no loss). Although these types of transactions are undertaken with the objective of earning profits, yet there always remains a risk of loss. These speculative risks are not insurable.

**(3) Dynamic and Static Risks**

Dynamic risks are the risks in the nature of speculative risks. These risks are the outcome of the changes taking place in the society due to economic, social, technology, environment and political changes. Static risks are those risks which exist in the absence of dynamic situations. These are similar to pure risks.

**(4) Fundamental and Particular Risks**

Fundamental risks are those risks that arise outside the control of any individual or even a group of individuals; the effect of such risks is felt by a large number of people. This includes the loss caused by earthquake, floods, famines, volcanoes and other natural disasters. Even the social changes (upheavals), political intervention under the provisions of UN Charter/International Law and war are also sometimes included in the fundamental risks.

In contrast to the fundamental risks, the personal risks are more of personal nature both in their cause and effect. These include many types of risks such as fire, theft, work related injury and motor accidents. All these risks arise from individual causes and affect individuals in their consequence.

It is interesting to note that the above mentioned classifications of risks are not water tight classifications. The risk classification may undergo a change due to legislative measures taken by the government or from country to country. For example, in many parts of the world, fundamental risks are regarded as not insurable, but in the United Kingdom, they are insurable.

## RISK MANAGEMENT OR CONTROL OVER RISK

Risk management is not a static concept; it is a continuous effort to be aware of operational uncertainties to minimize the loss potential to a company. Risk management is a plan to prevent happening of such events that destroy company's assets or contributing resources. The fiscal integrity and current position of the company is adversely affected by unplanned incidents or losses. Risk management provides a precise plan to handle various types of contingencies. In other words, risk management includes all efforts made by a company to minimize the outcome of uncertain events or risks. For example, Banks in India make provisions out of annual profits for possible losses due to Non-Performing Assets (Doubtful Loan Assets) in their investment portfolios.

We are now in a position to define risk management. It is as: The identification, analysis and economic control of those risks that can threaten the assets or earning capacity of an enterprise are part of risk management.

This articulated definition is important as it highlights the approach through which risks in the operating business environment are to be managed. These are as follows:

Risks must be identified before they can be measured, and only after their impact has been evaluated can we decide on the most effective control of risks.

To decide to control risk, it must be 'economic' preposition. There is no point in spending Rs. 100 to control a risk which can save only Rs. 40. There will always be a point where spending on risks control has to stop.

The definition mentions the assets and earning capacity of an organization.

These assets can be physical or human. Both are important, and risk management has a part to play in both of them.

Even so, risks do not only strike at assets directly and for this reason the definition also mentions the earning capacity of an enterprise.

Finally, the word in the definition uses enterprise rather than a more restrictive word such as company or manufacturer.

The principles of risk management are applicable in the services sector just as they are in the manufacturing sector.

### Control of Speculative Risks

Speculative risks can be controlled by adopting the modern management techniques, conducting market research, forecasting government policies, diversification of product portfolio, etc. A producer who manufactures more than one product is in a better position to face loss caused by uncertain market conditions.

Moreover, the application of all concepts and principles of risk management are equally applicable to all types of speculative risks in the same way as they are applicable in case of pure risks, which call for their identification, quantification and control. In practice, each speculative risk needs different areas of knowledge and skills and needs to be tackled as a part of respective specialized managerial function.

### Control of Pure Risk

Effects or outcome of the pure risks can be controlled only through the techniques of risk management. The techniques of controlling the pure risks are different from that of speculative risks. However, as a whole risk management is a specialized managerial function and therefore risks manager must take the following steps to minimize uncertainties and loss:

Steps in Risk Management are the following: Identification

of source of risk; Measurement of impact of risk; Treatment of risk; Selection of suitable methods of risks handling; Implementing the selected method; and Feedback and review.

### *(1) Identification of Source of Risk*

The risk manager is to locate the source or causes of risks. He is to determine where the source of risks for company lies. This includes fixed assets and property, other areas of potential loss like property borrowed, business interruption, natural risks like flood, earthquake, etc.; these risks may involve financial loss and may create financial liability to injured or affected third party.

### *(2) Measurement of Risk*

The risk manager makes a loss study using historical data to eliminate future losses. The past experience and historical data enable a manager to decide in advance how many and to what size of losses may occur in future as a result of outcomes of an uncertain event. It also helps all the parties to calculate volume of insurance, premium amount, etc.

### *(3) Treatment of Risk*

After the completion of the risk analysis, the next step is to decide what risks may be retained and what will be transferred onward to others.

### *(4) Selecting Suitable Method of Risks Handling*

There are various techniques of risks handling such as avoidance, prevention, assumption, reduction, transfer or assurance of risk. It is essential to select an appropriate method to take care of risk.

### *(5) Implementing the Selected Method*

After the selection of suitable method, it is necessary to implement the selected method to cover the risks, after taking into consideration of all important factors affecting its successful implementation. Various factors like cost of insurance, required information, amount of periodical premium, financial condition and amount of loss require proper attention while implementing the selected (appropriate) method.

*(6) Evaluation*

Feedback process helps in evaluation of results of selected method. It is appropriate that evaluation of result of adopted method is done after a certain interval and corrective actions or measures must be taken to eliminate the bad results or effects of implementation.

## RISK HANDLING TECHNIQUES

Risk is the happening of an uncertain event, which causes a loss. The following are the important techniques available to avoid the problem of risk:

**(1) Avoiding Risk**

Some human activities are risky. They may increase the possibility of loss. So, the best method to avoid risk is not to undertake such type of activity. For example, if there is certainty of accident while driving a car, best method to avoid accident is, not to buy a car or not to drive it yourself. Similarly, a risk of damage by floods may be avoided by moving to another place, less prone to recurring floods.

**(2) Risk Reduction**

Another important method of risk handling is risk reduction. Risk reduction includes all those efforts made by company management to reduce the risk creating events. There are a number of ways to handle risk, e.g. to avoid fire by using fire-proof materials, slogans/notice boards prohibiting smoking like 'no smoking', etc.

**(3) Assumption of Risk**

As risk is unavoidable to the full extent, we must assume some risk. It is the best method to retain the risk with self by creating some contingency reserves or funds to meet losses arising from those risks. The non-insurable risks are covered by maintaining funds (reserves) at own level.

**(4) Transfer of Risks**

Some of the methods of shifting non-insurable risks are as under:

*(a) Hedging*

One of the most important methods of shifting non-insurable risks (e.g. changes in prices) is hedging by entering into future contract. It involves shifting of the existing risk incurred in the cash or spot market by entering into another contract in the future market.

Therefore, hedging transaction involves two transitions simultaneously, one in the spot market and the other in the futures market.

*(b) Sub-Contracting*

The general and original contractor may shift most of his risk to other contractors by entering into sub-contracts with them for the work contracted for. It is mostly applicable in case of building industry. The main contractor, after getting a contract, enters into sub-contracts with other person(s) for the supply of raw material, labour or even for the construction of most of the parts of the building. Thus, original contractor shifts most of his risk to the sub-contractors.

*(c) Surety Bond*

This is an arrangement under which third party steps into the shoes of the person who furnishes surety bond. If the main person fails to meet the liability, the surety will have to meet the liability.

*(d) Limited Company*

Company form of business has a large number of shareholders. Total risk of failure of a business is divided among those large number of members of the company.

**(5) Insurance**

The unavoidable, insurable risks may be transferred to another insurance company (reinsurer) by purchasing suitable/ appropriate policy. Modern insurance system is capable of taking over the largest possible risks relating to business, property and other kinds of liability. This is the most widely used device of risk avoidance.

A business may adopt all or any of the methods of risk avoidance in the light of its organizational planning, policies and objectives and financial considerations.

## REASONS FOR RISE OF RISK MANAGEMENT PRACTICES

In the present era, there is a great increase in the amount and variety of risk due to industrial development and other economic factors. The main reasons for rise in risk management are as follows:

- Industries and business have grown in size, diversification, process and strategic alliances.
- Complication of evaluating risk of each and every aspect has increased.
- Increase in business relations with suppliers, consumers, employees and government.
- Physical hazards have increased and changed in shape due to raw material quality and sources, manufacturing processes, range of products, technology, etc.
- Increased trend in movement of large investments has also increased the importance of protection and prevention measures.
- Business operations face many contingencies due to tough competition between enterprises.
- Globalised economy has brought in many complications due to e-commerce, e-banking, global tendering, economic co-operation, technology transfers, increasing inter-dependence of nations for various goods and services.

# 3

# Insurance: Meaning, Definition and its Nature

## BACKGROUND

Many exploratory studies have been made to find out the exact factors responsible for evolving the concept of insurance and about the time and place of the origin of the concept of insurance. It is believed that the concept of insurance originated with the evolution of man. As nature teaches, human beings are used to take different types of risks in their daily life and they have an idea to get things insured against these risks. It is also believed that insurance system has existed even during the ancient India. The oldest form of insurance is the marine insurance which continues in the modern times though in much improved and transformed form.

## MEANING OF INSURANCE

Insurance may be defined as a form of contract between two parties whereby one party (insurer) agrees to compensate the other party (insured) against a loss (which may or may not arise) against a payment of a consideration (premium).

An ant is one of the tiniest creatures but it has taught man the lesson of co-operation. Well, insurance is a cooperative system; it takes the form of distributing certain risks over a group of persons, who are exposed to it. It is again a cooperative technique to spread the loss caused by a particular risk over a number of persons and who have agreed to insure themselves against such risk. In other words, insurance is a device which provides security and fearlessness to a common person. Insurance is a means of shifting risk to insurer, in consideration for a nominal cost called 'premium'. Insurance is an arrangement where the loss feared by a few persons is spread over a large number of persons who are exposed to similar risks. Insurance companies collect premium to provide security for this purpose. Therefore, the function of insurance is to spread the loss over a large number of persons who have agreed to cooperate with each other at the time of loss. This agreement is implicit and not expressed, not evident in concrete/physical form. But it must be clearly understood that insurance cannot stop an event from happening.

## DEFINITION OF INSURANCE

Two type of definitions of insurance are current:

Functional definitions
Contractual/Legal definition

### (I) Functional Definitions

Insurance is a cooperative device to spread loss caused by a particular risk over a large number of persons, who are exposed to a similar risk and who have agreed to insure themselves against that risk.

**According to John Megi,** "Insurance is a plan where all the persons collectively share the losses of risk".

**According to Rock Fell,** "Insurance is a source of distribution of loss of a few parsons into many persons".

**According to Reigal and Miller,** "The function of insurance is primarily to decrease the uncertainty of events".

**According to William Beviridge,** "The collective bearing of risk is insurance".

**According to D.H. Magee,** "Insurance is a plan by which large number of people associate themselves and transfer to the shoulders of all, risk attached to individuals".

**According to Mowbray and Blanchard,** "Insurance is a social device for eliminating or reducing the cost to society of certain types of risk".

**According to Allan H. Willett,** "Insurance is that social device for making accumulation to meet uncertain losses which are carried out through the transfer of the risk of many individuals to one person or to a group of persons".

On the basis of above definitions, it can be concluded that:

Insurance is a cooperative device by which risks are distributed among a large number of persons.

Insurance provides protection against uncertain events, losses and risks.

Insurance is based upon the law of probability.

Insurance is a plan in which losses of uncertain events are considered.

### (2) Legal/Contractual Definition

Insurance is also governed by Contract Act. Like other forms of business in which a sum of money (as a premium) is paid in consideration for the insurer's incurring the risk of paying a large sum upon happening of a given contingency.

**According to Reigel and Miller,** "Insurance is a contract, the insurer agreeing to make good any financial loss, the insured may suffer within the scope of the contract, and the insured agreeing to pay a consideration" (Premium).

**According to Dr. W.A. Dinsdale,** "Insurance is a device for transfer of risks of individual entities to an insurer, who agrees for a consideration (called the premium), to assume to a specified extent losses suffered by the insured."

**According to E.W. Patterson,** "Insurance is a contract by which one party, for a compensation called the premium, assumes particular risks of the other party and promises to pay to him or his nominee a certain or ascertainable sum of money on a specified contingency".

**According to Chief Justice, Tindal,** "Insurance is a contract in which a sum of money is paid by the assured in consideration of the insurer's incurring the risk of paying a large sum upon a given contingency".

On the basis of the above definitions, it can be concluded that the insurance is a contract whereby:

Certain consideration is paid by one party to another. Such consideration is known as "premium".
Against such consideration by the other party, a large sum is guaranteed to be paid by the insurer.
The payment will be made by the insurer either to the extent of the actual loss or amount of policy taken, whichever is less.
The payment is made only on the happening of certain risks having taken place.

## IMPORTANT TERMS USED IN INSURANCE

The terms used in insurance are: insurer, premium, compensation, insurance policy, insured amount, risk, contingency and peril.

### (a) Insured

Insured is a person whose risk is shifted to another party. As he faces a particular risk, he is the person who seeks protection.

### (b) Insurer

Insurer is the party or insurance company which undertakes the risk. It is the party which pays money on the happening of a contingency to the insured or his nominee. Generally, the insurers are the insurance companies like Life Insurance Corporation, General insurance companies, etc.

### (c) Premium

Premium is the amount paid by the insured to the insurer in consideration for shifting his risk to the insurer. It is the price of insurance cover.

### (d) Compensation

Compensation is the amount paid by the insurer to the insured on happening of any defined contingency. It is the amount of actual loss or the insured amount, whichever is less. The compensation is paid upon the happening of a contingency.

**(e) Insurance Policy**

Insurance contract in which terms and conditions of insurance are defined is called 'insurance policy'. It is the stamped document which contains the terms and conditions of the insurance contract. Usually, it is issued by the insurer, i.e. insurance Company.

**(f) Insured Amount**

It is the money value of risk. It is also the maximum amount which the insured may get in case of loss. It is also known as policy money or face value of a policy.

**(g) Risk**

It refers to the uncertainty about loss.

**(h) Contingency**

It is the actual happening of an event or not happening of an event on which the loss depends.

**(i) Peril**

It is an event that may cause a personal or property loss.

## CHARACTERISTICS OF INSURANCE

The following are the important characteristics of insurance:

**(1) Contract**

Insurance is a contract between the insurer and the insured wherein the insured makes an offer to the insurer to shift his risk and the insurer accepts his offer. The insurance contract is always made in writing. It must contain all the essentials of a valid contract under the Indian Contract Act of 1872.

**(2) Consideration**

Insurance is a contract under which one party, for a consideration called premium, undertakes or promises to pay a certain sum of money to the insured or his nominee on the happening of an uncertain event. Premium paid to the insurer is the consideration against the coverage of risk.

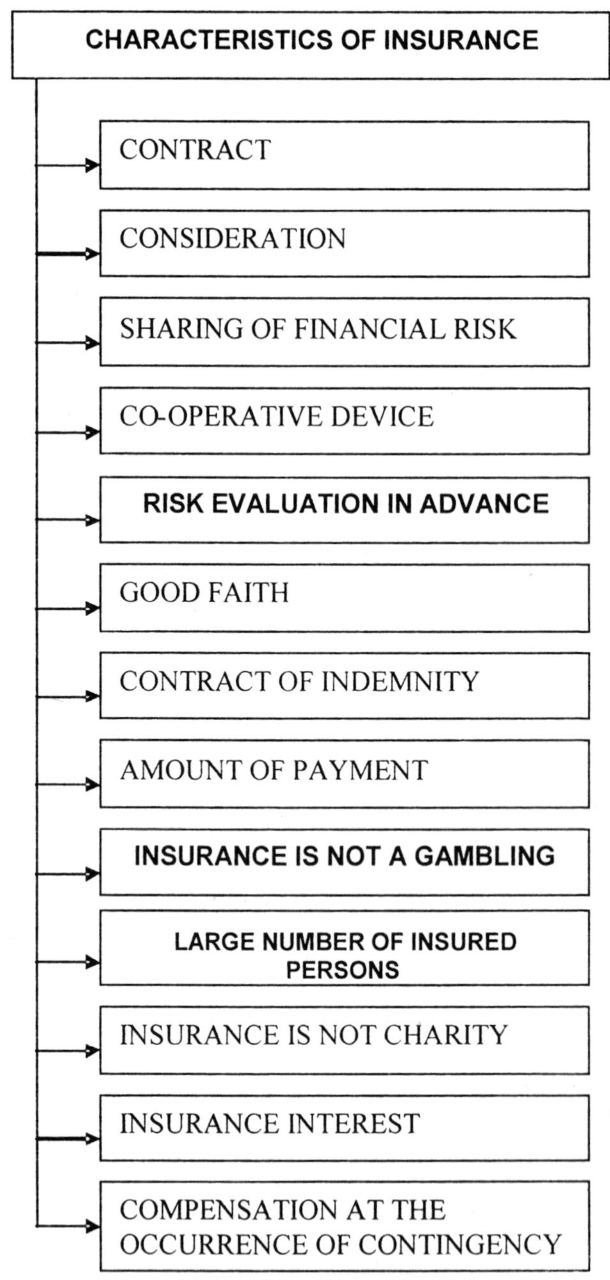
CHARACTERISTICS OF INSURANCE
CONTRACT
CONSIDERATION
SHARING OF FINANCIAL RISK
CO-OPERATIVE DEVICE
RISK EVALUATION IN ADVANCE
GOOD FAITH
CONTRACT OF INDEMNITY
AMOUNT OF PAYMENT
INSURANCE IS NOT A GAMBLING
LARGE NUMBER OF INSURED PERSONS
INSURANCE IS NOT CHARITY
INSURANCE INTEREST
COMPENSATION AT THE OCCURRENCE OF CONTINGENCY

**(3) Sharing of Financial Risk**

Insurance is a technique to share the financial loss which might fall on an individual on the happening of a particular event. The event may be death of a bread earner of the family, loss of asset due to fire, accident, etc.

**(4) Co-operative Device**

The most important feature of every Insurance plan is the co-operation of a large number of persons who agree to share the financial loss arising on account of a particular risk. Such a group of persons may come together voluntarily or through publicity. Like all co-operative techniques, there is no pressure on anybody to purchase the insurance policy.

**(5) Risk Evaluation in Advance**

The risk is evaluated before issuing the insurance policy. The amount of share of an insured called premium is decided on the basis of assessed risk. Several methods are used to evaluate the risks. If there is chance of more loss, higher premium may be charged or *vice-versa.*

**(6) Good Faith**

The insurance contract is based on the concept of uberima fiddie, i.e. utmost good faith, on the part of all the parties to the contract, i.e. insurer and insured. All relevant and important information and facts must be disclosed to each other before entering into insurance contracts.

**(7) Contract of Indemnity**

It is settled in law that all the contracts of insurance are contracts of indemnity except the life insurance. The payment is made on the happening of a certain contingency insured. If the contingency occurs, payment is made to the insured. The main objective of the insurance is to shift the loss of a person to the insurance company which can be easily shifted to a large number of persons. The insured is paid only the cash value of the loss so caused and nothing more. In case of life insurance, the death or expiry of term, will certainly occur, the payment is certain, that is why such contract is called 'contingent contract'. In other cases, if the contingency occurs, payment is made, otherwise no amount is given to the policy-holder.

### (8) Amount of Payment

The amount of payment by the insurer depends upon the value of loss occurred due to particular risk insured, provided insurance is taken up to that amount. The insurer promises to pay a fixed sum on the happening of an event. In case of property and general insurances, the amount of loss and happening of loss are required to be proved, but it is immaterial in life insurance as to what the amount of loss was at the time of happening of the specified contingency.

### (9) Insurance is not a Gambling

The contract of insurance is not gambling because the insured is to get his loss indemnified only in the event of occurrence of such uncertainty; there may be profit or loss.

### (10) Large Number of Insured Persons

A large number of persons should be insured to spread the loss immediately, smoothly and cheaply. It is essential to insure large number of persons or properties to make the insurance cheaper. The lesser is the cost of insurance the lower would be the premium. Therefore, insurance should be joined by a large number of persons in order for it to function successfully.

### (11) Insurance is not Charity

Insurance is not and cannot be treated as charity. While charity is given without consideration, insurance is not possible without premium. Premium payable under an insurance contract is the cost of risk so covered. Insurance provides security and safety to as individual in consideration for premium.

### (12) Insurable Interest

No person can make or enter into a contract of insurance unless he has insurable interest in the object or the life insured.

### (13) Compensation at the Occurrence of Contingency

The compensation is paid at the happing of certain contingency that is insured against. If the contingency occurs, payment is made otherwise not.

## FUNCTIONS OF INSURANCE

Insurance serves very useful purpose; it relieves worry. It is very important in the modern age. The importance can be judged from the various functions and services rendered by insurance. The different types of functions performed by insurance are as follows:

### (I) Primary Function

*(1) Insurance Provides Certainty*

The main function of insurance is to provide certainty by reducing the risks or uncertainties of events. Insurance is a means to compensate the losses caused by uncertain events. The insured can convert his uncertainties into certainties by paying premium to the insurer. Insurance also provides certainty of payment for the risk of loss actually happening. There is uncertainty of happening as regards time and amount of loss. Insurance removes all these uncertainties and the insured is given certainty of payment in case of loss. The insurer charges premium for providing the said certainty.

*(2) Insurance Provides Protection*

The other important function of insurance is to provide protection against the probable chances of loss. The insurance guarantees the payment of loss and thus protects the insured against suffering. The insurance cannot check the happening of the risk and/or event but can compensate for losses arising at the happening of the risk/event.

*(3) Risk Sharing*

The concept of insurance is based on the law of co-operation to share the loss. When risk takes place, the loss is shared by all the persons who are exposed to the same category of risk. The share is obtained from each and every insured person/entity in the shape of premium without which the insurer does not guarantee the protection.

*(4) Insurance Provides Security*

Another function of insurance is to provide security to the

persons against the risks of uncertain events. The insurance provides a feeling of security against the evil effects of the uncertain events, i.e. risks.

*(5) Assistance to Business Enterprises*

Insurance provides help to business houses. There is heavy capital investment by the companies/entities in modern industry, especially in building constructions and manufacturing and sale/purchase of machinery and plant, equipments, and so on. This investment is exposed to loss or damage by fire, theft, accident or other perils. The provision for these losses may be very costly. Insurance provides protection to these assets in return for a payment called 'premium'.

**(II) Secondary Functions**

*(1) Prevention of Loss*

The insurance companies extend financial assistance to the health organizations, fire brigades, educational institutions and other organizations, which are engaged in rendering essential and general welfare services to the society by preventing the losses of the masses from death or damage. Insurance not only secures those losses but also advises to adopt various methods and techniques which help in reducing losses.

*(2) Provides Capital*

Insurance provides capital to the industry. It provides funds for investments. The surplus amount, received on account of premium by various insurance companies is made available for the industrial development of the country. Investment is made in share capital of the companies, providing long-term loans to companies, and make advances by assignments of the insurance policies. The industry, business and individuals are benefited by both the investments and loans by the insurers.

*(3) Improves Efficiency of Industry*

The insurance companies help in asset formation in the economy by extending financial help for various purposes in the industry organizations, etc. These help government in mobilizing resources for execution of development plans.

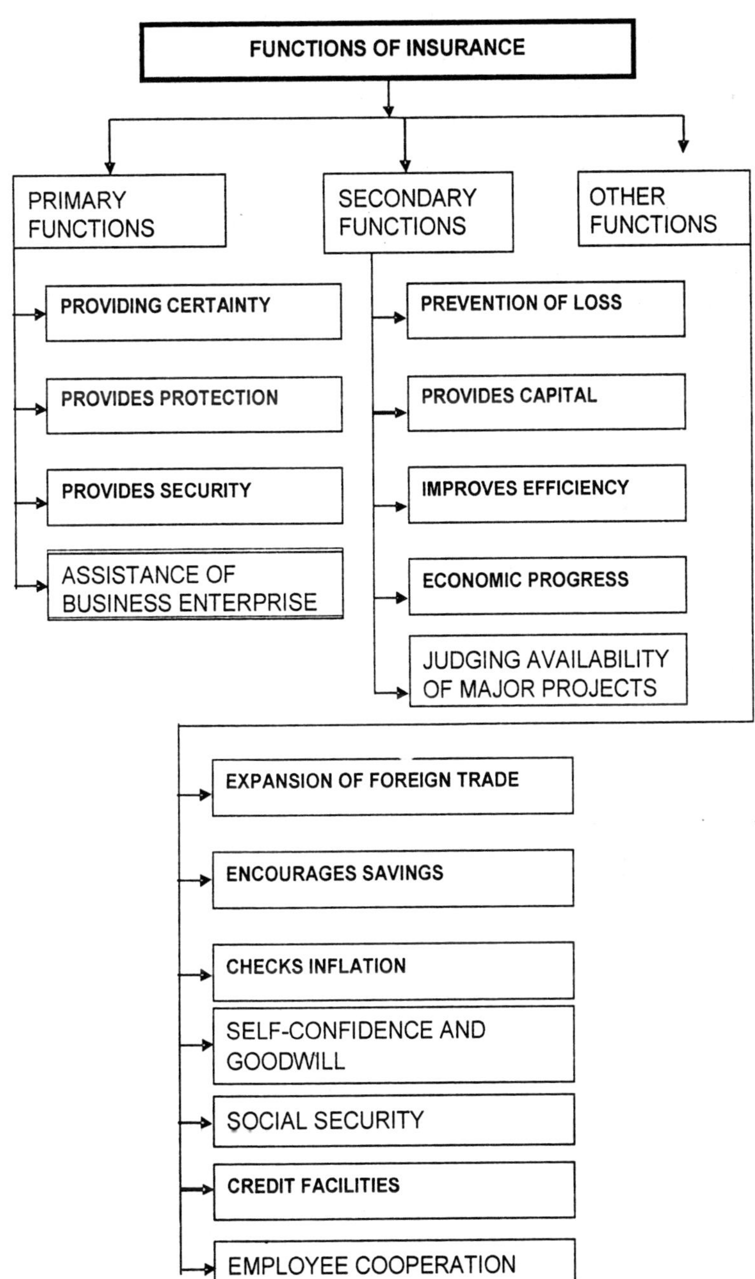
FUNCTIONS OF INSURANCE
PRIMARY FUNCTIONS
SECONDARY FUNCTIONS
OTHER FUNCTIONS
PROVIDING CERTAINTY
PROVIDES PROTECTION
PROVIDES SECURITY
ASSISTANCE OF BUSINESS ENTERPRISE
PREVENTION OF LOSS
PROVIDES CAPITAL
IMPROVES EFFICIENCY
ECONOMIC PROGRESS
JUDGING AVAILABILITY OF MAJOR PROJECTS
EXPANSION OF FOREIGN TRADE
ENCOURAGES SAVINGS
CHECKS INFLATION
SELF-CONFIDENCE AND GOODWILL
SOCIAL SECURITY
CREDIT FACILITIES
EMPLOYEE COOPERATION

*(4) Economic Progress*

The insurance provides an initiative to work hard for the betterment of masses by protecting the society from huge losses of damage, destruction and death.

*(5) Judging the Profitability of Major Projects*

Insurance also helps in judging the viability of major projects. Before insuring the assets or property of any organization, the insurer conducts a viability investigation of assets or project as a whole with a view to judge the profitability of the project.

**(III) Other Functions**

In addition to primary and secondary functions, insurance performs various other functions for the benefits of the common man, business community and the nation as a whole. These are as follows:

*(1) Expansion of Foreign Trade*

Insurance promotes foreign trade and helps in earning valuable foreign exchange by providing security to the international traders, shipping companies, banking and financial institutions, who work in the field of foreign trade. Indian insurance is transacted in overseas countries particularly in the Middle-East, Africa and South-East Asia through branches. Those branches also contribute towards earning foreign exchange.

*(2) Encourages Savings*

Insurance makes saving possible. These days insurance is considered to be a better alternative to investment of surplus funds. Money deposited as premium in insurance policies is for future use of saving and to get the benefits of income tax deductions under section 80 of Income Tax Act. Insurance premia are thus free of tax expenditure.

*(3) Checks Inflation*

Insurance also helps in checking inflation in the economy. Forced savings in the form of premium, reduces the spending of the individuals. The saved scarce resource of production (capital), is used for national development by investment in a better way.

*(4) Feeling of Self-Confidence and Goodwill*

Insurance creates self-confidence in the insured by providing a feeling of security and safety to them. Insurance provides protection against risks. It also provides capital to the insured on maturity of the policy, which becomes a source of financial stability and strength. Insurance increases self-confidence, reputation and goodwill of the insured.

*(5) Social Security and Pursuing Education*

Insurance proves an instrumental force to fight against evils of poverty, unemployment, disease, old age debility, fateful accidents of persons and damage to property, etc. Insurance also helps in spreading education among the masses regarding adoption of techniques for minimizing the happening of controllable uncertain events.

*(6) Credit Facilities*

It is possible for traders who are in a position to raise loans from various financial institutions and banks by assigning their insurance policies.

*(7) Seeking Employees' Cooperation by Employers*

The strategy of Employers to have good relations with their employees is by insuring employees against life, accident and sickness, etc. Group insurance policies are issued by the insurers in such cases. There is no exaggeration in the assertion that satisfied employees are the assets of an organization.

## USES/ROLE AND IMPORTANCE OF INSURANCE OR RELEVANCE OF INSURANCE IN DEVELOPING COUNTRY LIKE INDIA

The concept and process of insurance has been evolved to safeguard the interests of people from uncertainty, by providing certainty of payment on the happening of a given contingency. The principles of insurance come handy and more and more used and found useful in modern times in the conduct of affairs.

The relevance of insurance is inseparable from its role and importance. The role and importance of insurance can broadly be classified into three categories:

(i) Relevance to Individuals,
(ii) Relevance to business or industry, and
(iii) Relevance to the society.

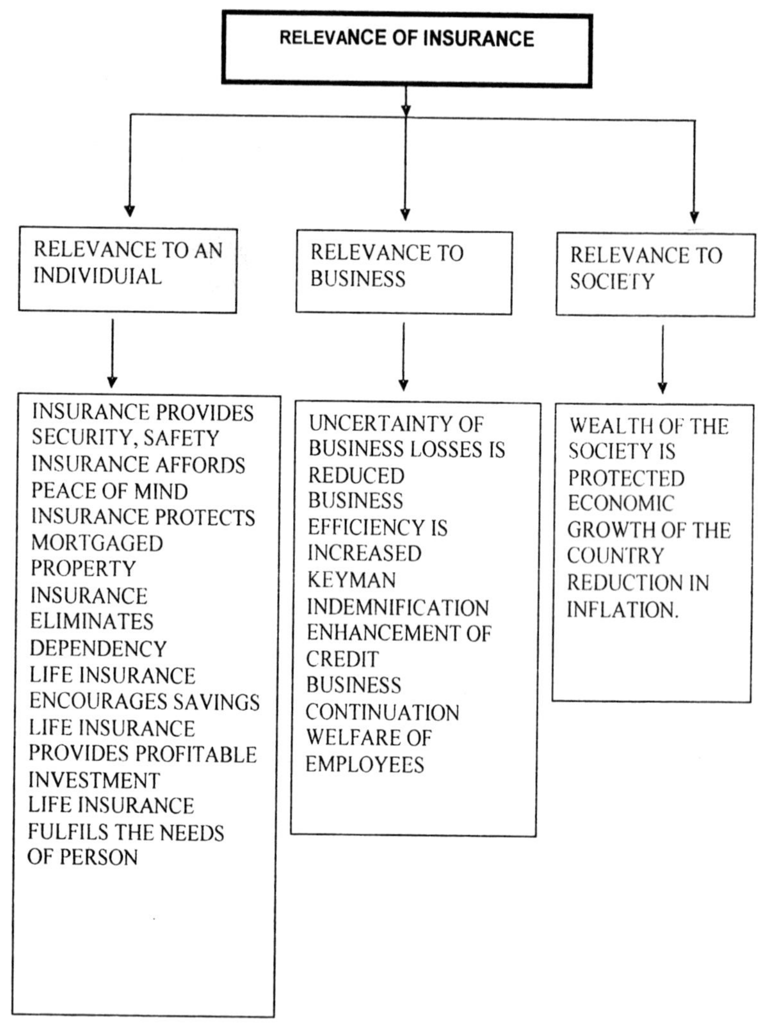

### (I) Relevance of Insurance to an Individual

*(1) Insurance Provides Security and Safety*

As said before, insurance provides safety and security to an individual against the loss of life or loss/damage to an asset or property on happening of a particular event. In case of life insurance, payment is made when death occurs or the term of insurance expires. The losses to the family due to premature death of bread-earner or payment in old age are adequately provided by life insurance. Similarly, the property of insured can also be secured against the loss by fire in fire insurance. In other types of insurance also, this security is provided against the loss at the happening of a given contingency.

*(2) Insurance gives Peace of Mind*

There is no doubt in the statement that insurance provides peace of mind to the insured by securing against various risks and losses. The security eliminates the fear and uncertainty of hazards like fire, accident, damage and death which are beyond the control of human beings and which may frustrate or weaken the human mind.

*(3) Insurance protects the Mortgaged Property*

At the death of the owner of the mortgaged property, the property is taken over by the lender of money and the family will be deprived of the uses of that mortgaged poverty. But thanks to the insurance device that insurance will provide adequate amount to the dependents in case of the early death of the property owner by paying-off the unpaid loans out of the proceeds of the insurance claim.

*(4) Insurance eliminates Dependency*

Every one knows that the economic independence of the family is reduced or lost totally at the death of the bread earner of the family. It results in reduced standard of living; the suffering may go to the extent of begging from the relatives, neighbourers or friends which is degrading and shameful. The insurance is here to assist them as it provides adequate amount at the time of sufferings of loss due to death or destruction of property. It eliminates dependence on others and the nominee or the insured can live with dignity.

*(5) Life Insurance encourages Savings*

Insurance makes savings possible. These days, insurance products/schemes are varied. Therefore, insurance is considered a better alternative to invest surplus funds. Moreover, the insurance premium provides rebate in income tax also.

*(6) Life Insurance provides Profitable Investment*

Life insurance policies are inherently better alternative of profitable investment. Various policies like endowment policies, multipurpose policies, deferred annuities, are certainly better forms of investment. In India, as per current Income Tax rules, the insurance policies carry a special exemption under income tax, wealth tax, gift tax, etc.

*(7) Life Insurance Fulfils the Needs of a Person*

*(a) Family Need*

Death is certain, but the time is uncertain. Therefore, there is uncertainty when the suffering and financial stringencies may fall on the family due to the death of bread earner in a family. All life policies provide a better means of meeting such requirements.

*(b) Old Age Needs*

The life insurance provides old age funds along with the protection of the family by issuing various policies after the retirement.

*(c) Re-Adjustment Needs*

At the time of reduction in income due to loss of employment, disability or death, adjustment in the standard of living of family is required. The life insurance helps to accumulate adequate funds to readjust the needs of family.

*(d) Special Needs*

There are certain special needs of the family, which are fulfilled by the earning member of the family. If the earning member become disabled to earn due to his old age or death, those needs may remain unfulfilled and family may suffer.

*(i) Need for Education*

There are certain insurance polices, and annuities which are useful for the education of children irrespective of the death or survival of the head of the family.

*(ii) Marriage*

The insurance also provides funds for meeting the expense of daughter's marriage, if an appropriate policy is taken for the purpose.

**(II) Relevance to Business**

The insurance is also useful to the business society in the following ways:

*(1) Uncertainty of Business Losses is Reduced*

In business world, i.e. commerce and industry a huge amount is invested in properties. The property may be destroyed with a slight slackness or negligence. A businessman can reduce the uncertainties of his business losses by obtaining a suitable insurances policy.

*(2) Business Efficiency is Increased*

When the businessman is free from the botheration of losses, he will certainly devote more time to his business. The carefree owner can work better for the maximization of the profit. The insurance stimulates the businessmen to work hard by removing the uncertainty.

*(3) Key Man's Indemnification*

Key man is that particular man who has capital expertise, experience, energy, ability to control. Goodwill and dutifulness make him the most valuable asset in the business. The death or disability of such valuable worker will prove more serious loss than fire or any hazard. The insurance policies can make up the loss, to compensate the dependents of such worker and appointing and training of new employees.

*(4) Enhancement of Credit*

The business can obtain loan by pledging the policy as security for the loan. In case of death of businessman, the cash value of policies can be used for setting-off the loan along with the interest.

*(5) Business Continuation*

In partnership, the business may discontinue on the death of any partner. The surviving partners can restart the business, if each partner is insured for an amount of his interest in the partnership and his dependents will get that amount on the death of the partner without economically affecting the firm.

*(6) Welfare of Employees*

The welfare of employees is the responsibility of the employer. The employer has to look after the welfare of his employee in case of early death, disability or old age. These requriemetns are easily met by the life insurance against accident, death, sickness, etc.

**(III) Relevance to Society**

*(1) Wealth of the Society is Protected*

The loss of a particular wealth can be protected with insurance. Life insurance provides loss of human wealth. The loss of damage of property due to fire, accident, etc. can well be indemnified by the property insurance. Insurance

*(2) Economic Growth of the Country*

Insurance proves a boon as it provides strong hand and mind for the economic growth of the country by providing protection against loss of property and adequate capital to produce more wealth. Insurance contributes to meeting all the requirements of the economic growth of a country by protecting the agriculture equipments and industrial tools and techniques.

*(3) Reduction in Inflation*

One of the instruments available to government to suck liquidity from the public to reduce inflation is through savings. In this matter, the insurance reduces the inflationary pressure by extracting money in circulation by the amount of premium collected and by providing sufficient funds for productive activities in the economy and thus narrow down the inflationary gap.

# Scope and Dimensions of Insurance

## INTRODUCTION

No body knows exactly the origin of Insurance. Its origin is lost in antiquity. The earliest traces of insurance in the ancient world are found in the marine trade loans or carrier contracts, which included an element of guaranteeing or underwriting or undertaking to compensate for the loss of merchandise lost in transit; it may be called insurance. At present, insurance occupies an important place in the modern business world. It also plays an important role in the life of every citizen, not only business. It has developed on an enormous scale leading to the evolution of many types of insurance. In fact, almost every risk can be made a subject-matter of contract of insurance now-a-days.

## CLASSIFICATION OF INSURANCE

The practice of insurance has evolved different types of insurance. Many insurance companies have been established. Insurances can be classified as follows:

### (I) Classification on the Basis of Nature of Insurance

On the basis of nature of insurance, it maybe divided into the following two categories:

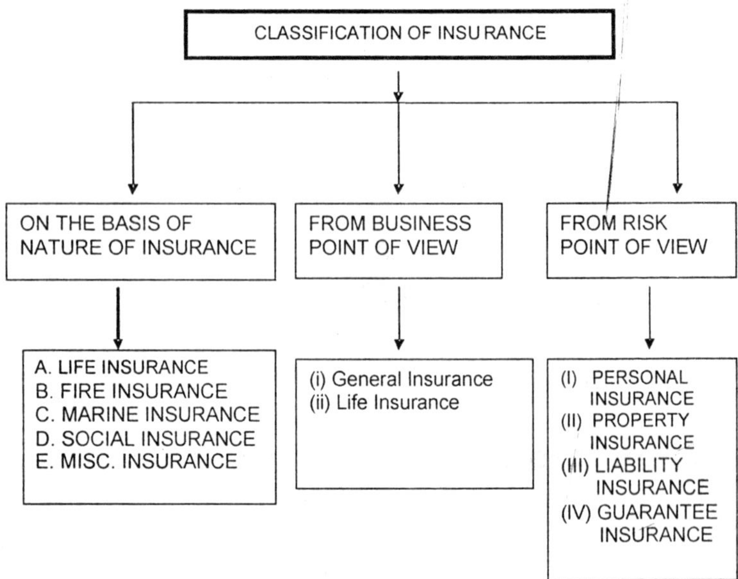


## LIFE INSURANCE AND NON-LIFE INSURANCE (GENERAL INSURANCE)

### (I) Life Insurance

Life insurance may be defined as a contract in which the insurer agrees to pay to the insured or his nominee the assured sum of money on the happening of a specified event contingent on human life, either on the death of the life insured or at the expiry of certain period, in consideration for a certain premium. In life insurance, the risk insured is death. The life insurance company pays the sum assured to the nominee of the insured in the event of death.

Life insurance enjoys at present the maximum scope because of the awareness that the human life is the most important property of society. Life insurance provides protection to the family at the premature death of family head or gives adequate amount at the old age when earning capacities get reduced. Life insurance is not only a protection but also a sort of investment because a certain sum is returnable to the insured at the expiry of a specified period. Bonus and other benefits are added to the sum assured.

Insurance provides financial protection against the risk of early death. Life insurance contract can be described as a contingent contract because the loss of life cannot be compensated and only a specified sum of money is paid if the insured dies during the currency of the policy.

**Definition of Life Insurance**

Under Section 2 of the Indian Insurance Act, 1938, "Life insurance business is the business of effecting contracts upon human life". Again, a life insurance contract may be defined as a contract whereby the insurer, in consideration for a premium paid either in lump sum or in periodical instalments, undertakes to pay an annuity or a certain sum of money, either on death of the insured or on the expiry of a certain number of years, as agreed upon.

According to J.H. Maggee:

> "The life insurance contract embodies an agreement, in which, broadly stated, the insurer undertakes to pay a stipulated sum upon the death of the insured, or at some designated time to a designated beneficiary.

Stated in simple words, insurance may be defined as a contract whereby the insurance company, in consideration for payment of periodical premium, agrees to pay a certain amount either on the death or on maturity of policy, whichever occurs earlier.

**Characteristics of Life Insurance**

The characteristics of life insurance contract are the following: outcome of an offer; payment of sum assured; payment of premium by the insured or by another person on his/her behalf; contract of contingency; insurable interest; provides financial help; encouragement of savings; and it has wide scope.

*(1) Outcome of an Offer*

Life insurance contract is the outcome of an offer made by the insured and its acceptance by the insurer. Life insurance contract is made in writing; it is called a proposal.

*(2) Payment of Sum Assured*

The insurer agrees to pay a certain sum of money either on the death of the insured or on the maturity of the policy, whichever occurs earlier.

*(3) Payment of Premium*

The insured is under an obligation to pay periodically the pre-fixed premium amount till the death of insured or expiry of the period of policy, whichever is earlier.

*(4) Contract of Contingency*

The contract of life insurance is a contract of contingency because the loss caused by the death cannot be calculated or reduced in money terms.

*(5) Insurable Interest*

Insurable interest of the insured must exist in the person insured at the time when the policy is taken in case of life insurance. It may or may not be present at the time of insured's death.

*(6) Provides Financially Help*

Life insurance extends the hand of protection to those who are left support-less and helps financially in case of death of the insured.

*(7) Encouragement of Savings*

Life insurance is also considered to be the best alternative for making savings. Premia payments are practically investments. Investments made in life insurance policies are tax-free.

*(8) Wide Scope*

Life insurance also covers other risks besides death which are related to human life, such as total or permanent disability, medical expenses incurred in hospitalization, etc.

**Procedure for Taking a Life Insurance Policy**

Any human being who wants to take a life insurance policy has to follow the following procedures:

(1) Proposal in prescribed format;
(2) Proof of Age;
(3) Medical Examination;
(4) Confidential Report by the Agent/counsellor;
(5) Acceptance of Proposal;
(6) Payment of First Premium; and
(7) Insurance Policy document issued and delivered.

*(1) Proposal*

The person who wants to get an insurance policy makes an offer to the agent/counsellor of the insurance company by filling up a prescribed proposal form, available free of cost from the insurance agents. Various types of information are furnished therein such as:

(i) Name, occupation and address of insured;
(ii) Family history and health of insured;
(iii) Facts about the income, life and habits of the insured;
(iv) Date of birth as age proof of the insured;
(v) Mode of payment of premium; and
(vi) Address, Telephone Number, Mobile Telephone Number, etc.

The above information must be filled in the application form. The insured is under an obligation to provide true and correct information in the form.

*(2) Proof of Age*

The insured is required to give proof of his/her age along with the proposal form at the time of entering into the contract of insurance. The age of the insured can be proved by a certified copy of an entry in the Birth Register of the Local Body, certificate of date of birth issued by the school or college or Education Board or the University, or service book maintained by the employer, etc.

*(3) Medical Fitness Report*

After the receipt of the proposal from in the office of insurance company, the proposer is required o get himself medically examined from the doctor approved by the insurance company. The expenses of medical examination are normally paid by insurance company.

*(4) Confidential Report by the Counsellor/Agent*

The life insurance counsellor/agent is required to prepare confidence report about the health, character, financial position and other personal information of the insured. This report is attached with the proposal form.

*(5) Acceptance of Proposal*

On the basis of information given in the proposal form, the insurance company considers the acceptance of the proposal. After determining the types of risk, amount of risk, premium rate, etc. it accepts the proposal. Acceptance letter is dispatched to the insured stating therein the conditions to be fulfilled by the insured

*(6) Payment of first premium*

On receipt of the acceptance letter, the insured pays the first premium and the insurance company becomes liable for loss from the day on which it is paid. The premium may be paid monthly, quarterly, half yearly or yearly as the insured at present, desires.

## General Insurance

*Fire Insurance*

Fire insurance is a contract of indemnity and the insured cannot claim anything more than the value of goods lost or damaged by fire or the amount insured, whichever is less. The contract of fire insurance does not help in controlling or preventing the fire but it is a promise to compensate the loss caused by fire.

Fire insurance is an agreement between the insurer and the insured, under which the insurer agrees to indemnity the loss caused by fire, to the insured, in consideration of certain payment, called premium.

## Definition of Fire Insurance

According to T.R. Smith:

> "Fire insurance may be defined as a contract whereby the insurers in return for a consideration, known as premium,

undertake to indemnify the insured against financial loss which he may sustain, by reason of certain defined perils against which the property is insured, being damaged or destroyed by fire within a stated period, the liability of insurer being limited to a specified amount, called the sum insured".

According to Section 2 of Indian Insurance Act, 1938—

"Fire insurance business means the business of effecting, otherwise than incidentally, some other class of insurance business, contracts of insurance against loss by or incidental to fire or other peril, the occurrence customarily included among the risks insured against in fire insurance policies".

According to V.R. Bhushan and R.S. Sharma—

"Fire insurance may be defined as an agreement whereby one party, in return for a consideration, undertakes to indemnify the other party against financial loss caused by fire or other defined perils upto an agreed amount".

**Characteristics of Fire Insurance**

(1) Contract of indemnity
(2) Offer and acceptance
(3) Premium
(4) Insurable interest
(5) Payment of premium
(6) Policy duration
(7) Principle of subrogation
(8) Outcome
(9) Claim settlement

*(1) Contract of Indemnity*

The contract of fire insurance is a contract of indemnity. The insured cannot claim anything more than the value of goods or properties lost or damaged by fire or amount of policy, whichever is less.

*(2) Offer and Acceptance*

The contract of fire insurance is the outcome of the offer made by insured and its acceptance by the insurer.

*(3) Premium*

Fire insurance policy is issued for a lawful consideration, i.e. premium.

*(4) Insurable Interest*

The insured must have insurable interest in the properties insured at the time when the policy is taken and loss occurs in regard to the same.

*(5) Payment of Premium*

Premium is required to be paid at the time of taking a policy.

*(6) Policy Duration*

Fire insurance polices are issued usually for one year. But in some cases, they are also issued for a shorter period.

*(7) Principle of Subrogation*

It is the principle of subrogation that the scrap or whatever is left of the goods or properties after damage by fire, automatically passes on to the insurer after the payment of the claim.

*(8) Outcome*

The loss must be the outcome or consequence of fire only.

*(9) Claim Settlement*

The claim may be settled in cash or by rehabilitating the goods or properties damaged by fire and covered under the fire insurance.

**Scope of Fire Insurance**

The scope of fire insurance can be divided into two parts:

(i) Ordinary scope of fire insurance.
(ii) Comprehensive or broader scope of fire insurance.

*(i) Ordinary Scope*

This type of insurance includes only those risks which define the narrower scope of fire insurance, i.e. the losses caused by fire only. Under the fire insurance contract, the claim for loss by fire must fulfil two basic conditions:

(a) There must be actual fire; and

(b) The fire must be incidental.

The property insured must be damaged or burnt or destroyed by fire.

*Risks covered under the fire insurance*: The main causes of risk must be mentioned in the fire insurance policy and only those risks are indemnified by the insurer in cases of loss. Main causes of fire insurances are fire, blasting of boiler, blast of gas cylinder, etc.

*Risks not covered under Fire insurance policies*: There are certain risks against which insurance companies do not indemnify the insured in case of loss, e.g. fire in jungle, theft during fire, etc.

*(ii) Comprehensive Scope of Fire Insurance*

These policies cover the various types of risks allied to the risks of fire. Coverage of such risks under the purview of fire insurance has widened the scope of fire insurance.

**Procedure for Taking a Fire Insurance Policy**

The insured desirous of taking a fire insurance policy has to follow the following procedure for taking out a fire insurance policy:

Selecting the Insurance Company

Submission of a Proposal Form

Evidence of respectability

Survey of properties to be insured

Acceptance of proposal by the Insurance Company

Issuing a Cover Note by the Insurance Company

Issue of Policy Document

*(1) Selecting the Insurance Company*

First of all, the insured selects a financially strong and efficient insurance company. The company which requires less formalities and easy terms for taking a policy is always preferred.

*(2) Proposal Form*

The insured has to fill up the proposal form to get the insurance policy. The insured is under obligation to give true and correct information about the details of property, its location and value of property. The insured is required to provide true and correct information in the proposal form as the contract of insurance is based on utmost faith.

*(3) Evidence of Respectability*

The insurance company collects the proofs of honesty, integrity and financial position of the insured from the third parties. The insured has to submit a certificate of respectability along with proposal form to the insurer.

*(4) Survey of Properties to be Insured*

The insurer has to assess the properties to be insured to determine the risk involved in the property against fire.

*(5) Acceptance of Proposal*

On the basis of the information furnished in the proposal form, certificate of respectability and the reports of surveyors, the insurer-company gives its acceptance to the proposal submitted by the insured. The insurer sends an intimation of acceptance to the insured, mentioning the premium payable. Proposal is always accepted subject to the payment of premium.

*(6) Cover Note*

The insurer issues a cover note which is in the nature of an interim protection note before the final form/document of policy is prepared. Cover note is not equal to policy, but if a fire occurs in the mean time, the cover note will cover the risk and the insurer will be liable to indemnify the risks covered under the cover note.

*(7) Issue of Policy*

Finally, a fire insurance policy is prepared in a proper form, duly stamped and signed, containing the terms and conditions of the insurance. The policy contains the name and address of the insured, value/amount insured, contents and subject matter of properties, period of insurance, amount of premium, mode of payment of premium, etc. This insurance policy is issued by the insurer to the insured in due course of time.

## MARINE INSURANCE

Marine insurance is the oldest form of insurance. It is concerned with the foreign trade conducted through sea routes. Marine risks are usually related to the ship or cargo or both. The businessman and the owner of ship always want to ensure the safe arrival of their cargo and ships.

Marine insurance covers a large number of risks including sinking, burning of ship, standing or going astray of the ship, accident, stormy winds, collision of ships, jettison, explosion, sea dacoities (piracy), etc. causing losses to the ship and/or cargo due to many other perils of the sea.

Therefore, marine insurance is an arrangement by which the insurance company agrees to indemnify the owner of the ship or cargo or both against the risks involved in marine venture.

Marine insurance provides protection against loss due to marine perils. These perils cause damage, destruction or disappearance of the ship and cargo and non-payment of freight. Thus, marine insurance insures ship (Hull), cargo and freight. Marine insurance insures all types of risks which can occur during transportation on the high seas.

### Definition of Marine Insurance

Under Section 3 of Marine Insurance Act, we can find the definition which is as under:

> "A contract of marine insurance is a contract whereby the insurer undertakes to indemnify the insured in a manner and to the extent thereby agreed, against marine losses, i.e. to say, the losses incidental to marine adventures".

Under Section 2 (13) of Insurance Act, 1938, the definition is as under:

> "Marine insurance business means the business of effecting contracts of insurance upon vessels of any description, including cargoes, freight and other interest which is legally insured in or in relation to such vessels, cargoes, freights, goods, wares, merchandise or property of whatever description, insured for any transit by land or water or both and whether or not including warehouse risks or similar risk in addition to or as incidental to such transit and includes any other risks customarily included among the risks insured against in marine insurance policies".

According to Arnold,

> "A marine insurance is a contract whereby one party, for an agreed consideration, undertakes to indemnify the other against loss arising from certain perils and sea risks to which a shipment and other interest in a marine adventure may be exposed during a certain voyage or a certain time".

On the basis of the above reproduced definitions, it may be concluded that marine insurance provides protection and security against the sea and inland risks relating to cargoes, ship, freight, etc.

**Characteristics of Marine Insurance**

The main features of marine insurance are as under:

Marine insurance is based on the contract between insured and insurer.

The insured is under an obligation to pay certain amount of premium as consideration.

Cargo, ship and freight can be insured under marine insurance policy.

The insurance may be for a single journey or a number of journeys during a specific period of time.

Under marine insurance, the insurer guarantees only to compensate the loss caused by sea uncertainties.

Marine insurance may be inland also, i.e. for railway, road transportation, of course, as part of sea voyage.

## Scope or Subject Matter of Marine Insurance

Marine Insurance may be classified into three categories:

(1) *Cargo Insurance*: when goods loaded on a ship are insured, it is called cargo insurance. Any loss of cargo during journey is indemnified by the insurance company. The cargo and ship is exposed to risks arising from an act of enemy, fire, gales or other perils of sea, etc.

(2) *Ship Insurance*: Ships on the high sea-waters are also exposed to some risks. The owner of ship may insure the ship against the risk of sea transportation. It is known as "Hull Insurance".

(3) *Freight Insurance*: In case both the cargo and the ship get destroyed, the shipping company will also lose the freight on the carriage of cargo. Therefore, freight insurance is taken. The policy covering such a risk is called "freight insurance".

## Procedure for Taking Marine Insurance Policy

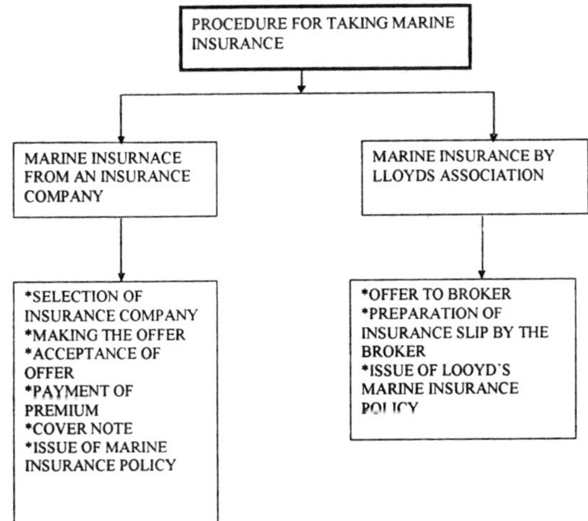


Marine insurance can be effected either by a Joint Stock Co. or a Lloyd's Association.

### (I) Marine Insurance from an Insurance Company

The General Insurance Companies and their subsidiaries are undertaking marine assurance business in India. The following procedure is adopted.

*Selection of Insurance Company*

The insured has to select one of the best companies out of various available companies doing same kind of insurance business. Generally, such company should be preferred that provides quick service and makes prompt payment of the compensation.

*Making the Offer*

The insured is required to fill up an application form. It is prescribed by the insurance company for making an offer of insurance. The application form is given in the form of questionnaire in which the insured is required to give information about his name, address, occupation, business, name of ship, amount to be insured, etc.

*Acceptance of Offer*

The Insurance Company may accept or reject the application or proposal. Proposal is checked thoroughly before it is accepted by the insurance company.

*Payment of Premium*

If the insurance company accepts the proposal, it determines the amount of premium payable on the policy. The amount of premium is determined on the basis of goods, ship, type and mode of packing, route, etc.

*Cover Note*

On the payment of the premium by the insured, a cover note is dispatched by the company. The company will be legally liable for the risk covered under the contract with the issue of cover note and from the date of the cover note.

*Issue of marine Insurance Policy*

In the mean time, the insurance company prepares a marine insurance policy in a proper form containing terms and conditions of marine insurance contract.

### (II) Marine insurance by Lloyd's Association

*Offer to Broker*

The insured has to select or contact a broker for making an offer to get insurance policy. These brokers must be recognized by Lloyd's Association.

*Preparation of Insurance Slip by the Broker*

Any recognized broker to whom an offer is made collects necessary information from the insured and prepares a slip, quoting the facts, e.g. rate of premium, amount to be insured, and name of ship, type and nature of risk. Every insurer signs on the slip, puts the amount which he wants to insure and the rate of premium. The slip is forwarded to another broker to insure the remaining amount. Then the broker prepares a policy on the basis of information and acceptance made by various insurers.

*Issue of Marine Insurance Policy (Lloyd's or other)*

After the acceptance by the insurer of the offer made by the insured in full, the broker prepares a policy on the basis of the facts and information or acceptances of insurers, given in the slip. He gets it signed from different insurers who have accepted the offer in full or in parts. Then he affixes proper stamp duty on it and then the policy is forwarded to the insured.

## SOCIAL INSURANCE

Social insurance has developed to provide economic security to the weaker sections of society who are unable to pay the premium for an adequate insurance. Various forms of social insurance are pension plans, disability benefits, unemployment benefits, sickness insurance, etc. The social insurance is an obligatory duty of the nation with the belief in the socialistic philosophy of the country.

Due to international social cohesion and constant contact and connectivity through satellite technology as spurred by the concept of globalization and with Information Communication Technology as its wings, social content is impregnated in all human activities. As such, the main aim of social insurance is to help the community to fight against the risks of disease, old age, industrial accidents, unemployment and above all the evils of poverty.

**Forms of Social Insurance**

Sickness Insurance
Accident Insurance
Disablement Insurance
Maternity Insurance
Old Age Insurance
Unemployment Insurance

In response to the above, the insurers have worked out products to offer to the society. The following are some of the current social insurance schemes currently operative though there is effort to evolve new schemes to suit each interest and pocket:

*Sickness Insurance*

Under this scheme, the insured is provided with financial help in addition to medial facilities during the period of sickness. In India, Employees' State Insurance Corporations have been set-up under the respective state insurance acts.

*Accident Insurance*

Under accident insurance scheme, the insured is provided with financial help in case of accident, causing loss to the insured. In case of death of the insured in accident, insurance company undertakes to pay a certain sum of money to the dependents of the insured. The insured is under obligation to pay certain amount regularly, called premium.

*Disablement Insurance*

Under this, the insured is given financial help if he becomes disabled in an accident, other than the industrial accidents. The insured has to pay premium regularly in order to get security from such risks.

*Maternity Insurance*

The insured women workers are compensated by the

insurer for the expenses incurred on getting medical treatment, medicines and balanced diet/food during the period of pregnancy/maternity. Compensation is paid at a fixed rate in consideration for premium paid by the insured.

#### *Old Age Insurance*

Under old age insurance scheme, the insured persons are given pension or fixed amount when they become old enough, not being able to earn their livelihood.

#### *Unemployment Insurance*

This is the scheme under which, the insured person is given financial help until he gets employment again.

## MISCELLANEOUS INSURANCE SCHEMES

As the process of fast development of the society gives rise to a number of risks in our daily life, many other types of insurance schemes have also been developed to provide security against such risks. The important schemes are:

Motor Insurance
Duty Insurance
Erection all risks Insurance (EAR)
Contractor's All Risk Insurance (CAR)
Machinery Breakdown Insurance
Product Liability Insurance
Cash Insurance
Business Premises Burglary Insurance
Shopkeeper's Insurance Policy
Rural Insurance
Householder's Insurance Policy (HHI)
Rajeshwari Mahilla Kalyan Bima Yojna
Sports Insurance

### Motor Insurance

Motor insurance has been classified according to types of vehicles, i.e. scooter/motor cycles, private cars, commercial vehicles as well as private and public goods or passenger and miscellaneous vehicles. No motor vehicle can ply in a public place unless it is insured against third party liability prescribed under Motor Vehicles Act, 1988.

### Export/Import Duty Insurance

This policy is normally taken by an exporter or importer to cover the payment of excise/import/export duty on the imported/exported goods.

### Erection All Risks Insurance (EAR)

Erection is the installation of Plant and Machinery and undertaking civil works. Therefore, E.A.R. insurance has become an important part of insurance business in all industrialized countries. Large projects like erection of Thermal Power Stations, Fertilizer Plants, Oil Refineries, etc. bring many risks for both the contractor (as agent) and the principal (the company putting up the project), i.e. it is possible to bear these risks in an economical manner by taking out an EAR Insurance.

### Contractor's All Risk Insurance (CAR)

Insurance products are tailor-made to suit all situations where human activities are concerned. So, this insurance has been specially designed to protect the interest of civil contractors against damage to or destruction of various civil engineering projects (undertaken) by them and in progress.

### Machinery Breakdown Insurance

The machinery break-downs are usual occurrences. Therefore, insurance scheme was tailor-made/developed to grant industry specific insurance cover for expensive plant, machinery and mechanical equipment.

### Product Liability Insurance

This is a variant of liability insurance. It is effected by the insurers for the producers of products, traded commercially when they are susceptible to claim on account of defect. This is a specialized policy as security for legal liability of producers if defective products are found by the buyers.

### Cash Insurance

Cash insurance policy intends to protect banks and

industrial or business establishments against loss of money in transit. Such money may be carried by their messengers or couriers and that may be in transit from one place to another.

**Business premises' Burglary Insurance**

There are goods kept in the stores or shops or halls/malls of business establishments. These are exposed to various risks, more particularly the risk arising from burglary and dacoity or even house-breaking. This policy covers contents of business premises against all risks of loss or damage by burglary and house breaking.

**Shopkeepers' Insurance Policy**

This policy is tailor-made to cover various risks and contingencies faced by small shopkeepers under single policy. It provides protection for property and interest of the insured and his partners in the shop.

**Rural Insurance (Agricultural/Allied Activities)**

The various important schemes under rural insurance category are Cattle insurance, Sheep and Goat insurance, Plantation/horticulture insurance, Poultry insurance and in fact it covers all farm and non-farm activities in agriculture. Banks advance loans to the farmers against crops and so, crop insurance policy is taken for securing their interest in case of fire or other damage to the crops. The government has brought out scheme of insurance for the farmers to insure their crops. Details of some schemes of rural insurance are given below.

**Milch cattle and/or Draught Animal Insurance**

This policy is meant for milk cows, milk buffaloes, bullocks. It provides risk cover of death due to accident including natural calamities, strikes, riots, etc. Maximum sum assured cannot be in excess of market value of the insured cattle.

**Sheep and Goat Insurance**

This policy covers the risk of death from diseases or accidents including natural calamities to sheep and goats.

### Plantation/Horticulture Insurance

This policy covers grapes, citrus fruits, chickoo, bananas, rubber, teak wood, tea, apple, oils, palms, floriculture, kadam and coconut. The policy shall cover and compensate the insured to the extent of loss or damage to the insured trees/fruits due to any one or more of risks like fire, lightning, storm, earthquake, cyclone, floods, riots, etc.

### Householder's Insurance Policy (HHI)

HHI policy is designed to cover various risks and contingencies faced by householders under a single policy. It provides protection to property and interest of the insured and his family members who permanently reside with the insured.

### Rajeswari Mahilla Kalyan Bima Yojna

This insurance scheme is framed for women. The policy under this scheme has been designed to provide relief to the family members of insured women in case of their death or disablement arising due to all types of accidents or death or disablement arising out of problems incidental only to women.

### Sports Insurance

This policy insures a comprehensive cover available to amateur sportsmen covering their sporting equipment, personal effects, legal liability and personal accident risks.

### *(2) Classification of Insurance from the Business Point of View*

Insurance can be classified into two broad categories from business point of view – Life Insurance and General Insurance:

#### *Life Insurance*

Life insurance may be defined as a contract by virtue of which the insurer, in consideration of payment of a certain amount of money, called premium, paid either in a lump sum or by periodical payments (in instalments), agrees to pay to the insured, or the person for whose benefit the policy is taken, an assured sum of money, on the happening of a specified event contingent on the human life or at the expiry of certain period, whichever is earlier.

### *General Insurance*

General insurance business refers to fire, marine and other insurance business, excluding life insurance, whether carried on singly or in combination with one or more of them.

### ***Classification of Insurance from Risk Point of View***

Insurance can be classified into the following four categories from risk point of view:

Personal Insurance

Property Insurance

Liability Insurance

Fidelity guarantee Insurance

### *(i) Personal Insurance*

Under personal Insurance, there is reference to the loss to life by accident or sickness to individual, which is covered under the policy. The insurer undertakes to pay the sum insured on the happening of certain event or on maturity of the period of insurance. Life insurance contains both the element of investment and protection while the accidental, sickness or health insurance contains the element of indemnity only.

The subject-matter of personal insurance is the person who is in the centre-stage. The life or health of a person is insured under personal insurance. Under personal insurance policy, the insured or his nominee is compensated financially in the event of death, or total or partial disablement of the insured.

The Law of Indemnity does not apply to life and other type of personal insurance. The partial or total disablement of a person cannot be evaluated in terms of money. Money cannot be any compensation for such losses or for the death of the insured. A fixed sum is undertaken to be paid on the occurrence of risk causing personal/physical loss to the insured persons.

### *(ii) Property Insurance*

Property insurance is a contract of indemnity. Under this contract, the insurer undertakes to compensate the other party against financial loss caused by a certain risk in consideration for a certain periodical payment, called premium.

Property is the subject-matter of the contract of property insurance. The insured cannot claim anything more than the value of property lost or the amount of policy, whichever is lower. Important types of property insurance are based on the kind of loss or damage: (a) Fire insurance, (b) Marine insurance, (c) Motor insurance, (d) Live-Stock Insurance, (e) Theft Insurance, and (f) Agriculture Insurance, etc.

*(iii) Liability Insurance*

Liability insurance is the major field of general insurance whereby the insurer promises to pay the damage to property or to compensate the losses suffered by the third party. The amount of compensation is paid directly to the third party. The areas of liability insurance include workmen's compensation insurance, third party motor insurance, etc. There may be various reasons for liability to arise, i.e. accident of a worker at the workplace, defective goods supplied/detected, and explosion in the factory during the process of production and formulation of poisonous gases within the factory due to the uses of chemicals and other such substances in the manufacturing process.

Liability insurance can be classified as follows:

*(i) Re-Insurance*

When an insurance company takes upon itself greater liability on account of insured risks than the limit which it itself is able to bear, then the insurance company may shift the excessive part of such risk to another insurer. This means that the insurance company (insurer) gets certain risks insured with another insurer and such an arrangement is called 'Re-insurance'.

*(ii) Workmen's Compensation Insurance*

This scheme was introduced with the objective of helping the employers in the events when they become liable to pay compensation to the workers under the provisions of labour laws. The insurance company undertakes to compensate the loss of employer which arises on account of liabilities towards the payment of compensation to the workers under the provisions of Fatal Accidents Act, Workmen's Compensation Act.

*(iii) Public Liability Insurance*

This is the type of insurance under which the insurance company undertakes to compensate the loss caused to third party. The concept of third party includes the public at large and a large number of risks are involved in daily life.

*(iv) Fidelity Guarantee Insurance*

Fidelity means loyalty, faithfulness and honesty. This insurance enables the insurance company to undertake to indemnity the insured against loss caused on account of dishonesty of the employees. Insurance company indemnifies the loss arising out of fraud, embezzlement, etc.

## Distinction between Life Insurance, Fire Insurance and Marine Insurance

It is important at this stage to know the distinction between Life Insurance, Fire Insurance and Marine Insurance. A table is furnished below depicting the difference between these types of insurance:

**Table showing the Differences between Life Insurance, Fire Insurance and Marine Insurance**

| *Sr. No.* | *Basic Parameter* | *Life Insurance* | *Fire Insurance* | *Marine Insurance* |
|---|---|---|---|---|
| 1. | Risk | Risk is certain but the time of happening is uncertain. | The occurrence of risk is uncertain. | The happening of an event is uncertain. |
| 2. | Period | Life insurance is effected for a longer period say 10, 15 years, etc. | It is generally for a year or lesser period. | It is also for a year or for a voyage |
| 3. | Insurable Interest | It must exist when policy is purchased. | It must exist both time i.e. when policy is purchased as well as when the loss occurs. | It must exist only when the loss occurs to the subject insured. |
| 4. | Premium | Premium is based upon nature of risk and tables are prepared. | Premium is based upon the types of risk insured. | Here also premium is calculated on the basis of risk involved. |
| 5. | Mode of payment of Premium | Premium can be paid in monthly, quarterly, half yearly or yearly instalments. | The whole premium is payable at the time of insurance | In marine insurance also, premium is paid in single instalment at the time of effecting insurance. |
| 6. | Indemnity | The principle of indemnity is not applicable as the loss in case of death cannot be determined. | In fire insurance, principle of indemnity is applicable. In case of floss, either the actual loss or sum insured, | In certain policies, amount of compensation may be more than the actual loss. |

*(Contd.)*

| *Sr. No.* | *Basic Parameter* | *Life Insurance* | *Fire Insurance* | *Marine Insurance* |
|---|---|---|---|---|
| | | | whichever is less, is paid to the insured. | |
| 7. | Object | The object is security as well as investment. | It provides protection against loss only | It is also effected for protection purposes. |
| 8. | Surrender Value | The life policy can be surrendered. On surrender, the insured gets the surrender Value. | These policies can not be surrendered and hence there is no question of receiving surrender value | These policies also cannot be surrendered. |
| 9. | Double Insurance | A person can purchase more than one policy for the same life. On death, loss will be paid on all policies. | Double insurance can be effected. But the actual loss cannot be claimed on all policies. | Here also, double insurance is possible. But the loss compensation cannot exceed the actual loss suffered. |
| 10. | Value of Policy | There is no question of under or over valuation of life policies. | The value of policy cannot be taken for more than the actual value of property or goods. | Under this insurance (except valued policy) also, the policy amount cannot exceed the actual value of property insured. |
| 11. | Determination of Premium | Premium payable can be determined with reference to life tables Easily. | Determination of premium is difficult on account of variety of risks involved. | Under marine insurance also, premium determination is a bit difficult. |

# 5

# Principles of Insurance

## INTRODUCTION

Insurance has been evolved by wise men, based on their life experience, as the mantra to broaden the cause of a particular risk over a number of persons who are exposed to it and who agree to insure themselves against it. Conceptualization requires imagination, creativity and quest to explore and devise new methods, ways and systems and procedures. Salute to those who did this marvel of the schematic framework to add one more class of institution in society!

Insurance helps to manage risks of various types. Risk is defined as uncertainty of a financial loss. The main functions of insurance include providing certainty, protection, risk sharing, and prevention of loss and capital formation.

As has been discussed in the previous chapters, the term 'insurance' has been defined as the technique in which a sum of money as premium is paid in consideration for the insurer's undertaking to incur the risk of paying a large sum upon happening of a particular uncertainty.

Insurance is a contract whereby—

(a) Certain sum, called premium, is charged as consideration,

(b) Against the payment of the said premium, a large sum is guaranteed to be paid by the insurer,

(c) The payment will be made in the shape of a certain/ definite sum, i.e. the loss incurred or the policy amount, whichever is less, and

(d) The payment is made only upon the happening of the contingency.

Therefore, insurance may be defined as a contract in which one party (insurer) agrees to pay to the other party (insured or beneficiary under the policy), a certain sum upon a particular unforeseen event (risk) taking place against which insurance was sought.

Every subject or discipline has certain generally accepted and systematically laid down standards or principles to achieve the underlying objectives. Insurance is also not an exception to this general rule. There is a body of doctrines commonly associated with the theory and procedures of insurance, guiding all stakeholders about the explanation and application of current policies and for making the best choice among the available alternatives.

These principles may be defined as the rules of action or code of conduct that are universally accepted by the different stakeholders involved in the business of insurance.

These are given in the table on next page for better and quick understanding due to visual effect:

## PRICIPLES OF INSURANCE

### (I) General Principles (or Essentials of Insurance Contract)

All agreements are contracts if they are made by the free consent of parties, competent to contract; for a lawful consideration, for a lawful object and are not expressly declared to be void. As we know, an agreement enforceable by law is called a contract. Like all general contracts, a contract of insurance is also required to fulfil all basic requirements as prescribed under section 10 of the Indian Contract Act, 1872. These requirements are given below:

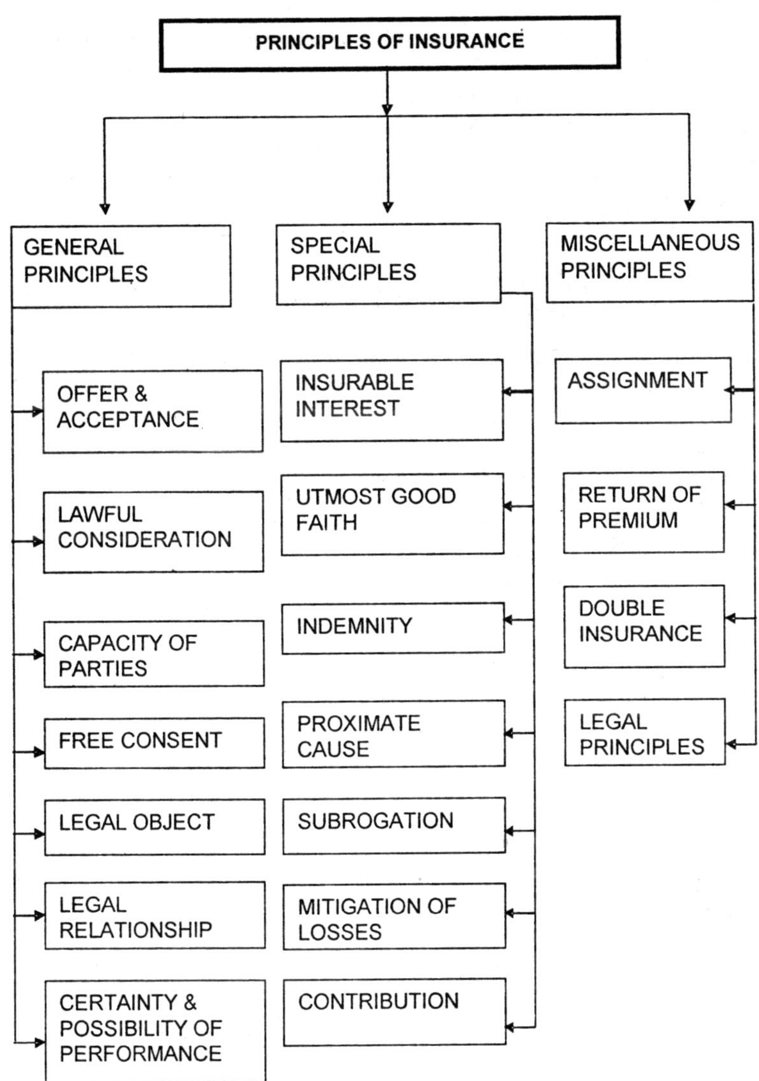


*(1) Offer and Acceptance*

It is the first requirement in the formation of a valid contract. The offer in insurance is intimation of the proposer's intention to purchase an insurance policy. When the insurer is ready to undertake the stated risk, it is called acceptance. In insurance, 'offer' is known as 'proposal'. It generally comes from the insured. If the insurer accepts the proposal, it is transformed into an agreement.

Therefore, when one party (potential policyholder) makes a proposal to another party (insurance company) and the latter accepts it, the proposal is said to be accepted. The moment the notice of acceptance is communicated, it would be a valid acceptance and valid contract is born instantaneously.

The procedure goes like this: potential policyholder who wants to get his risk insured is required to fill a prescribed proposal form in an insurance contract. The insurance company studies the offer made in the proposal form. It may accept it. To complete offer and acceptance as conditions precedent for creating valid contract, the notice of acceptance must be communicated to the insured along with the information regarding the premium payable and first premium receipt is issued.

*(2) Intention to Create Legal Relations*

The second basic principle of valid insurance contract is that both the parties must have common intention and act to create the legal relationship between them. It needs to be reiterated that the intention of both the parties is to create the legal relationship between themselves. Under the insurance contract, an insured expresses his intention while making a valid offer and the insurer expresses his intention on the acceptance of that offer which will bind both the parties in accordance with the terms and conditions of the insurance policy.

*(3) Parties Competent to make Contract*

Both the parties to insurance contract should be competent/capable of entering into contract, Section II of Indian Contract Act, 1872, lays down that every person is competent to contract—

Who is of the age of majority according to the law governing majority (under Indian Majority Act);
Who is of sound mind (can understand the full implications of the terms and conditions of contract); and
Who is not disqualified from entering into contract by any law to which he is subject (undischarged insolvent, etc.).

A valid contract requires that both the parties should understand the legal implications of each other's conduct as obligants (rights and duties/obligations) under the contract. A minor is not competent to contract. A person is said to be of sound mind, who can understand the contract at the time of making the contract. An alien enemy, an insolvent and criminal cannot enter into contract. Contract made by incompetent party/ parties will be void. Therefore, minor, persons of unsound mind and those with criminal background cannot take an insurance policy because they cannot enter into valid contract.

*(4) Free Consent*

It means when both the parties have agreed to a contract on the terms and conditions of the agreement in the same sense and spirit, they are said to have a free consent. Under Section 14 of Indian Contract Act, 1872, the consent is to be free when it is not caused by: coercion; undue influence; fraud; misrepresentation; and mistake.

Contract without free consent is voidable at the option of the party whose consent is not free except when there is fraud. In case of fraud, the contract is void.

*(5) Lawful Consideration*

It means when a party to an agreement promises to do something, he/she must get something in return. This is called 'consideration' in law. In insurance contract, the payment of premium is the consideration on the part of the insured. The contract of insurance is the contract of indemnity under which an insurance company, in consideration of premium, undertakes to compensate the loss of the stated insured against a specified risk, e.g. fire, marine hazard, accident or death. The consideration for which the insurance company undertakes to compensate the risk of insured is called the 'premium'. Premium may be paid either in lump sum or in periodical instalments spread over the specified period of policy. The insurance contract cannot be initiated without the payment of premium.

*(6) Lawful Object*

There is another important basic principle of insurance contract and that is the legality (or lawfulness) of objects. The object of the insurance contract should be lawful. It is lawful when:

It is not forbidden by law, or
It is not immoral, or
It is not opposed to public policy, or
It is not against the provisions of any law.

An unlawful object of any contract shall make it unenforceable at law. If the object of insurance, like the consideration, is found to be unlawful, the policy is void.

*(7) Certainty and Possibility of Performance*

Also important is the factor and that is the parties to a contract must agree on the terms of their mutually arrived agreement. They have to make their intention clear in their contract. The terms of contract must be definite or certain and capable of performance. If the agreement does not make it possible to ascertain its meaning and is impossible to perform, it cannot be enforced.

**(II) Specific or Fundamental Principles of Insurance Contracts**

Insurance contracts, to whichever category they may belong, they are based on the following fundamental principles:

*(1) Principle of Utmost Good Faith*

The contracts of insurance are, therefore, included in the category of the contracts uberima fiddie, i.e. those contracts which require absolute and utmost good faith on the part of the parties concerned. In this respect, such contracts are different from the ordinary business contracts; the latter are based on the rule of Caveat Emptor (let the buyer beware). For instance, in an ordinary sale of goods contract, the buyer is expected to take reasonable care to satisfy himself as to the genuineness and quality of goods intended to be purchased. If the goods turn out to be otherwise, the buyer will have no remedy against the seller and will have to bear the loss.

This principle compels both the parties to the contract to make full disclosure of all martial facts. The material facts mean those facts which may affect the decision of either party whether to enter or not to enter into the contract. Both the parties should have the same state of mind when entering into contract, only then the correct risk, rights and obligations can be ascertained. It also means that there should not be any concealment, misrepresentation, half-disclosure or fraud regarding the subject matter to be insured. Otherwise, the contract would be null and void. Under the contract of insurance, greater degree of good faith is expected from the proposer.

Therefore, the insured must disclose the following facts in a life insurance contract:

> Name, address and his occupation; date of birth, age, height, weight, etc.; facts about his life and habits; family history; information about health; quantum and nature of his income; and a certification by the proposer that he has answered all questions truly and correctly and agrees that the proposal and declaration shall be the basis of contract.

The breach of obligation of disclosing material facts may arise in the following:

> Non-disclosure of material facts; intentional non-disclosure of facts; non-disclosure of material facts by negligence or through oversight; and misrepresentation of material facts with fraudulent purposes/intention.
>
> In case of marine insurance, the offer-maker is required to disclose the following information about the subject matter of insurance:
>
> Nature of goods; method of packing; particulars of vessel carrying the goods; the port of shipment and destination along the route of journey; insurance cover required and condition of insurance; sum to be insured; and past claims information and experience.
>
> Section 20 of the Marine Insurance Act prescribes that in the following cases, the insured is not required to disclose the information:
>
> Facts already known to insurer; facts which the insurer is expected to know in the normal course of his business; facts which may tend to reduce the risk; and facts covered under the warranty.

It generally happens, and it begins a controversy and promotes litigation, that the insurance company finds it a better way to cancel the contract or dismiss the claim on account of non-disclosure of material facts and as a consequent breach of utmost good faith. Similarly, the insured may also avoid contract, in case the insurance company does not conduct in good faith in disclosing the scope of insurance.

In the case of fire insurance also, this principle is applicable. But this duty lies more on the offer-maker, who is in possession of all material facts relating to the subject matter to be insured. The insurer is also required to disclose important facts of policy to the prospective offerer. The following material facts are required to be disclosed in contract of fire insurance:

Location of property; details of construction and description of property; particulars of occupier, i.e. whether used for office, residence, shop, godown, manufacturing unit or service undertaking, etc.; nature of goods or material; and particulars of previous loss, if any, suffered.

*(2) Principle of Insurable Interest*

No person can enter into a valid contract of insurance unless he had insurable interest in the object to be insured. If it were not so, and if everyone were at liberty to take out an insurance policy on any object or life in the world, irrespective of his insurable interest, the contracts of insurance would have been reduced to mere gambling. In such conditions, insurance contract would be reduced to wagering contracts, which are not valid and cannot be enforced in a court of law as wagering is unlawful activity.

It is important to understand insurable interest. It is understood as an interest in the preservation of a thing, or continuation of a life, recognized by law. Whoever has such interest in an object or a life may insure that object or life. Truly speaking, insurable interest is in the nature of pecuniary or financial interest in an object or a life. It follows that a person can have an insurable interest only when he would stand to benefit financially by the continuation of object or life insured. In other words, he would be put to a financial loss by the happening of the event against which an object or the life of the person has been insured. Moreover, insurable interest is not a mere sentimental interest in the object insured. It is a pecuniary interest and it follows that the loss caused by the risk insured against must be capable of measurement in term of money. It is important to know the views expressed by Prof. Mehr, "If the happening of the event insured cannot cost the insured in terms of money, then there is no insurable interest".

### *Essentials of Insurable Interest*

The essentials of a valid insurable interest are as under:

There must be a specific subject matter to be insured; the insured should have the monetary benefit in the subject matter; the insured should have the legal relationship with the subject matter and it must be recognized by law; the insured must be the owner or possess the legal right or interest in the subject matter; the insured should be economically benefited by the existence of the subject mater; and the insurance-maker should suffer an economic loss on its non-existence or at the damage/death of the insured thing/person.

Insurable interest in a life insurance should exist when a policy is purchased. In a life insurance policy, the insurable interest is as follows:

A child has an insurable interest in the life of his father; a person has unlimited interest in his own life; a husband has an insurable interest in the life of his wife; a wife has an insurable interest in the life of her husband; a creditor has an insurable interest, to the extent of his debt, in the life of his debtor; a partner in a business has an insurable interest in the life or lives of his co-partner or co-partners; a company has an insurable interest in the life of a senior officer whose death may affect the profit of a business; and a servant has an insurable interest in the life of his employer.

Insurable interest in case of fire insurance must exist when insurance is effected as well as when the loss occurs. In fire insurance, however, insurable interest is as under:

The owner of the property has in his property; every

partner has an equitable interest in the properties of the firm; and an agent has an insurable interest in the property of his principal.

In marine insurance, insurable interest must exist only when the loss occurs. In Marine Insurance, the following persons have insurable interest:

The owner of a ship has an insurable interest in the ship; the cargo owner has in its cargo; the master and the crew of the ship have it in respect of their wages; a creditor who has advanced money on the security of cargo or ship, upto his claim; a ship owner in the freight to be received on the completion of journey; a mortgagor has an insurable interest to the full value of the property; a mortgagee has it to the extent of the sum due to him; and a trustee holds property in trust up to the extent of value of such property.

*(3) Principle of Indemnity*

All contracts of insurance, except for life insurance, are contracts of indemnity. The basic principle of insurance is to transfer the loss of a person to the insurance company which can easily be spread over a large number of policy holders. It is, therefore, necessary that a person will get exactly the same amount as he has lost due to the loss of his goods or damage to the property. The insured cannot be permitted to make profit out of his loss. If insurance company were to agree to compensate a higher sum than the actual loss, there would be a constant temptation on the part of the insured to destroy his goods or property intentionally and thus to reap profit out of insurance. If it is so, it will be against the basic principle and also an anti-social act. For example, if the goods are insured for Rs. 10,000 and the insured suffers a loss of Rs. 5000, he will be compensated for Rs. 5000 only. But if the insured has taken a policy for a smaller value than the actual loss, the insurance company is bound to pay only the amount of policy and not the actual loss (assuming that average clause is not applicable). This is so because by insuring his goods for a lesser value, the insured has expressed his intention of transferring only a part of his actual loss to the insurance company. The balance of loss will justifiably be met by the insured himself. Thus, for a policy of Rs. 4000 instead of Rs. 10,000 and the actual loss being Rs. 6000, insurance company will pay only Rs. 4000 and no more.

*Merits of Principle of Indemnity*: There are merits in the principle of indemnity which are as follows:

*(1) Avoidance of Under or Over-Insurance*

If this principle were not there, there would be tendency on the part of the insured to get things over-valued and then intentionally cause a loss and gain profit through enforcing insurance claim. Since in insurance only the actual loss is compensated, the insured would be discouraged to under or over value the policy's amount.

*(2) To Avoid Anti-social Activity*

This principle avoids anti-social act on the part of the insured. If the insured is allowed to make profit (which is against the principle of indemnity), there would be a constant temptation to destroy the property after it is insured. Therefore, the whole society will be doing only anti-social act to get easy money. But in insurance, only the cash value of loss of the insured is compensated even if it might have been insured for a greater amount.

*(3) To Maintain Premium at Low Level*

This principle helps the insurance company to maintain premium at low level because very few claims will be made and those will be genuine (within the actual value). If this principle is not made applicable, large amount of compensation will be required to be paid for a small loss. This will increase the cost of insurance and the companies would be forced to raise the premium. This will defeat the purpose of insurance.

**Main Features of Indemnity**

The following are the main features of the principle of indemnity:

(1) All contracts of insurance are contracts of indemnity except life insurance.
(2) There is an indirect relationship between the principle of indemnity and insurable interest because the insured is required to prove the amount of his actual loss and his interest therein in order to get compensation.

(3) The amount of compensation cannot exceed the amount of actual loss or the value of policy, whichever is less.
(4) After the compensation of loss, the insured cannot hold the ownership right on the things insured, i.e. the ownership right will shift to the insurance company.
(5) Valued policies are not covered under the principle of indemnity.

**Conditions for Indemnity**

The following conditions are required to be satisfied in full for the application of the principle of indemnity:

> Insured has to prove that he has suffered a loss on the subject matter insured and it is the actual monetary loss; the compensation cannot exceed the amount insured; insurer has a right to get back the extra amount, if any, paid to the insured; the insurer has a right to get back all amount received by the insured from the third party if the loss is fully indemnified by the insurer; and the principle of indemnity is not applicable in case of life insurance as the actual loss on death cannot be calculated.

**Liability of Insurer to Pay Compensation**

According to the application of the principle of indemnity, the insured can get only the actual loss of goods or property destroyed, or the insured amount, whichever is less. The loss payable is calculated after considering the following factors:

*(a) Sum Insured or the Value of Policy*

Every insurance policy is issued for a specific sum, called sum insured, which is the maximum limit or liability of the insurer in respect of goods insured. But the actual amount payable is calculated with reference to his actual loss or the sum insured, whichever is less.

*(b) Excess and Franchise Clause*

It is a practice that certain insurance polices are issued subject to excess or franchise clause. This clause says that under certain conditions a part of the loss shall be borne by the insured himself. The liability of insurer is limited by the imposition of excess or franchise clause. In case of imposition of this clause, if the loss does not exceed the limit, it is not paid at all and if it exceeds the limit, only excess is paid under 'Excess clause' and total loss is indemnified under the franchise clause.

*(c) Pro-Rata Average*

Sometimes, the policy contains an average clause. This condition is incorporated with two objectives, i.e. to penalize the insured for taking a policy for a lesser sum than the actual value of property and secondly, to limit the liability of insurer. According to the provision contained in this clause, the compensation payable by the insurer is proportionately reduced in case of under-insurance of goods or property. For example, a person may insure his property for Rs. 75,000. While the actual loss is assessed at Rs. 40,000 and the market value of the property at the time of loss is Rs. 1,00,000, the claim will be settled at Rs. 40,000 × 75,000/1,00,000 = Rs. 30,000. Obviously, in this case, the insured is penalized for Rs. 10,000 for under-insurance of his property. Formula is as under:

$$\text{Liability of Insurer} = \text{Actual Loss} \times \frac{\text{Insurance Policy Taken}}{\text{Market value of property at the time of loss}}$$

*(d) Salvage*

In the event of loss of insured property, it may be partially destroyed, not completely. Anything left after the occurrence of loss is known as 'Salvage'. The salvage or scrap left of the damaged or destroyed goods or property is to be reduced from the amount of indemnity payable to the insured.

*(e) Subrogation*

The doctrine of subrogation is an extension and corollary of the principle of indemnity. According to the principle of indemnity, the insurer steps into the shoes of the insured and becomes entitled to all the rights of the insured regarding the subject matter of insurance after the claim of the insured has been fully and finally settled. In some cases, there may be possibility of his getting something in addition to what he has received from the insurer. If the goods are not fully destroyed, the insured may try to obtain some amount of scrap in addition to the money received by him in the settlement of his claim. This will be against the principle of indemnity because the insured will get more than what he lost. Therefore, whatever is left of the damaged or destroyed goods or property will automatically pass on to the insurance company after the claim of the insured has been settled.

*(f) Contribution*

Sometimes, the insured may get his goods or property insured with more than one insurer. This is referred to as 'Double Insurance'. In the event of loss, the insured will be indemnified only against actual loss incurred against the risk insured. In such cases, the companies concerned will follow the principle of contribution for the payment of compensation. According to this principle, each insurance company will contribute that proportion of the loss which the policy issued by it bears to the total amount for which insurance has been effected with all the insurance companies. But in case where the insured chooses to get the amount of loss from one particular company or two of them, the paying company or companies can later on adjust loss paid with other insurer by receiving their contribution according to the proportion of their insured amount.

## Methods of Indemnifying

There are four alternative methods to indemnify an insured in the event of loss, damage or destruction of subject matter insured. These are as follows:

*Cash Payment*

Cash payment of the amount of claim of insurance is the easiest and a very common method of indemnification. After making proper enquiries of loss, the insurer accepts the claim by making cash payment through cheque to the insured.

*Repairs*

In some cases, where the subject matter of insurance is

partially damaged and is capable of being repaired, the insurer, instead of making cash payment, prefers to settle claim of the loss or damage by means of getting the damaged subject matter, repaired. The repair is authorized to the insured and the insured has to submit bill of repairs alongwith a note of satisfaction and then the repair bill is paid by the insurer.

*Replacement*

In case the subject of the insurance policy is damaged, lost or destroyed to such an extent that it is not possible and feasible to get it repaired, the insurance company may arrange the replacement of the property. Generally, this practice is followed in case of theft of property.

*Reinstatement*

Reinstatement is a method rarely used. In this case, the property damaged is reinstalled in its original position.

**Principle of Subrogation**

This principle is also known as 'Doctrine of Rights Substitution'. It is an extension of the principle of indemnity. Subrogation is the transfer of rights and remedies of the insured in the subject matter (property) to the insurer after indemnification.

In other words, the insurer steps into the shoes of the insured and becomes entitled to all rights of action against the third party to cover the loss from the responsible person regarding the subject matter of insurance after the claim of the insured has been fully settled and paid.

The principle of subrogation refers to the right of the insurer to stand in the place of the insured after the settlement of a claim. The insurer can recover the loss from the third party. There always exists a possibility of getting something in addition to the claim received from the insurer by the insured, e.g. value of scrap, damages from the person responsible for the loss and several other alternatives.

**Definition of Subrogation**

According to Federation of insurance Institutes, "Subrogation is the transfer of rights and remedies of the insured to the insurer who has indemnified the insured in respect of the loss".

According to Dinsdale—

"Subrogation may be defined as the insurer's right to receive the benefit of all the rights of the insured against third parties which, if satisfied, will extinguish or diminish the ultimate loss sustained".

## Essentials of Subrogation

*(i) Extension of Principle of Indemnity*

It is the extension and corollary of the principle of indemnity. According to principle of indemnity, only the actual loss is compensated to the insured. If the goods or property are partially damaged or destroyed, the insurer can recover some amount after the claim is fully and finally settled with the insured. The loss to property may be caused by an act of a third party. Accordingly, the insured is required to subrogate all his rights in favour of the insurer to reduce his paid compensation.

*(ii) Subrogation is the Substitution*

All rights and remedies available to the insured are transferred to the insurer after the settlement of claim. Insurance company is substituted in place of insured for all matters concerning the loss.

*(iii) Subrogation is only up to the Amount of Payment*

The insurer is substituted only up to the amount of compensation paid to the insured. If the insured has been compensated by the third party after he has been indemnified by his insurer, he (insured) is liable to compensate the insurer for the amount received by him from the third party.

*(iv) Subrogation may be Applied before Payment*

If the insured is compensated to some extent by the third party before being fully indemnified by the insurer, then the insurer can pay only the balance amount of the loss.

*(v) Personal Insurance*

The principle of subrogation is not applicable in case of personal insurance.

**Need of Subrogation**

The principle of subrogation has been introduced with the aim to protect the interest of insurers. In case of loss without it, the insured may be in a position to collect more money than his actual loss by selling the salvage. According to this principle, since the insured is required to subrogate all his rights in favour of the insurer after the loss is settled, cannot make profit out of insurance policy. Moreover, the insurer has a right to claim loss if it is caused by the act of third party.

**Features of Subrogation**

Subrogation has the following features:

(a) It is a corollary to and outcome of the principle of indemnity and is applicable in all contracts of indemnity.

(b) It is applicable only after the payment of loss by the insurer.

(c) It may also arise even before indemnification of loss except in case of marine insurance policies.

(d) The insured is required to provide all help to insurer while enforcing the claim against the defaulters.

(e) The insurer has a right to sue the third party in the name of the insured. But all expenses of litigation are to be borne by the insurer.

(f) The insured will hold the amount of compensation received from the third party in trust for the insurer if he has already been compensated by the insurer.

(g) The right of subrogation arises from the acts of torts, contract, salvage, etc.

(h) The principle of subrogation is automatically applied even without any express condition in the contract in this regard.

(i) Under this principle, the insurer cannot recover from the defaulter party anything more than the amount of compensation paid to the insured. The right of recovery is limited to the amount of claim paid to the insured.

## How Right of Subrogation Arises?

Subrogation rights arise in the following ways:

### *Tort*

Where the insured has sustained some damage, lost right or incurred liability due to atrocious acts of some other person and the insurer has indemnified the loss, the insured is entitled to take action to recover the loss from the wrong doer.

### *Contract*

Subrogation relates to rights, which arise out of certain contracts. This may arise where there is a custom of the trade to which the contract applies. Subrogation right may arise from contract where a person has contractual right to compensation regardless of fault.

### *Subject Matter of Insurance*

Sometimes, a situation may arise, where an insured has been indemnified and the subject matter treated as lost. Once the claim has been compensated, the insured cannot claim the salvage or scarp.

## Principle of Causa Proxima (Immediate and the Nearest Cause)

The principle of proximate cause is also called 'causa proxima'. The term causa proxima is a Latin term which means, the nearest cause or proximate cause or immediate cause. Causa proxima is the real cause of loss and not the distant cause. It is helpful in deciding the actual cause of loss when a number of causes have contributed to the occurrence of loss. The maxim used in this regard is 'Sed Causa proxima non remote spectator' which means that 'see the nearest or direct cause and not the remote or distant cause'. The real, nearest and direct cause of loss must be seen while making payment of the loss. If the real cause of loss is insured, the insurer is liable to compensate the loss, otherwise the insurer may not be responsible for loss.

In other words, while deciding the liability of the insurer, the direct, nearest or proximate cause and not the remote or indirect cause of the loss is to be taken into account.

### Meaning and Definition of the Doctrine of Causa Proxima

The doctrine of causa proxima is in fact based on the law of cause and effect which means that having proved that cause and effect thereof, there remains no need to proceed further.

In case of Pawsey *Vs*. South Union and National Insurance Co., it was observed that:

> "Proximate cause means the active and efficient cause that sets in motion a train of events which bring about result, without the intervention of any force started and working activity from new and independent source".

Thus, the cause must be 'immediate cause' to be 'proximate'. The expression 'immediate' should be understood in terms of effectiveness or efficiency. In other words, proximate cause is the cause, which is effectual in producing that result.

The proximate cause means that direct, the most dominant and most effective cause of which the loss is the natural consequence. It is the cause, which is most closely and directly connected with the loss, not necessarily in time but in efficiency and effectiveness.

### Practical Aspects of Doctrine of Causa Proxima

There is no problem in deciding the question of liability of the insurer if the loss is the outcome of only one event. But the loss may be the result of two or more events or causes. It becomes necessary to locate the effective and most powerful cause of loss. It is not easy to decide the proximate cause when it is caused by a large number of events.

Events or causes for the purpose of determining the practical use of doctrine of causa proxima may be divided into three categories:

#### *(1) Operation of a Single Cause*

Where there is a single event which causes the loss, it will be a clear case of proximate cause and the insurer will be held liable for the event if it is insured under the policy, e.g. if a person dies in road accident, the accident will be the proximate cause under the personal accident policy.

*(2) Concurrent Causes*

In case of concurrent causes, i.e. causes occurring simultaneously, and the policy has not excluded perils, there arises liability of insurer if one of the causes is 'insured peril' and other causes may be ignored. The concurrent causes may be separable and inseparable causes. Separable causes are those causes which can be separated from each other. The loss caused by a particular separable cause, if insured against peril, will be compensated by the insurer. In case the circumstances are such that causes are inseparable, then the insurer is not liable at all when there exists any expected event.

*(3) Successive Causes*

Where there is a chain of events causing a loss to the subject matter insured, the liability of insurer would arise if the original cause event is an 'insured peril'.

**Principle of Mitigation of Loss**

Mitigation of loss means to minimize or to decrease the severity of the loss. Under this doctrine, it is prescribed that whenever the event insured against occurs, it will be the duty of the insured to take all such steps to minimize the loss as he would have taken when the subject matter was not insured. The logic behind the principle of mitigation of loss is that the insured should not become careless and passive at the time of loss simply because his property had been insured. He must act like any uninsured prudent person.

Accordingly to this principle, the insured must act reasonably to make the loss less severe and try to make each and every effort and arrangement to minimize the loss in the event of loss occurring.

**Principle of Contribution**

Sometimes, the same subject matter of insurance could be covered by different policies. It is possible that these policies are taken in different contexts under different portfolios or even multiple policies for extra protection. Here, as we saw in the case of subrogation, there is a possibility that the insured might get compensated more than once from different sources for the same loss, thereby making a profit. The principle of contribution is relevant in this context.

In the event of multiple policies covering the same subject matter of insurance, the principle of contribution provides for an equitable sharing of any loss between all the insurers according to their respective insurances. (Denis Riley, 1967) In cases where a risk is insured vide more than one insurance policy (for example, loss of luggage on both a trivial and household policy), the two insurers concerned may share that cost of any claim. When a loss is insured under more than one insurance policy, for example, a travel policy and a household policy, in the event of a claim the two insurers share the cost. The principle of contribution like that of subrogation seeks to prevent the insured from getting compensations from different sources for the same loss, thereby violating the principles of indemnity.

Contribution is the right of an insurer who has paid claim under a policy, to call upon other insurers for the same loss, to contribute. This principle is applicable to all contracts of indemnity except the life insurance.

**Definition of Contribution**

According to the Federation of Insurance Institutes, Mumbai—

> "Principle of contribution refers to the right of an insurer who has paid for a loss under a policy to recover a proportionate amount from other insurers who are liable for the loss".

Therefore, contribution is the right of an insurer, to call upon other insurers liable for the same loss to contribute the payment to the one who has paid the loss under a policy. This doctrine ensures an equitable distribution of losses between different insurers.

*Need of Principle of Contribution*

Sometimes, a person may get his goods insured with more than one insurer. This is known as double insurance, in the event of loss if he got his loss indemnified from all insurers, he will receive more compensation than his actual loss. It is against the principle of indemnity. In case of loss, he may choose to get his loss compensated by one or more insurers taken together. In such a case when an insured chooses to collect his loss from one or two of them, the paying company or companies can later claim proportionate amount from other insurers.

*Pre-Requisites of the Principle of Contribution*

The principle of contribution is not applicable in all cases of 'double insurance'. The following are the pre-requisites for the application of principle of contribution:

(a) The subject matter or property of insurance must be common to all insurers. In simple words, it means that the goods or properties to be insured must be the same in case of all policies issued.
(b) The risk event which causes the loss must be common to all policies in order to attract the principle of contribution.
(c) The policies must be legally enforceable which means that the policies must be valid. These/none of these must not be invalid, void, null or defective at the time of loss.
(d) The policies must be in force at the time of loss. The principle of contribution is applicable only to those polices which shall be in force at the time of occurrence of loss.
(e) The insurable interest must be the same under all policies. All policies must be effected in favour of an insured.

## Miscellaneous Principles

There are also certain miscellaneous principles of insurance beside the general and specific principles. These are as under:

*(i) Principle of Assignment*

Principle of assignment is also known as transfer of interest. It is necessary to distinguish between assignment of the subject matter of property of insurance; the policy and the policy money when payable.

In case of marine and life insurance policies, assignments can be made freely without the prior consent of the insurer. But in case of fire insurance and accident insurance policies, assignment without advance consent of insurer is not valid.

The life insurance policy can be assigned freely for a legal consideration or even without consideration in case of love and affection.

Assignment refers to transfer of interest of policy to third party by the insured. The assignment shall be complete and effective only on the execution of such endorsement either on the policy itself or on a separate deed. Notice for this purpose must be given to the insurer who will acknowledge the assignment. Once the assignment is complete, it cannot be revoked by the assignor. The life policies are the only policies, which can be assigned whether the assignee has an insurable interest or not. A marine cargo policy is freely assignable unless it contains conditions expressly prohibiting assignment. It may be assigned either before or after loss. It may be assigned through endorsement or in any other customary manner.

Assignment of fire insurance cannot be done without prior consent of insurer. Change in insurable interest in fire insurance policies is not valid unless the consent of the insurer has been obtained.

### (II) Principle of Return of Premium

The amount of premium once paid cannot ordinarily be refunded. However, in the following cases the premium paid is returnable.

#### *By Agreement in the Policy*

The insured may pay full premium while effecting the insurance but it may be agreed in policy to return it wholly or partly on the happening of certain events.

#### *For Reasons of Equity*

Equity implies a condition that the insured shall not receive the price of running a risk he bears. So, the contract does not come into effect in this case or it is held to be void. It can be established by the following points:

#### *Non-attachment of Risk*

Where the subject matter insured or part thereof, has never

been imperiled, e.g. such policy is term insurance with returnable premium. Again, the premium is returned to the policy-holder if death does not occur during the period of insurance.

*Undeclared Balance of an Open Policy*

Policy may be cancelled and premium may be returned for short interest allowed provided there was no further interest in the policy.

*(i) Payment of Premium is Apportional*

The apportioned part of the consideration is refundable when a part of policy interest is not involved. For example, insurance may be taken for a voyage in stages, each stage being rated separately. In such a case if some stages are not completed, the premium, relating to the journey not completed, is returnable.

Where the assured has no insurable interest throughout the currency of risk, the premium is returnable provided the policy was not attached by way of wagering.

Unreasonable delay in commencing the voyage may also entitle the insurer to cancel the insurance by returning the premium.

*(ii) Principle of Over-insurance by Double Insurance*

If there is over insurance by way of double insurance, a proportionate part of several premium is returnable provided that if the polices are taken at different times and any earlier policy has at any time borne the whole risk or if a claim has been paid, premium on the first policy cannot be returned. When double insurance is effected knowingly by the insured, no premium is returnable.

*(iii) Legal Principles*

Life insurance is a contract and, therefore, the provisions of the Contract Act, 1872 are applicable. The provisions of other Acts like Transfer of Property Act, Estate Duty Act, Indian Stamp Act, Law of Limitation, Succession Act, etc. are applicable to life insurance.

**New for Old Part(s) Principle**

When a part of a machine or a vehicle is replaced

following an accident, the insurer pays for the cost of a new part to see that the machine is reinstated to its working condition. Here, indemnity is seen as the process of putting the machinery back to working condition and not like replacement of the old part with another old part. In the bargain, the insured gets a new part instead of the old part and the insurer would be meeting the cost of new spare parts.

It is a term used to describe a basis of cover, usually within property insurance, whereby the insurer agrees to pay the full replacement cost of the damaged insured item and not what the actual item is valued at the time of the loss. This principle is used in areas such as marine hull, machinery parts, vehicle parts and the like.

In other words, it denotes replacing old damaged parts or equipment with new ones rather than repairing them. In an insurance cover for property or equipment, an item lost or destroyed is replaced by the equivalent new item without deduction for age or wear and tear of the old item and regardless of price inflation. Items lost or damaged beyond repair will be at the present purchase price. The advantage is that the insured will not be left out of pocket when replacing items. However, new for old does not apply to item like clothing, household linen and pedal cycles where wear and tear needs to be taken into consideration. New for old or replacement cost option is usually offered at the proposal stage of arranging insurance and will carry a higher premium charge than a strict indemnity only policy, which will take into account a deduction for wear and tear.

**Reinstatement**

Reinstatement is a claim settled on option agreed between the insured and the insurer, stating that the insurer would make good the damaged property of the insured, rather than pay a monetary amount. Reinstatement valid is the cost of making good the insured damaged property accordingly the reinstatement clause or memorandum is usually used within a property policy that states the duty of the insurer if they decide to reinstate the property in the event of an insured loss. For this benefit, the insurer would usually charge a policyholder an additional premium.

However, reinstatement of the loss by the insurer is not followed strictly due to various practical issues. Reinstatement would be a costly exercise for the insurer. Again, if he were not able to reinstate to the satisfaction of the insured, his work would have to be abandoned. The insured may not practically prefer reinstatement, as he would like to have better buildings or newer technology or higher capacity equipment to replace the loss. In practical terms, the insured would prefer receiving the full cost of reinstatement in lieu of actual reinstatement. This cost would comprise of (i) the indemnity *per se,* (ii) wear and tear, depreciation, and (iii) cost of inflation between date of loss and probable time of reinstatement, this clause helps in bringing the insured closer to his start prior to the loss, instead of getting a lump sum in the event of the loss. However, there is a possibility of an insured getting away with a lower sum insured (and lower premium) utilizing this clause. Hence, the condition of average (or adjusting the claim payable to the sum insured chosen by the insured) is applied. Reinstatement at 85 per cent average is only applied to a claim settlement, if the building's sum insured is less than 85 per cent of the reinstatement value.

Apart from the above reinstatement that is applied in the case of a loss, there is a concept of reinstatement of premium. Under property insurance, reinstatement premium is the amount of premium payable by the policyholder to restore the sum insured to its original level, following an insured loss.

## Agreed Value

Agreed value policies or valued policies are considered a practical way out in many cases where assessing the value of a loss post the event can pose problems. There could be different reasons for such situations and in the context of different types of policies. Moral and morale hazards may be involved in areas such as health insurance. In case of marine cargo, there could be difficulty in finding out the value at the location of the loss. In such cases, the value would be the invoice price plus some other objective measure such as freight, which seldom violate the principle of indemnity. In fire and engineering project insurance, the value of stock may have changed due to some processes involved, or by market conditions, inflation or currency fluctuations. In the case of rarities and personal possessions such as paintings, fitted items or prizes, sentimental reasons would make objective evaluation unacceptable. Values of such items can be extremely difficult to assess post loss. In areas like personal accident, measuring personal losses post event may be painful.

As situations of over insurance and total losses can cause overpayments, the reasonableness of fixing the agreed value becomes important. The agreed value concept has pitfalls as well. If the value reduces between the date of agreeing and the date of loss causing an over-indemnification, the valuation in case of partial losses can be difficult. In some cases, partial losses may have to be treated on a different basis. In total losses, the value of salvage may vary widely between the insured and an objective assessor.

### Material Fact

Any information that could affect the underwriter's assessment of the risk is regarded as a material fact. The underwriter's assessment can include fixing the insurance premium, framing the condition that would operate in the event of a claim, or even the decision to accept the risk itself. The Marine Insurance Act, 1906 defines the concept as follows:

> "Every circumstance is material which would influence the judgment of a prudent insurer in fixing the premium or determining whether he will take the risk".

Failure by the policyholder or proposer to inform insurers of all relevant material facts that affect the insured risk is referred to as non-disclosure. Non-disclosure of material facts could normally result in a reduced indemnity depending on the level of non-disclosure. However, if the material facts that were not disclosed are found to be very crucial or if there is any serious misrepresentation of facts, insurers are entitled to treat it as a serious matter and refuse to deal with any claims or void the policy from the start of cover.

### Reciprocal Duty

Reciprocity is another guiding principle in insurance. Fundamental principles that are binding on one party call for reciprocal behaviour from the other party as well, whether stated or otherwise. While the insured is expected to disclose all material facts, the insurer should also disclose to him benefits under the policy that he normally may not know about. For instance, an insured has to inform the insurer that the old wiring in a block of the factory has caused short circuits in the recent past and due to insufficient budget allocation, rewiring has not been done yet. Reciprocally, the insurer should inform the insured that the automatic fire protection system he has installed in the block would entitle him to a discount, or that as a fire safe door had been fixed in the block, the loading for improper electrical installations would be applicable only to that block and not to other communicating blocks.

## Condition of Average

The principle of average requires the amount of a claim payment to be reduced proportionately if a policyholder has not insured his property for its full value, or full replacement cost. The insurer has to meet the losses of a few from the money pooled from many. If an insured opts for a lesser sum insured and consequently pays a less than adequate amount as premium, it is only logical that the loss also gets reduced proportionally. An insured who contributes less to the common pool is allowed to reap only lesser benefits from the pool. If a policy is subject to average and if the sum insured at the time of a loss is less than the actual value of the property insured, the amount of claim under the policy will also be reduced in proportion to the under-insurance. In mathematical terms:

$$\text{Allowable Claim} = \frac{\text{Loss} \times \text{Sum Insured}}{\text{Value at Risk}}$$

The concept of average is applied by dividing the sum insured by the actual value at risk and applying the same proportion on the loss by multiplying the amount of loss by the result, making the loss proportionate to the sum insured. The remaining part of the sum insured is treated as actually covered by the insured himself who has retained the premium with him. Hence, he has to pay to himself the proportionate amount of the loss as well.

**General Average**

Concepts of general and particular averages are not to be confused with the condition of average stated above.

General average is a contribution made by all parties involved (usually) in a sea adventure, towards a loss occasioned by the sacrifice of the property of some of the parties in the common interest for the benefit of all. In order to save a ship in peril of sinking during a storm, some of the cargo may have to be thrown overboard. In the exigencies of hazards faced at sea, crew members often have precious little time to determine precisely whose cargo they are jettisoning. Thus, to avoid quartering that could waste valuable lives/goods, there arose the equitable practice whereby all the merchants whose cargo was on board would be called on to contribute a portion, based upon a share or percentage, to the merchant or merchants whose goods had been tossed overboard to avert imminent peril. The ship owner and the owners of the saved cargo obviously benefit at the expense of the owners of the jettisoned cargo. It is called general average, because the loss is applicable in general to all the ship, the cargo and the freight at risk saved by the sacrifice. This was demand unfair and the principle of general average evolved so that all parties would contribute in such a situation.

It is believed that the inhabitants of Rhodes invented the concept of the general average. Merchants whose goods were being shipped together would pay a proportionally divided premium that would be used to reimburse any merchant whose goods were jettisoned during storm or sinkage. While general average traces its origins in ancient maritime law, it still remains a part of the admiralty law of most countries. The first condition of general average was the York Antwerp Rules of 1890. American companies accepted it in 1949. General average requires three elements as stated by Justice Grier in Barnard *Vs.* Adams.

- "A common danger: A danger in which vessel, cargo and crew all participate, a danger imminent and apparently "inevitable, except by voluntarily incurring the loss of a portion of the whole to save the remainder".
- "There must be a voluntary jettison, jactus, or casting

away, of some portion of the joint corner for the purpose of avoiding this imminent peril, periculi imminent is evitandi causa, or in other words, a transfer of the peril from the whole to a particular portion of the whole".

- "This attempt to avoid the imminent common peril must be successful".

In simple words, the law of general average is a legal principle of maritime law, according to which all parties in a sea venture proportionally share any loss resulting from a voluntary sacrifice of a part of the ship or cargo to save the whole in an emergency. Thus, if one ships cargo on a vessel that is involved in a loss, he may face a claim against him even though his goods are not damaged. This aspect is questioned by some insured as unfair. However, actually it is not unfair because all the insured are part of the same marine venture, went through the same situations, and anyone could have suffered the loss.

**Particular Average**

Particular average is the damage or partial loss happening to the ship or cargo or freight, in consequence of some fortuitous or unavoidable accident, and it is borne by the individual owners of the articles damaged or by their insurers. The term is usually used in marine insurance. In contrast to general average, particular average does not deal with damage voluntarily incurred in case of a cargo consignment, the measure of indemnity varies depending on whether there was a total loss to some of the cartons sent, or whether damage was sustained by some part of the consignment. The value is derived as an average of the CIF invoice value (comprising cost, insurance and freight) for the entire consignment. As particular average means a partial loss insurance cover, policies issued on total loss cover are said to be on free of particular average (FPA) which means excluding partial losses (or total loss only). FPA is a set of marine insurance conditions providing a very narrow cover. Another term relating to average that is used in marine insurance is petty averages that are sundry small charges, which occur regularly, and are necessarily defrayed by the master in the usual course of a voyage. These include port charges, common pilotage, and the like, which could be borne partly by the ship and/or partly by the cargo.

**Sue and Labour/Particular Charges**

Sue and labour/particular charges are charges incurred by or on behalf of the insured for the safety and preservation of the subject mater insured. These are different from general average, particular average and salvage charges. In practice, particular average is treated synonymously with sue and labour.

The principles stem from the theory that the insured should at all times, act as if he/she were uninsured. That is, he should take all reasonable care that he would have taken had the subject matter been uninsured. The sue and labour clause requires the ship owner to make every attempt to reduce or save the exposed interest from loss. Under the terms of the values, the insurer pays for any necessary costs incurred in carrying out the requirements of the sue and labour clause. Thus, if a ship is stranded, under the sue and labour clause, the hull owner would be required to hire salvers and get it towed to the nearest port. In case of fragile cargo such as bottles of jam, this logic applies in taking due care of the consignment, say, with adequate packing and proper labelling. If a heavy machine tilts and damages the cartons containing the jam bottles, the cartons may have to be shifted to a safer place on the ship. Also, the damaged cartons may have to be opened and broken bottles removed so that the leaking contents do not rot and damage the remaining jam bottles by spoiling the labels or by attracting ants and insects. Such insuring costs are reasonably incurred short of destination. In averting or minimizing the loss, these are termed sue and labour charges and are payable by the insured if these costs are incurred after the goods reach their destination, such as some additional costs are incurred for cleaning up the remaining bottles and re-labelling them to make them saleable, these are treated as particular charges. Sue and labour follows a loss or damage making incident, whereas particular average can be incurred to avoid or avert the threat of an imminent loss. Differences like these are treated as academic by many authors, and in actual practice both the terms are treated almost synonymously.

## Excess and Deductibles

In an insurance policy, the deductible or excess is the portion of any claim that is not covered by the insurance provider. That is, only the amount that is in excess of the deductible is recoverable. It is normally quoted as a fixed amount and is a part of most policies covering losses to the policyholder. The deductibles must be met by the insured, or in other words, paid by the insured before the benefits of the policy can apply. An excess can apply is two-ways: either as a voluntary excess at the instance of the insured to obtain a discount on the premium, or as a compulsory excess imposed by the insurer for underwriting reason such as avoiding larger number of small claims and their associated administration costs. Often, the second case is specifically referred to as a deductible.

Either way, the excess or deductible is the amount of a claim that is the responsibility of the insured or where he is his own insurer. In simple terms, it is the amount of the claim that you have to pay out of your own pocket. In a typical automobile insurance policy, a deductible will apply to claims arising from damage to or loss of the vehicle, caused by accidents for which the holder is responsible, or by theft. If a person has an insurance policy for his car with Rs. 5000 as deductible for damages, in the event of an accident costing Rs. 8000 worth of damage to the car, the insurance company would pay not Rs. 8,000 but Rs. 3,000 only. The insured is responsible for the first Rs. 5000 worth of damage (the deductible). Most health insurance policies and some travel insurance policies have deductibles as well. Generally, for a higher deductible, the premium is lower and *vice-versa*. Some medical insurance policies have a deductible that does not cover the cost of routine outpatient visits (e.g. to a doctor's clinic). The concept can operate on per event (per condition) basis or a per year basis, explained below:

### *Per Event Basis*

This most common form of deductible is applied on a per event basis. The deductible amount is agreed upon between the insurance company and the policyholder on each occasion that a claim arises for each medical condition that requires treatment, the insured will be required to pay a percentage over fixed sum of the treatment costs. For example, a deductible of Rs. 1000 is applied for the treatment of an illness. If the total bill comes to Rs. 5000, then the insurance company reimburses Rs. 4000. If the total bill from three occasions of treatment comes to Rs. 15,000 in a year, the insurance company reimburses Rs. 12,000 (Rs. 15,000 less Rs. 3000 as deductibles for three occasions @ Rs. 1000 per occasion).

*Per Year Basis*

In a per year form of deductible, an annual limit for deduction applies instead of a per event basis. The insurance company and the policyholder agree upon an annual limit of deductible and not a claim by claim deductible. Once the claims have reached this limit, the insurance company reimburses all further expenses in full. The insured will be required to pay for their treatment up to the agreed annual limit and the insurance company will be responsible for all further costs. In the above case, if Rs. 1000 is agreed as the deductible, the insured will be required to bear the first Rs. 1000 for the treatment he receives in the year. If the total bill comes to Rs. 5000 for the first occasion of treatment, the insurance company reimburses Rs. 4000. If there are two more occasions of treatment of Rs. 5000 each in the same year, the insurance company does not make any further deductions and the full claim is reimbursed on these subsequent two occasions.

**Co-insurance or Co-pay**

This is a form of excess used in some markets, where the insurance company requires the policyholder to pay a certain amount, most often expressed as percentage of the total cost. Co-insurance usually applies for dental, maternity treatments and outpatient treatment where the client will bear a percentage of the total expenses. For example, if an insurance company requires 20 per cent co-insurance and the total bill comes to Rs. 1000 the policyholder will bear Rs. 200 and then the insurance company will pay the remaining Rs. 800.

*Franchise*

This concept is similar to excess and deductibles in that the insurer makes no settlement if the total claim is below the franchise figure. In case of excess, deduction is made when a loss crosses an agreed figure. Franchise is different from excess in that no deduction is made once the loss crosses the agreed figure. This figure, however, applies as a threshold level for a claim to be considered. If the claim is more than the franchise figure, the claim is paid in full. In the above example, if the franchise figure is Rs. 1000, no claim under Rs. 1000 is payable, just as in the case of excess. However, if a loss exceeds Rs. 1000, the entire amount is paid without any deduction. Franchisees are becoming less and less common in modern insurance practice though machinery breakdown covers sometimes use time franchise.

### *First Loss*

First loss denotes a policy where the sum insured is accepted to be less than the value of the property but the insurer undertakes to pay claims up to the sum insured, without application of average. It is a contract written on such an amount as to cover only an insured's expected loss during the policy period with no other insurance in existence. It is a type of partial insurance (which covers less than the full value of goods or property at risk) where both the insured and the insurer acknowledge that the 'subject to average (see average) rule' does not apply. 'First Loss Policies' cover only the estimated largest possible loss and are often used in theft insurance, covering high value goods that would be physically impossible to steal in a single burglary, that is where the possibility of total loss is extremely remote (such as in case of a large store).

In other words, it is an accepted form of partial insurance where the insured decides he would not suffer a total loss and selects a maximum insured sum for any loss that is probable. The sum insured is often decided by calculating the maximum probable loss (MPL) or probable maximum loss (PML). The PML of a particular risk is the estimate of the maximum loss that would occur as a result of damage caused by the most destructive peril to be insured, in regard to the location, construction, occupation and protection of the risk. PML is usually expressed as a percentage of the sum insured. It is important that first loss sums insured are used only on first loss policies where average does not apply. In the usual insurances if the sum insured does not represent the full value, the insured will not get a full settlement of any loss. In some markets, first loss is used to refer to a policy whose limits are reduced (and not reinstated) by loss payments. There are also contexts where the term first loss is used to denote a policy that covers only a single loss during the policy period or that provides coverage of multiple locations for only the first loss at each location during the policy period.

**Performance Ratios**

Insurance companies have to constantly assess and reassess the effectiveness of their various strategies and readjust them based on their findings. The assessments have to be objective, scientific and based on quantifiable parameters so that they are reliable. Performance is assessed essentially from three angles, the company's exposure, the company's actions, and its results.

*(1) Exposure Ratios*

These ratios essentially assess where the company is placed in the insurance market and in comparison to the other companies. In other words, it indicates the relative position of the insurer in the environment in which it operates.

*Market Share*

It indicates the insurer's share in the total pie (market). That is considering the total market as 100, how much of it the company has been able to capture for itself. This is often expressed as line graph or in table or in pie chart.

$$\text{Market Share} = \frac{\text{GDP of the particular company}}{\text{Total GDP of the market}} \times 100$$

The pie chart enables an insurance company to visualize its standing in terms of the share of the market that it controls.

Relative Market Share is another term used for comparison purposes. The comparison can be with the share of the biggest player or with an average share.

Relative Market Share (against biggest share)

$$\text{RMS} = \frac{\text{GDP of the particular company}}{\text{Total GDP of the market}} \times 100$$

In the line graph given in figure the market share of the company, the largest market share (the highest market share) is taken to be 100 per cent. The company that wants to compare itself with the largest company works out its share as compared to that of the largest company's share.

Similarly, an average company is taken as 100 for comparison to find out where the company comparing its share stands as compared to the Average Company:

$$\text{Average GDP share} = \frac{\text{Total GDP of the market}}{\text{Number of Players}}$$

Relative market share (Against average shares)

$$= \frac{\text{GDP of the particular company}}{\text{Average GDP share}} \times 100$$

Persistence Ratio is considered a yard stick to evaluate the market performance of the company *vis-à-vis* a past period. The most common comparison is between the premium collection of the current month and the premium collection of the corresponding month of the previous year, i.e. premium amount of January 2011 *Vs.* premium amount of January 2012. Comparison is also made between the current month's premium incomes as a percentage of the total Gross Direct Premium (GDP) *Vs.* the corresponding month's premium of the previous year as a percentage of that year's total GDP. For example, only 5 per cent of this year's GDP came from this January premium, whereas 15 per cent of last year's GDP had come from the business done in last January.

Premium Persistence Ratio refers to the tendency of the policyholders to renew the insurance with the same company. It is taken as an indication of the trust the market reposes in the company. It represents a level of satisfaction of policyholders towards their policies. This indicator is often used as an important reference when evaluating the potential growth of business. As most general insurance policies are one-year policies, substantial thrust is given on the ability of the company to retain existing customers. Customers often seek best rates and services at the point of renewal. Hence, retaining customers is taken as a barometer for the company's ability to keep its rates reasonable, give good service and maintain a healthy level of credibility in the market. It is often indicated as the amount of the premium coming from renewed business *Vs.* the premium expectation as per the company's renewal register.

Premium Persistence Ratio (PPR) works as under:

$$\text{PPR} = \frac{\text{Premium in respect of renewed business}}{\text{Premium expected as per renewal register}} \times 100$$

Insurers take pride in stating that they have a premium/policy persistence ratio of 95 per cent, indicating a high level of satisfaction among its customers. In some markets, the terms Policy Persistence Ratio/Policy Retention Ratio are used to make similar comparisons between the number of policies issued in a given period and those issued in a previous period (same season). The gap between the policy retention ratio and the ideal ratio of 100 per cent is referred to as the Policy Lapse Ratio. That is, if 98 per cent of the policies due for renewal have been renewed, it indicates a policy retention ratio of 98 per cent and a policy lapse ratio of 2 per cent.

Policy Lapse Ratio (PLR):

$$\text{PLR} = \frac{\begin{array}{c}\text{Number of Policies not renewed}\\ \text{as per renewal register}\end{array}}{\begin{array}{c}\text{Number of Policies expected to be renewed}\\ \text{as per renewal register}\end{array}} \times 100$$

Reinsurance Retention Ratio (net premiums/gross premiums) is different from the policy retention ratio mentioned above. This retention ratio indicates a company's dependence on reinsurers and the potential scope of reinsurance cover purchased. This is done by comparing the amount of premium paid for reinsurance protection *vis-à-vis* the gross amount received by the company.

$$\text{Re-insurance Retention Ratio} = \frac{\text{Net Premium Written}}{\text{Gross Premium Written}} \times 100$$

It is a rough measure of how much of the risk is being carried by an insurer rather than being passed on to reinsures.

Loss Retention Ratio (LRR) is calculated by dividing net claims incurred by gross claims incurred. If this ratio is materially lower than the premium retention ratio, for consecutive years, it indicates a potential excessive reliance upon reinsurers' support for generating underwriting profits. Heavy dependence on re-insurance support for meeting claims for continuous period can impact an insurer's reputation among reinsures.

$$\text{Loss Retention Ratio} = \frac{\text{Net Claim Incurred}}{\text{Gross Claim Incurred}} \times 100$$

*(2) Action Performance Ratios*

These ratios relate to the various activities carried out by the insurers as part of their business actions or activities. These are often direct indicators of the company's efficiency and customer satisfaction. Ratios relating to the expeditious settling of claims, claim amount carried forward from previous years, the company's preparedness for settling claims by maintaining solvency margins, keeping sufficient liquid reserves, etc. are often considered indicators of the company's efficiency. An insurer's underwriting performance is measured by a set of ratios. Some such ratios are discussed below.

Claims Ratio is one of the most commonly used ratios. Claims ratio is often used synonymously with loss ratio. It is the percentage of the premium paid towards settlement of claims. In other words, the total losses of the company are divided by the premium collected during the same period; it is expressed as a percentage. This is worked out as under:

$$\text{Claims Ratio} = \frac{\text{Claims}}{\text{Gross Premium}} \times 100$$

A loss ratio of 60% indicates that out of Rs. 10,000

premium collected, Rs. 6000 has been paid towards claims in the particular period. This ratio does not reflect the costs or expenses that are necessarily incurred by the insurers, and refers purely only to the premium and claim, this is more appropriately called as burning cost or pure risk cost.

Incurred Claims Ratio is an accounting mechanism of apportioning the claims ratio to a particular year as closely as possible. As the insurer continues with the process of settling claims all through the year and claims constantly spill over to one or more future years, it becomes difficult to apportion claims to a particular period and calculate such ratios. Incurred claims ratio is an accounting mechanism of appropriating claims to a year. The amount of claims paid in a year and the amount of claims outstanding at the end of the year are added, from which the amount of claims outstanding at the beginning of the year is deducted. This figure is called incurred claims.

**Incurred Claims** = claims paid during the year
+ Claims outstanding at the end of the year
– Claims outstanding at the beginning of the year

Gross Premium is the total amount of premium that comes in from the policies issued. Net written premium or net premium refers to gross premium less premium on re-insurance ceded to re-insurers plus premium on re-insurance accepted.

**Net Premium** = Gross Premium
+ Premium on reinsurance accepted
– Premium on reinsurance ceded.

When amount of incurred claims is divided by the net written premium, we get the incurred claims ratio that gives a closer picture of the insurer's performance.

$$\text{Incurred Claims Ratio} = \frac{\text{Incurred Claims}}{\text{Net Premium}} \times 100$$

This exercise primarily tries to allocate claims to a particular year to ensure that the claims are more or less matched to the premiums received during the period. In other words, there is no mis-match between assets and liabilities (or tolerable mis-match).

Claims Coverage Ratio is a relative term that seeks to compare the company's claim experience *vis-à-vis* the industry's claim experience in a particular portfolio or a given market segment. This analysis would give insight into having a disproportionate share of claims *vis-à-vis* the market share, if such be the case. For instance, a company can find that it has only 10 per cent share of the industry's own damage insurance in respect of goods carrying vehicles, whereas it is paying 20 per cent of the claims paid by the industry on the particular segment.

Claims Duration Ratio helps in finding out the company's internal effectiveness in settling claims. Claims due to certain occupations and use of certain products take a long time to get noticed. In some cases, the courts take long periods of time, for instance 10-15 years, for settling liability claims (when there is litigation). The types of claims that get settled fast are called short tailed claims and those that take a longer settlement time are referred to as long tailed claims. While making provisions and allocating reserves, actuaries deal with these claims differently based on their devolvement period and duration ratios.

Complaints Ratio of a company is another core indicator. This figure indicates how a company's track record for satisfied customers stacks up against the competition. The common practice is that a ratio less than 0.3 indicates good performance *vis-à-vis* the median for a particular insurance market (marked by a score of "1"). A number higher than 1 suggests a relatively large number of complaints per customer served. Another thumb rule is to count the number of established complaints for every 1,00,000 customers served.

Capital Risks Ratio or Solvency Ratio tries to assess whether an insurer is solvent. In other words, if an insurer has adequate assets (over its liabilities) that can be utilized to pay the claims that can arise, it is solvent. It should have adequate technical reserves to meet the obligations entered into, and adequate capital as security. In simple terms, solvency margin can be defined as the surplus of assets over liabilities. A company's ability to pay claims denotes its solvency. Regulators expect that a certain minimum level of solvency margin is maintained so that the fluctuations in the overall results of a year are sufficiently cushioned without directly affecting the company. Solvency ratio from the Indian regulatory perspective is dealt with as a separate topic a little aftrerwards.

*(3) Result Performance Ratios*

These ratios indicate the end-product or the final result of all the performance parameters of the insurers. This includes concepts such as management expenses ratio and combined ratio. However, before dealing with them directly, we have to be clear about a few more terms.

Net Claims Paid is worked out by adding the claims paid on the re-insurances accepted and reducing the claims received on re-insurance ceded, to the gross claims paid. (Gross Claims paid refers to the total claims paid, including all claim-related expense and interest). When net claim paid is adjusted to the current accounting year, by reducing the effect of the previous year's accumulated claims, we get Net Incurred Claims.

Net incurred claims = Net claim paid
+ Amount of claims outstanding at the end of the year
– Amount of claims outstanding at the beginning of the year

**Net Earned Premium**

In respect of almost all policies, (other than those effective from April 1 of the year), some part of the premium received and accounted in an particular year would relate to the same accounting year while the remaining part would relate to the un-expired part of the policy falling in the next accounting year. Claims on the un-expired part of these policies would fail in the next year whereas the premium would not. Insurers use the term Earned Premium to refer to the proportion of the premium pertaining to the policy period in which it was received. The part of the premium proportionate to the un-expired period which would fall in the next accounting year is called Unearned Premium (or premium received in advance). The net premium received in a year is apportioned on a 1/365 days basis to take care of the risks that the company is exposed to within the same year, i.e. excluding the premium on the un-expired part of the policies that would spill over to the next accounting year. This share is called net earned premium. On a thumb rule basis, instead of the 1/365 day basis, insurers usually apportion 50 per cent of the previous year's net written premium and the current year's net written premium to work out the current year's net earned premium. (There is a view that as the company continues in business for many years and premiums keep coming every year, the simple written premium and incurred claims are good enough indictors for all practical purposes, as the premium and claims experience tend to even out over long periods, even without such apportionments. However, such simplistic stands do not find favour with actuaries who find that these indicators do not support the kind of precise calculations required in the modern day's competitive environment).

NIC NEP Ratio tries to give a more accurate ratio than the ones seen above. However, one needs to understand the following concepts to appreciate this ratio. Net incurred claims (NIC) divided by net earned premium (NEP) is referred to as Loss ratio or NIC – NEP ratio in common parlance. It may be observed that both the denominator and numerator in this calculation are business figures duly appropriated to a specific year. (It may be noted that loss adjustment expenses are considered part of incurred losses for such calculations).

$$\text{NIC} - \text{NEP Ratio} = \frac{\text{Net Incurred Claims}}{\text{Net Earned Premium}} \times 100$$

Insurers have to take care of various overheads other than settlement of claims. They incur business promotion expenses, agency commissions, administrative expenses, establishment costs, etc. The main variable costs having a direct bearing on the insurer's performance are management expenses and agency commissions. The sum total of all such expenses incurred in a year is compared with the net written premium of a given year to assess the insurer's performance. Expense ratio is a commonly accepted term indicating the sum total of management expenses plus commissions, divided by net written premium. Here, it may be borne in mind that as the expenses relate to the payments made in the current year only, the net written premium, i.e. the premium received in the current year is taken into consideration. Both the denominator and numerator are, therefore, actual figures relating to the inflow/outflow in the particular year.

Management Expenses Ratio =

$$\frac{\text{Management Expenses} + \text{Commissions}}{\text{Net Written Premium}} \times 100$$

In some markets, expenses ratio refers specifically to management expenses divided by net written premium, while commission ratio is calculated separately as commissions divided by net written premium.

Combined Ratio is obtained when

NIC = NEP Ratio + Expense Ratio

The combined ratio is a reflection of the company's overall underwriting profits ability. A combined ratio of less than 100 per cent indicates profitability, while anything over 100 indicates a loss. These ratios are used to assess an insurance company's performance. Over and above these performance indicators, insurers make reserves/provisions for catastrophic losses as well. The insurer has to provide for his company's profit as well. The insurer's profit in the simplest terms can be stated in the form of the following equation:

Profit = Earned premium + Investment Income – Incurred Loss – Underwriting Expenses – Provisions

**Solvency Margin**

Solvency margin is important for an insurance company. It explains as having sufficient assets in terms of capital, surplus and reserves, and being able to satisfy financial requirements to be eligible to transact insurance business and meet liabilities. Certain mathematical comparisons of different components of an entity's financial statement have been prescribed to determine its solvency. Solvency ratios are calculated in India by a three-step method as prescribed by the regulator (IRDA) in the IRDA (Assets, Liabilities and Solvency Margin of Insurers) Regulation, 2000.

The first step that is prescribed for the calculation of the Required Solvency Margin (RSM) is based on (a) net premiums, termed RSM-1, and (b) net incurred claims, termed RSM –2. RSM on net premiums (i.e. RSM-1) is determined as 20 per cent of the amount, which is the higher of (i) the gross premiums multiplied by a set of factors prescribed for the purpose, and (ii) the net premium. In other words, the RSM on net incurred claims (i.e. RSM-2) is determined as 20 per cent of the amount, which is the higher of (i) the gross net incurred claims multiplied by a set of prescribed factors, and (ii) the net incurred claims. The Required Solvency Margin (RSM) for the company is the higher of the two. The second step is to calculate the Available Solvency Margin (ASM), which is the net assets in the policyholder's funds plus the net assets in the shareholder's funds. The third step is to calculate the solvency ratio, which is the total ASM divided by the total RSM.

Stated in simple terms, solvency margin denotes the surplus of assets over liabilities. A company's ability to pay claims denotes its solvency. As already stated, it should have adequate technical reserves to meet the obligations entered into, and adequate capital as security. Regulators expect that a certain minimum level of solvency margin is always maintained so that the fluctuations in the overall results of a year are sufficiently cushioned without directly affecting the company.

### IAIS Core Principles

Like other professional associations, the International Association of Insurance Supervisors (IAIS) sets standards that are fundamental to developing effective insurance regulation and supervisory practices. IAIS has prescribed a set of legally accepted standards called Insurance Core Principles that are fundamental in developing effective regulation and supervisory practices for the insurance sector. IAIS principles, standards and guidance papers provide the basis for evaluating insurance legislation, supervisory systems and procedures. The IRDA in India has successfully taken care of most of the 28 core principles (which are in seven clusters). However, in its adherence to standards, India needs to focus on certain perceived gaps that are based on internationalization of the Core Principles (Core Principles by Dr. K.C. Mishra). For a core principle to be regarded as being "observed", the essential criteria must be met without any significant shortcomings. We may refer to the Basel Committee on Banking Supervision (BCBS) which has formulated the Core Principles of Banking Supervision, which ensure best supervisory practices in the area of banking supervision.

### Insurance Core Principles and Methodology

(International Association of Insurance Supervisors (IAIS)—October 2003).

*ICP-1: Conditions for Effective Insurance Supervision*

Insurance supervision relies upon:

- A policy institutional and legal framework for financial sector supervisions.
- A well developed and effective financial market infrastructure.
- Efficient financial markets.

*ICP-2: Supervisory Objectives*

The principal objectives of insurance supervision are clearly defined.

*ICP-3: Supervisory Authority*

The supervisory authority:

- Has adequate powers, legal protection and financial resources to exercise its functions and powers.
- Is operationally independent but accountable in the exercise of its functions and powers.
- Hires, trains and maintains sufficient staff with high professional standards.
- Treats confidential information appropriately.

*ICP-4: Supervisory Process*

The supervisory authority conducts its functions in a transparent and accountable manner.

*ICP-5: Supervisory Cooperation and Information Sharing*

The supervisory authority cooperates with other agencies and shares information with other relevant supervisors subject to confidentiality requirements.

*ICP-6: Licensing*

An insurer must be licensed before it can operate within a jurisdiction. The requirements for licensing are clear, objective and public.

*ICP-7: Suitability of Persons*

The significant owners, board members, senior

management, auditors and actuaries of an insurer are fit and proper to fulfil their roles. This requires that they possess the appropriate integrity, competency, experience and qualifications.

*ICP-8: Change in Control and Portfolio Transfers*

The supervisory authority approves or rejects proposals to acquire significant ownership or any other interest in an insurer that results in that person, directly or indirectly, alone or with an associate, exercising control over the insurers.

The supervisory authority approves the portfolio transfer or merger of insurance business.

*ICP-9: Corporate Governance*

The corporate governance framework recognizes and protects rights of all interested parties. The supervisory authority requires compliance with all applicable corporate governance standards.

*ICP-10: Internal Control*

The supervisory authority requires insurers to have in place internal controls that are adequate for the nature and scale of the business. The oversight and reporting systems allow the board and management to monitor and control the operations.

*ICP-11: Market Analysis*

Making use of all available sources, the supervisory authority monitors and analyses all factors that may have an impact on insurers and insurance markets. It draws conclusions and takes action as appropriate.

*ICP-12: Reporting to Supervisors and Off-site Monitoring*

The supervisory authority receives necessary information to conduct effective offsite monitoring and to evaluate the condition of each insurer as well as the insurance market.

*ICP-13: On-Site Inspection*

The supervisory authority carries out on-site inspections to examine the business of an insurer and its compliance with legislation and supervisory requirements.

*ICP-14: Preventive and Corrective Measures*

The supervisory authority takes preventive and corrective measures that are timely, suitable and necessary to achieve the objectives of insurance supervision.

*ICP-15: Enforcement or Sanctions*

The supervisory authority enforces corrective action and, where needed, imposes sanctions based on clear and objective criteria that are publicly disclosed.

*ICP-16: Winding-up and Exit from the Market*

The legal and regulatory framework defines a range of options for the orderly exit of insurers from the marketplace. It defines insolvency and establishes the criteria and procedure for dealing with insolvency. In the event of winding up proceedings, the legal framework gives priority to the protection of policyholders.

*ICP-17: Group-wide Supervision*

The supervisory authority supervises its insurers on a solo and a group-wide basis.

*ICP-18: Risk Assessment and Management*

The supervisory authority requires insurers to recognize the range of risks that they faced and to assess and manage them effectively.

*ICP-19: Insurance Activity*

Insurance is a risk taking activity. The supervisory authority requires insurers to evaluate and manage the risks that they underwrite, in particular, through re-insurance, and to have the tools to establish an adequate level of premiums.

*ICP-20: Liabilities*

The supervisory authority requires insurers to comply with standards for establishing adequate technical provisions and other liabilities, and making allowance for re-insurance receivables. The supervisory authority has both the authority and the ability to assess the adequacy of the technical provisions and to require that these provisions be increased, if necessary.

*ICP-21: Investments*

The supervisory authority requires insurers to comply with standards on investment activities. These standards include requirements on investment policy, assets-mix, valuation, diversification, asset-liability matching, and risk management.

*ICP-22: Derivatives and Similar commitments*

The supervisory authority requires insurers to comply with standards on the use of derivatives and similar commitments. These standards address restrictions in their use and disclosure requirements, as well as internal controls and monitoring of the related positions.

*ICP-23: Capital Adequacy and Solvency*

The supervisory authority requires insurers to comply with the prescribed solvency regime. This regime includes capital adequacy requirements and requires suitable forms of capital that enable the insurers to absorb significant unforeseen losses.

*ICP-24: Intermediaries*

The supervisory authority sets requirements, directly or through the supervision of insurers, for the conduct of intermediaries.

*ICP-25: Consumer Protection*

The supervisory authority sets minimum requirements for insurers and intermediaries in dealing with consumers in its jurisdiction, including foreign insurers selling products on a cross-border basis. The requirements include provision of timely, complete and relevant information to consumers both before a contract is entered into to the point at which all obligations under a contract have been satisfied.

*ICP-26: Information, Disclosure and Transparency Towards the Market*

The supervisory authority requires insurers to disclose relevant information on a timely basis in order to give stake-holders a clear view of their business activities and financial position and to facilitate the understanding of the risk to which they are exposed.

*ICP-27: Fraud*

The supervisory authority requires that insurers and intermediaries take the necessary measure to prevent, detect and remedy insurance fraud.

*ICP-28: Anti Money Laundering, Combating the Financing of Terrorism (AML/CFT)*

The supervisory authority requires insurers and intermediaries, at a minimum those insurers and intermediaries offering life insurance products or other investment related insurance, to take effective measures to deter, detect and report money-laundering and the financing of terrorism consistent with the Recommendations of the Financial Action Task Force on Money Laundering (FATF).

**Summary**

The foregoing description has provided the reader/student with a detailed understanding of the fundamental principles of insurance. It would have been realized that insurance as a branch of learning uses its own set of terms and principles. The terms used are numerous and it may not be possible to cover them here. Suffice it to say that this account has familiarized readers with a good number of principles and terms used in the insurance market so that a reasonably good understanding of all the important aspects of insurance is obtained. Effort has been made to give a brief idea of the core principles developed by the International Association of Insurance Supervisors (IAIS).

(1) Although trust or good faith is cardinal to all financial transactions yet the position in insurance emphasizes greatly the importance of trust. As the underwriter knows nothing of the risk and the proposer knows everything about it, it is the duty of the proposer to make a full disclosure of all the material circumstances and facts to the underwriter without being asked. That is expressed by saying that it is a contract of utmost good faith.

(2) When a ship is proposed for insurance, if the proposer does not state the factual negative details

such as the ship's machinery being worn out, or that repairs are needed to make it seaworthy, or that it is carrying hazardous goods that it is not designed to carry, the insurer will not be reasonably expected to know of these. If the insurer had come to know of these details, he might have insured it only with some additional conditions or with an additional premium or he might not have insured the ship at all. In such cases, the withholding of these vital details from the insurer is a breach of the principle of utmost good faith.

(3) Insurance does not allow anyone to insure or get an insurance claim on any risk. It is important that the insured has a real interest in the subject offered for insurance. This is termed 'insurable interest' and is a prime requirement for an insurance contract to be valid.

(4) The requirement of 'insurable interest' is to ensure that the insured does not insure the risk with an intention of speculation, i.e. to make a profit out of the loss.

(5) The importance of 'insurable interest' can be made clearer by the following example. If a person insures his neighbourer's car, he is not at any financial loss if some damage happens to that car. Primarily, he has no financial interest in the car and his contract can only be a bet or wager on someone else's property. Further, as any damage happening to the car, it is to his advantage (with no loss to him). It is possible that he causes to become instrumental in causing damage to the car. The requirement of insurable interest is to ensure that the insured does not indulge in wagering or making a profit out of the loss.

(6) The principle of indemnity goes hand in hand with insurable interest and implies that the insured will be compensated only to the extent of the financial loss he has suffered or only up to the value previously agreed as the cost of the loss. The principle ensures that an insured should get a full indemnity and that he should get no more, i.e. he does not make a profit from the transaction.

(7) In the cases of health and personal accident insurance where the principle of indemnity does not strictly apply, the insurer promises to pay a predetermined amount to the insured on account of a disability due to an accident and/or to reimburse his medical expenditure. Although indemnity can not be possible for physical suffering yet the unfortunate or their families are moved closer to their former economic position.

(8) Subrogation is a provision by which the insurer is placed in the position of the assured to ensure that the assured is prevented from recovering more than the indemnity from any source. By this principle, on payment of the loss, the insurer is entitled to be placed in the position of the insured and success to all his rights and remedies against third parties in respect of the subject matter of insurance.

(9) In a road accident, if an insured vehicle gets totally damaged beyond repair, the insurer would pay the full sum insured of the vehicle to the insured. However, if the accident was caused entirely due to the fault of another vehicle, the insured has the legal right to claim compensation from the owner of the vehicle that caused the accident. The debris of the damaged vehicle can also be sold as scrap for some amount of money. Such a situation can give opportunity to the insured to recover more money than his loss. By the principle of subrogation, on payment of the loss, the insurer takes over the right of the insured to sue and to recover from any third party in respect of the loss that occurred.

(10) Proximate cause is explained as the active, efficient cause that sets in motion a chain of incidents which brings consequences without the intervention of any force and working actively from a new and independent source. It indicates the proximity or closeness of a loss to its cause or *vice-versa*. It refers to the most dominant and most effective cause from which the loss emanated.

(11) A vessel was insured for marine perils but not

against war like operations. The vessel was torpedoed and had to berth at a neighbouring harbour. When the tide fell, she grounded in the shallow waters and later became a total wreck. The insured claimed for a loss of perils of the sea. As the proximate cause of the loss was the torpedoing, which was not covered under the policy, the claim was not paid.

(12) When a part of a machine or a vehicle is replaced following an accident, the insurer pays for the cost of a new part to see that the machine is re-instated to its working condition. Here, indemnity is seen as the process of putting the machine back to its working condition and not for a like replacement of the old part with another old part. In the bargain, the insured gets a new part instead of the old part and the insurer would be meeting the cost of new spare parts.

(13) 'New for old' is a term used to describe a basis of cover, usually within property insurance, whereby the insurer agrees to pay the full replacement cost of the damaged insured item and not what the actual item is valued at the time of the loss. This principle is used in area such as marine hull, machinery parts, vehicle parts, and the like.

(14) Sometimes, the same subject matter of insurance could be covered by different policies. Here, there is a possibility that the insured might get compensated more than once from different sources for the same loss, thereby making a profit. In the event of multiple policies covering the same subject matter of insurance, the principle of contribution provides for an equitable sharing of any loss between all the insurers according to their respective insurance amount.

(15) Re-instatement is a claim settlement option agreed between the insured and the insurer, stating that the insurer would make good the insured damaged property, rather than pay a monetary amount. For this benefit, the insurer would usually charge the policyholder an additional premium.

(16) Re-instatement of the loss by the insurer is not strictly followed due to various practical issues. Re-instatement would be costly for the insurer. Again, if he were not able to re-instate to the satisfaction of the insured, his work would have to be abandoned. The insured may not practically prefer reinstatement, as he would like to have better buildings or newer technology or higher capacity equipment to replace the loss. In practical terms, the insured would prefer receiving the full cost of re-instatement in lieu of actual re-instatement. This cost would comprise (i) the indemnity *per se,* (ii) wear and tear and depreciation, and (iii) cost of inflation between date of loss and probable time of re-instatement.

(17) In some contexts, there can be practical difficulties in finding out the value of the loss due to change of value of stock due to processing, market conditions, location of the goods (especially in cargo insurances), inflation or currency fluctuations. In the case of rare objects and personal possessions, objective evaluation values can be extremely difficult to assess post-loss. In areas such as personal accident, measuring personal losses post-event may be offending and painful. Agreed value policies or valued policies are considered a practical way out in many cases where assessing the value of a loss post the event can create difficulties.

(18) Any information that could affect the underwriters' assessment of the risk is regarded a material fact. The underwriter's assessment can include fixing the insurance premium, framing the conditions of acceptance. Framing the conditions that would operate in the event of a claim or the decision to accept the risk itself.

(19) Reciprocity means that principles that are binding on one party call for reciprocal behaviour from the other party also whether stated or otherwise. While the insured is expected to disclose all material facts, the insurer should also disclose the benefits under the policy that the insured normally may not know.

(20) The principle of 'average' requires the amount of a claim payment to be reduced proportionately if a policyholder has not insured the property for its full value. If an insured opts for a lesser sum insured and consequently pays a less than adequate amount as premium, the loss also gets reduced proportionately. The concept of average is applied by dividing the sum insured by the actual value multiplied by the loss incurred. If the sum insured is only 50 per cent of the value, the loss will also be reduced to 50 per cent.

(21) General average is a contribution made by all parties involved (usually) in a sea adventure towards a loss occasioned by the sacrifice of the property of some of the parties in the common interest/for the benefit of all.

(22) The law of general average is a legal principle of maritime law according to which all parties in a sea venture proportionally share any loss resulting from a voluntary sacrifice of part of the ship or cargo to save the whole in an emergency. Thus, if an insured ships' cargo on a vessel that is involved in sea hazard/unworthy sea and meets with a loss, he may face a claim from the insurer against him even though he was lucky that his goods are not damaged. This aspect is criticized by some insured as unfair. However, actually it is not unfair because all the insured were also part of the same venture, went through the same situation and all could have suffered the loss.

(23) Particular average means a partial loss. Insurance cover is taken and policies issued on total loss cover only are said to be free of particular average, which means excusing partial losses. 'Sue and Labour' denotes charges incurred by or on behalf of the insured for the safety and preservation of the subject-matter insured.

(24) In an insurance policy, the deductible or excess is the portion of any claim that is not covered by the insurance provider. That is, only the amount that is

in excess of the deductible is recoverable from the insurer.

(25) This most common form of deductible is applied on a per event basis. The deductible amount is agreed upon between he insurance company and the policyholder on each occasion that a claim arises.

(26) In a per year form of deductible, an annual limit is applied instead of per event basis. The insurance company and the policyholder agree upon an annual limit of deductible and not go by claim deductible.

(27) This concept is similar to the excess/deductible, in that the insurer makes no settlement if the total claim is below the franchise figure. In the case of excess, a deduction is made when a loss crosses an agreed figure. The difference is that in franchise, no deduction is made once the loss crosses the agreed figure. It rather applies as a threshold level for a claim to be considered.

(28) Usually the sum insured is the limit of indemnity and in case of under-insurance, the condition of average applies. The Probable Maximum Loss (PML) of a particular risk is the estimate of the maximum loss that would occur as a result of damage caused by the most destructive peril to be insured with regard to the location, construction, occupation and protection of the risk. PML is usually expressed as a percentage of the sum insured. Where the sum insured is decided based on the PML, as in the case of First Loss Policies, the sum insured is accepted to be less than the value of the property, but the insurer undertakes to pay claim up to the sum insured, without application of average.

(29) The simplest form of loss ratio or claims ratio is the total loss divided by net premium. It is expressed as a percentage. As this ratio does not reflect all the costs or expenses that are necessarily incurred by the insurers, this is more appropriately called as the burning cost or pure risk cost.

(30) Incurred claims ratio is an accounting mechanism of appropriating claims to a year. The amount of claims

paid in a year and the amount of claims outstanding at the end of the year are added, from which the amount of claims outstanding at the beginning of the year is deducted. This figure is called the incurred claims which are divided by the net premium to get the incurred claims ratio.

(31) The loss ratio (incurred loses and loss adjustment expenses divided by net earned premium) is added to the expense ratio (underwriting expenses plus commissions divided by net premium written) to determine the company's combined ratio. Thus, combined ratio = loss ratio + expense ratio.

# 6

# Life Insurance: Nature and Uses of Life Insurance

## HISTORY

Historical records show that Insurance appeared in the 16th century in the United Kingdom. As per evidence available, Willian Gybbon got the first life insurance policy from Richard Martin. The Gybbon's life policy gave greater publicity for life insurance. The private insurers entered into the insurance business and gathered in Exchange Alley where the insurance business was settled.

Afterwards, two life offices started their formal business, i.e., Hand in Hand Society and the Mercers' Company in 1696 and 1698, respectively.

This concept travelled to other European countries. In France, life insurance was allowed in 1787. In Germany, the first insurance company came into existence in 1806. In the USA, insurance was started in 1721 by Maher and Oster.

### Life Insurance in India

It is interesting to note that some types of protections have been mentioned in Hindu scriptures. Modern types of insurance covers were devised only in the 18th century when foreign insurance companies started their business in India.

In 1818, the first foreign insurance company started in India was 'Oriental'. Oriental was liquidated but it reappeared as the 'New Oriental'. In 1853, Medical Invalid and General absorbed the New Oriental.

In 1823, a Company named 'Bombay Life' started issuing short-term policies. Madras Equitable came up in 1921. These companies failed due to improper management of valuation, wrong depreciation of investment and defective ratings.

By 1956, there were 229 Indian insurers and provident societies and 16 non-Indian insurers carrying on life business in India. But on January 19, 1956, the life insurance business came under the control and ownership of the government. In June 1956, a Bill was passed in Parliament for establishing Life Insurance Corporation of India (LIC), which started functioning with effect from September 1, 1956.

The LIC is a body corporate, wholly owned Corporation of the government of India, having perpetual succession and a common seal with powers to purchase, hold and dispose of property and may sue and be sued by its own name. It has one central office, five zonal offices and several divisional and branch offices. The corporation is charged with the main function to carry on life insurance business in India.

## Meaning of Life Insurance

Life insurance provides assurance to the insured to pay him/her certain sum of money, in lieu of periodical payment of premium by the insured , on the death of the insured (to his/her nominee or legal representative) or on the maturity of policy (to him/her), whichever occurs earlier. Life insurance provides financial protection to the beneficiary against the risk of early death.

Life insurance includes both the element of protection and investment. In case the insured lives up to the maturity of the policy, the premium paid becomes investment. This accumulated investment made by the insured in the form of periodical premium payments is paid back to the insured on the maturity of the policy.

At present, life insurance enjoys maximum scope of business due to higher awareness level and because of multiple risks as a consequence of modern living. The human life is the most valuable property of society. The life insurance provides protection to the family at the pre-mature death of family head or gives adequate amount at the old age when earning capacities of the insured are reduced and diseases start attacking.

The life insurance contract can be defined as 'contingent contract' because the loss of life cannot be compensated (human life is invaluable, priceless) and only a specified sum of money is paid in case of death of the insured".

## Definitions

Section 2 of the Indian Insurance Act, 1938 has defined it as: "Life Insurance business is the business of effecting contracts upon human life".

According to J.H. Maggee, "The Life insurance contract embodies an agreement, in which, broadly stated, the insurer undertakes to pay a stipulated sum upon the death of the insured, or at some designated time to a designated beneficiary.

On the basis of above definitions, we may safely conclude that life insurance is a contract requiring payments of periodical instalments; it undertakes to pay an annuity or a certain sum of money, either on the death of the insured or on the expiry of a certain number of years. Thus, life insurers (Insurance Company), in consideration of periodical premium payments, agree to pay a certain amount either on the death or on the maturity of the policy, whichever occurs earlier. Under Life insurance, the sum assured under the policy is paid to the insured if policy matures during his/her lifetime and to his/her nominee(s) in case of death. The premium is paid by the insured or by the policyholder to insurance company either in lump sum or in monthly, quarterly, half-yearly or yearly instalments.

## Characteristics of Life Insurance

The following are the noticeable characteristics of life insurance:

Insurable Interest; as an outcome of an offer; being contract of contingency; payment of Premium by the insured; payment of sum assured by the insurer; provides financial help; encouragement of savings; tax exemption for amount assured and paid by insurer; wide scope; and it provides protection.

The characteristics of life insurance, named above, are now explained below for better and clearer understanding:

*Outcome of an Offer*

The life insurance contract is also the outcome of an offer made by the potential insured and its acceptance by the insurance company.

*Payment of Sum Assured*

The insurance company agrees to pay a certain sum of money to the insured on the maturity of the policy or, on the death of the insured, to his/her dependents, whichever happens earlier.

*Payment of Premium*

There is an obligation placed upon the insured to pay periodical premium to the insurance company till his death or up to the period of policy, whichever is earlier, as per the type of the policy taken.

*Contract of Contingency*

It is clearly understood without any misunderstanding that a contract of life insurance is a contract of contingency. It is not a contract of indemnity like other types of insurance because loss of human life caused by death of the insured cannot be calculated in monetary terms. Human life is unique and priceless and varies widely between individuals, hence complex entity. Therefore, the loss caused by death is not measurable in money value.

*Insurable Interest*

Insurable interest must be present in the person insured at the time when the policy is taken in case of life insurance and it may or may not be present at the time of death of insured. If it is not present at the time of death of the insured, the dead can not be sued and the beneficiary, once admitted to the benefit under the policy, can not be deprived of the benefit because of the fault or omission on the part of the insured, since dead.

*Provides Financial Help*

Life insurance assists those who are left behind by the insured (now no more). Supporters are few or none; dependent may be alone and helpless in case of death of the insured. Life

Insurance, therefore, extends financial help to the dependents of insured after the death of the insured.

*Encouragement of Savings*

Life insurance is considered to be the best alternative for making savings for future.

*Tax Exemption*

Investment made by means of premium in different policies of life insurance is exempted from income tax, etc.

*Wide Scope*

Life insurance has a wide scope. A large number of risks to human life, apart from the death, are covered under life insurance. In case of total and permanent disability and/or temporary disability, medical expenses are covered, so is compulsory retirement from service due to disability, etc. under life insurance.

*Provides Protection*

Life insurance relieves the insured from various risks and uncertainties, which may occur before and/or after the death of the insured.

**Procedure for Taking a Life Insurance Policy**

Any person wanting to take a life insurance policy has to fulfil the following policy conditions governing life insurance:

*(1) Proposal*

The person desirous of getting a life insurance policy makes a proposal to the counsellor/agent of the insurance company by filling-up a prescribed proposal form which is available free of cost from the counsellors/agents or the branches of insurance companies. The form is in the form of a questionnaire which contains the questions requiring various types of information from the applicant such as:

Name, occupation and address of the proposer and insured; family history and health of the proposer; facts about the income, life and habits of the proposer; date of birth and age of the insured; mode of payment of premium; and sum to be insured.

The proposer is under obligation to furnish true and correct information in the form because the contract of life insurance, unlike other contracts, requires absolute and utmost good faith on the part of both the parties, i.e. the insurer and the insured. The proposer must not conceal any material information, which is required to be given in the proposal form. The proposal form requires the prospect (to be insured) to give at least two names as references who know about the health, life and whereabouts of the proposer. This enables the insurance company for verification of the antecedents and to establish identification and confirm particulars furnished in the proposal form.

*(2) Proof of Age*

The proposer whose age is below 25 and above 50 years is required to give proof of age along with the proposal form; others may give it at the time of making claim. Many companies have started getting age proof in all cases in the beginning. The age proof of the proposed insured can be provided by certificate of date of birth issued by the Registrar of Births, school or college or service book maintained by the government department for its employees, etc. There are many source-documents of date of birth.

*(3) Medical Examination*

After the receipt of proposal form in the office of insurance company, the proposer is required to get himself medically examined from a physician (doctor) approved by the insurance company. The proposal form is sent to the approved doctor for medical report on the health of the prospect/insured and the insured is asked to appear before the doctor for medical examination. The doctor prepares a report on the basis of medical examination of the proposer and forwards it to the company's office.

*(4) Confidential Report by the Counsellor/Agent*

The life insurance counsellor/agent is required to furnish a confidential report about the proposer in the prescribed form. This report contains the facts about the proposer, his health, character, financial position and other confidential particulars having bearing on the risk profile; this report is usually attached with the proposal.

*(5) Acceptance of Proposal*

On the basis of the information given in the proposal form, personal facts about the proposer, counsellor's/agent's report, enquiries from the references and report of doctor, the acceptance of the proposal is considered by the company. The company determines the type of risk, volume of risk, probability of risk, premium rate, etc. and if it seems favourable (fair business risk) then it accepts the proposal. Acceptance letter is dispatched to the insured, stating the terms and conditions to be fulfilled by the insured in due course.

*(6) Payment of First Premium*

On receipt of acceptance letter containing a request for payment of the first premium, the insured deposits the amount of the first premium. The company becomes liable from the day on which the first premium is paid. But practically, the first instalment of premium is paid along with the proposal form. Subsequently, the premium may be paid monthly, quarterly, half-yearly, or yearly as the insured desires.

*(7) Insurance Policy*

On payment of the first premium, the policy comes into operation and risk is covered then onwards. Insurance policy is prepared in prescribed form, duly stamped and signed by authorized persons in the company and is finally issued to the insured. The life insurance policy bears the seal of the company along with the signatures of two of its directors. A copy of the proposal form is attached to the policy document these days.

## Nature of Life Insurance

The fundamental function of Life Insurance is to provide protection against the financial losses caused by disability, old age and death. Life insurance deals with permanent stoppage of earning capacity/power due to death or sickness.

Every life insurance plan is a method of spreading a possible financial loss over a large number of persons. Life insurance seeks to reduce the financial uncertainties, perils or risk events arising from the natural contingencies, i.e. old age, illness, death, etc.

Life insurance is also called "Income replacement insurance". This is so because it provides alternative source of income in case of death of bread earner of the family.

Life insurance is one of the most important methods evolved/developed to provide family security on voluntary basis through individual initiative. The concept of life insurance is born out of a human motive of self-prevention or self-preservation.

Life insurance cannot stop death but can manage to stop the suffering of financial loss caused by death. Life insurance may be defined as a guarantee by one person (insurer) to another (insured) against accidental loss by death or disease. Life insurance undertakes to protect the insured's family, creditors or others against pecuniary loss resulting out of death of the insured.

Under life insurance, an insurance company agrees to pay a stipulated sum upon the death of the insured or on the maturity of policy in consideration for the payment of a certain amount of premium, either in lump-sum or in instalments.

Life insurance is a contract between the insurance company and the person insured in return for a consideration (called premium). The nature of life insurance may be of two types, i.e. (i) Economic nature of Life Insurance; (ii) Legal nature of Life Insurance.

## (I) Economic Nature of Life Insurance

There are five basic economic thoughts underlying the need for life insurance:

(a) *Family life depends on Income*: Everyone of a family has requirements of food, clothing and shelter; these have to be paid from out of income.

(b) *Current income depends on Earnings*: At present, no one is self-sufficient enough to live solely on income from inherited wealth. So, everyone has to be dependent on earnings.

(c) *Earnings will cease sometime*: One cannot avoid reaching an age when one will cease to earn any money, unless it be by dying in the prime of life where one has no choice.

(d) *To meet future necessities*: Savings of the insured provide food, shelter and clothes for tomorrow.

(e) *Savings*: It can provide new source of income for his dependents when the earning stops due to the death of insured. From the above, it can be concluded that the fundamental principle of life insurance is to meet the unfortunate economic results which arise due to contingencies of life whether these are premature death, old age, permanent or temporary disability.

**(II) Legal nature of Life Insurance**

According to Sec. 2(11) of the Life Insurance Amendment Act, 1950, "Life Insurance is the business of effecting contracts of insurance upon human life, including any contract whereby the payment of money is insured, on death or the happening of any contingency dependent on human life and any contract which is subject to the payment of premium for a term dependent on human life and shall be deemed to include:

(a) The granting of disability or double or triple compensation accident benefits if so provided in the contract of insurance.

(b) The granting of annuities on human life. Pay once in lump-sum or in instalments for a defined period and get back in periodic instalments over a long period, especially when income source dries up.

(c) The granting of superannuating allowance and annuities payable out of any fund applicable solely to the relief and maintenance of persons engaged or who have been engaged in any particular profession, trade or employment or to the dependents of such persons.

Thus according to Insurance Act, granting annuities and/ or superannuating allowance under occupational pension schemes are also a part of life insurance business.

*Uses of Life Insurance*

Uses of Life Insurance are the following:

*It covers the Risk of Death*

It encourages compulsory savings; Easy settlement and protection against creditors; Provides security and safety; It eliminates dependency; Profitable Investment; Facilitates Liquidity; Tax Relief; Loan Facility; Helpful in Re-adjustment; Helpful in Education; Assists in Marriage; and extends help in Family Requirement. These uses of life insurance are explained hereunder:

*Life Insurance Covers the Risk of Death*

The risk of death is covered under life insurance. In case of death, insurance company pays full sum assured, which would be several times larger than the total of the premium paid.

Insurance encourages compulsory savings: the element of protection and investment both are present in case of life insurance. In most of the life policies, element of savings predominates. After taking insurance policy, if the premium is not paid within the time stipulated plus grace period, if any, allowed, the policy lapses. Thus, the insured is forced to go on paying premium. In other words, it encourages compulsory saving to pay premium.

*It is means of Easy Settlement and Protection against Creditors*

In case nomination or assignment is made, a claim under life insurance can be settled in a simple way. The policy money becomes a kind of trust, which cannot be taken away by the creditors.

*Insurance Provides Security and Safety*

Payment is made under life insurance, in case of death of the insured or when the term of insurance expires. The loss of the insured to the family at premature death, and payment for old age, are both adequately provided by life insurance. Stated in other words, security against premature death and old age sufferings both are provided by life insurance.

*It Eliminates Dependency*

On the death of husband or father, the suffering due to the destruction of family needs no elaboration. The family is affected by unending sufferings. It brings down the standards of living and the suffering may go to any extent—begging from the relatives, neighbourers or family friends. The economic freedom of the family is totally lost. The life insurance is here to help the wife and children and it provides adequate amount at the time of need.

*Insurance is Profitable Investment*

Life insurance policies provide practically the best alternative of investment to individuals. There are better forms of investment like endowment policies, multipurpose policies and deferred annuities.

*Insurance Facilitates Liquidity*

Life insurance provides liquidity. If a policyholder is not in a position to pay the premium, he can surrender the policy for cash to meet his cash requirement in time.

*Insurance provides Tax Relief*

In India, insurance policies carry a special exemption from income tax, wealth tax, gift tax and estate duty. The insured obtains significant relief in income tax and wealth tax by paying the insurance premium which is treated as saving.

*There is Loan Facility against Life Policy*

The insured can also take a loan for a temporary period to tide over his/her monetary difficulty against assignment of the policy. A life insurance policy is also acceptable as security for a commercial or personal loan.

*Insurance is Helpful in Re-adjustment in Living Standard*

The life insurance helps to accumulate adequate funds to make adjustment in standard of living, at the time of reduction in income due to loss of employment, disability, death, retirement, etc.

*It is Helpful in Education*

There are several life insurance policies and annuities which are useful in meeting expenses for education of children irrespective of the death or survival of the family head.

*Insurance Assists in Marriage of Daughter*

The life insurance can provide funds for the marriage of daughter if an appropriate policy is taken for this purpose. Otherwise, the daughter may remain unmarried in case of death of father due to inadequate provision for meeting the expenses on marriage.

*It is Source of Help in meeting Family Requirement*

After death, ritual ceremonies, payment of wealth tax and income tax, are certain requriements, which decrease the amount of funds of the family members, left behind, and insurance comes to help for meeting these requirements.

The above description makes it abundantly clear that Life Insurance is a kind of investment and saving. The insurer-company invests funds collected in the form of premia in developmental outlays of the government through equity or bond investment. The funds are also invested in government securities. There are regulations how the investment portfolio of insurers should be planned so that policy-holders' money remains safe and properly secured, of course, with low level of risk, as much as possible.

7

# Nature of Life Insurance Contract

## INTRODUCTION

Life insurance contract may be defined as the contract in which the insurer, in consideration for a premium, undertakes to pay a certain sum of money, on the death of the insured or on the expiry of certain (pre-determined) period of time. Under the life insurance contract, an assured sum of money is paid to the insured on the expiry of policy period or to his nominee in case of his/her death (death of the insured). In life insurance, the risk insured against is death.

It should be clearly understood that the life insurance contract is not a contract of indemnity because the insurer agrees to pay definite sum on maturity of policy or at the death, whichever occurs earlier. The life insurance contract is a contract of contingency.

Features/Characteristics/Nature of Life Insurance Contract is depicted on next page.

In view of what is stated above, Life insurance provides protection to the family at the premature death of the insured and makes payment of an adequate amount at the old age when earning capacities are reduced due to the biological life cycle.

The features of life insurance contract as depicted above are described on next page.

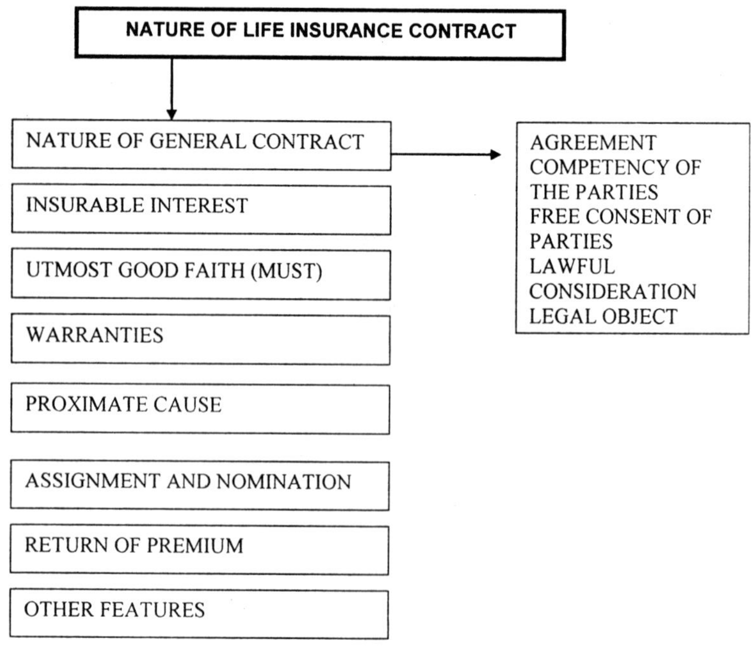


## (I) NATURE OF GENERAL CONTRACT

The life insurance contract must have all the essentials of a valid contract as provided in the Contract Act. According to Indian Contract Act, 1872, a valid contract must contain the following essentials:

### (1) There must be an Agreement

The life insurance contract includes 'offer' and 'acceptance'. An offer is a proposal. It is an intimation of intention to the other person to do or to abstain from doing anything with a view to obtaining the consent or assent of that other person to such an act or abstinence.

The person to whom the offer is made signifies his assent to it. At that point, the offer is said to have been accepted. The 'offer' and 'acceptance' in life insurance is of typical nature. A proposal form is filled up by the offerer. Payment of the first premium is also made along with the proposal form. Submission of proposal form alongwith the premium is an effective, constructive and complete offer. The dispatch of acceptance letter by insurer is the acceptance of the offer. The risk under the policy (proposal) will commence as soon as the acceptance letter is dispatched by the insurer. Policy document may be issued and supplied in due course.

A situation arises when the proposal form is not accompanied with the first premium. In that case, it would merely be intimation by the prospective insured (invitation to go through and consider proposal). A letter of insurer in response may ask the offerer to pay the first premium without any change in offer. The payment of first premium by the prospective insured is the acceptance by the insurer. This completes the agreement.

In other words, offer is an intimation of offerer to purchase the insurance policy. The readiness of insurer to undertake the stated risk in offer (proposal) is the acceptance. The offer in case of insurance is called 'proposal'. If the other party accepts this proposal, it is transformed into an 'agreement', complete in all essentials.

Section 2(b) of Indian Contract Act, 1872, defines offer as—

> "When one person signifies his willingness to do or not to do an act with the intention to obtain the assent of the other to do or not to do the act, is known as offer".

If the other party accepts this proposal, it is known as 'acceptance'. When a person to whom the proposal is made, signifies his assent, the offer is said to be accepted.

### (2) Competency of the Parties to Contract

The general rule of contract is that all natural persons are competent to contract. The essential element of a valid contract is that the parties to it must be legally competent to contract. Otherwise, if all is well, every person is competent to enter into contract. There are infirmities with which some persons are afflicted and law recognizes such as aberrations or inabilities. Let it be known who such persons can be. These are minor, persons of unsound mind, persons disqualified by law from contracting, etc. A description of these categories of persons is given below:

Who is not a minor; who is not of unsound mind and who is not disqualified by law from entering into a contract.

Section II of the Indian Contract Act, 1872 lays down that every person is competent to contract who is of the age of majority according to law to which he is subject and who is of sound mind, and is not disqualified from contracting by any law to which he is subject.

So, under the life insurance contract, both the insurer and the insured must be capable of entering into a valid contract.

The insurer will be competent if he has got the license from Insurance Regulatory and Development Authority (IRDA) to carry on insurance business and type of ownership (partnership, limited liability partnership, limited liability company) is lawful and legally constituted, etc. In other words, as per the law, the prospect must fulfil the following criteria:

*(i) Majority Status*

Majority is attained when a person completes the age of 18 years. If a guardian is appointed for a minor by a court in India, the age of attaining majority gets extended to 21 years. A minor is not competent to contract. A contract by a minor is void. The minors can repudiate the contract at any time during his/her minority. If life insurance policy is issued to a minor, the insurance company cannot repudiate it (as the benefit to minor is legally recognized as valid) but the minor can repudiate it during the minority.

*(ii) Person of Sound Mind is Incapable of Entering into Valid Contract*

Only the person of sound mind can enter into a valid contract. A person is said to be of sound mind for the purpose of making a contract when he/she is able to understand the implications of it including obligations and rights fully. A person may usually be of sound mind, but occasionally of unsound mind, may not make a contract when he is of unsound mind. He/she can do so only when he/she is in lucid interval. An intoxicated person cannot enter into a contract as he/she can not understand fully the terms and conditions, rights and obligations and all the implications of a contract.

*(iii) Other Disqualifications of a Person as Party to a Contract*

A contract with an alien enemy is void. An alien enemy is disqualified from and is not capable of entering into contract or enforcing it either. When an alien with whom an insurance contract has been entered into becomes an enemy afterwards, the contract is either suspended or terminated as from the declaration of war or belligerent status.

**(3) Free Consent of the Parties Essential for a Valid Contract**

When both the parties have agreed to a life insurance contract on the terms and conditions of the agreement in the same sense and spirit without coercion, undue force or any kind of pressure inhibiting independent judgement, they are said to have a free consent. Under Section 14 of Indian Contract Act, 1872, the consent is to be free when it is not caused by:

Coercion; undue influence; fraud; misrepresentation; and mistake.

Life insurance contract without free consent is voidable at the option of the party whose consent is not free, except fraud. In case of fraud, the contract would be void.

**(4) Lawful Consideration is Necessary Element in Contract**

When a party to an agreement promises to do something, he must get something in return. This is called consideration. In life insurance contract, the payment of premium is the consideration on the part of the insured. The presence of a lawful consideration is essential for a legal life insurance contract. The insurer must receive some consideration in return of his promise to pay a fixed sum at maturity or on the death of insured, as the case may be.

The consideration for which the insurance company undertakes to compensate the risk of insured is called the premium. Premium may be paid in lump-sum or in periodical instalments spread over a specified period (life) of policy. The life insurance contract cannot be initiated without the payment of premium.

**(5) Legal Object is the Foundation of a Valid Contract**

Another important basic principle of life insurance contract is the legality of objects for a valid contract. The object of life insurance contract should be lawful. A lawful object is that which is not forbidden by law; or not immoral or opposed to public policy; or not against the provision of any law. Unlawful object of any contract shall make it unenforceable at law. If the object of an insurance proposal, for example, consideration, is found to be illegal, the policy is void.

## (II) INSURABLE INTEREST

Insurable interest is the most essential characteristic of life insurance contract. The insured must have an insurable interest in the life to be insured. For a valid contract, insurable interest arises out of the pecuniary relationship that exists between the policyholder and the life insured so that the policyholder stands to lose by the death of the insured and continues to gain by his survival. If such relationship exists, then the policyholder has insurable interest in the life of the insured. The loss should be monetary or financial. The insurable interest in life insurance contract may be divided into two categories:

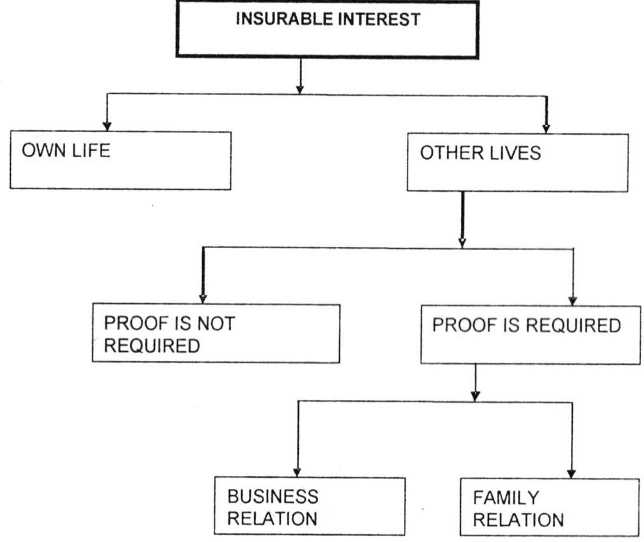


**(I) Insurable Interest in Policyholder's Own Life**

An individual always has an unlimited insurable interest in this own life. It is not required to be proved. According to Bunyon, "Every man is presumed to possess an insurable interest in his estate for the loss of his future gains or savings which might be the result of his premature death".

It is clear from the above definition that the individual will continue to gain financially while he is surviving and will suffer loss if he is dead because he will be unable to earn or protect the property and family. The insurable interest in own life is unlimited because the loss to the insured or his dependents cannot be measured in terms of money and, therefore, no limit can be placed to the amount of insurable interest that one may take on one's life. Thus, a person can take a policy to any unlimited amount on his own life. Of course, his income should be adequate to spare money for the payment of premium.

It is this aforesaid reason that the insurer will not issue a policy for an amount larger than the amount that seems suitable to the circumstances and means of the applicant. A general rule that is practised is that one cannot purchase life insurance policy more than ten times of his one year's income.

### (2) Insurable Interest in the Life of Others

Life insurance can be effected/contracted on the lives of third parties provided the proposer has insurable interest in those third parties. There are two types of insurable interest in the lives of others: in the first case, proof is not required, and in the other case, proof is required.

#### *(a) Cases where Proof is not Required*

The following are the two cases where insurable interest is not required to be proved.

*(i) Wife has insurable interest in the life of her husband and vice-versa*

It is presumed and decided by law that wife is presumed to have insurable interest in the life of her husband and *vice-versa*. It is because husband is legally bound to support his wife. The wife will suffer financially if the husband is dead and will continue to gain if the husband is surviving. Therefore, wife has unlimited insurable interest in the life of her husband. The reverse is also true where wife is the bread earner and the husband is either incapable of earning or is unemployed.

*(ii) Husband has insurable interest in the life of his wife*

Like insurable interest of wife, there also exists an insurable interest of husband in the life of his wife to an unlimited extent. This is not required to be proved. The husband has insurable interest in the life of his wife because domestic services are performed by the wife. If the wife is dead, husband has to employ some other person to render the domestic services including rearing children, if infants/small/school going/handicapped, etc. and has to incur financial expenditure. Therefore, the husband is benefited by the survival of his wife. The husband has unlimited insurable interest in the life of his wife because monetary loss at her death cannot be measured.

### *(b) Case where Proof is Required*

Insurable interest is to be proved in the following cases:

#### *(i) In Business Relationship*

The policyholders may have insurable interest in the life of the insured (prospect) due to business or contractual relationship as illustrated below:

A creditor has insurable interest in the life of his debtor: The creditor may lose money if the debtor dies before the repayment of loan. The survival of debtor is financially meaningful to the creditor because creditor will get all his money repaid at the survival of debtors. The maximum amount of loss to a creditor may be the amount of outstanding loan plus interest thereon and the amount of premium paid. The full amount of policy is payable irrespective of the payment of loan and interest because it is life insurance.

*Partners have insurable interest in the life of each other (as partners)*

At the death of a partner, the partnership will generally be dissolved and the surviving partners will suffer loss financially. Some partners may be having more experience and business contacts. At least, all partners form a cohesive team and such a team may not easily be formed again; there is risk. Therefore, all the partners have an insurable interest in the life of each partner because they will financially suffer at the death of any partner.

*An employer has insurable interest in the life of a key person*

A key person is the person whose presence, capital, capacity, etc. cause profit to the business. If the key person is dead, the employer may suffer a financial loss. The business has to incur extra expenses involved in appointing and training of new person in his place. Thus, business has insurable interest in the life of key-person.

*(ii) Family Relationship*

The insurable interest may arise due to family relationship if pecuniary interest exists between the policyholder and life assured because of blood relationship, e.g. a son can insure his father's life only when he is dependent on him and father can take insurance policy on his son's life only when he is dependent on his son. Insurable interest in these cases takes a wider view. There is emotion involved. Father, Mother and son or daughter are members of the same family and there is emotional bonding together. Each has insurable interest in the other or others and is keen to provide for the rainy day.

## General Rule Relating to Insurable interest Applicable in Life Insurance

*Time of Insurable Interest*

The insurable interest must exist at the time of the proposal. It is not essential that the insurable interest must be present at the time of claim.

*Service*

Services provided by other relatives will not essentially form insurable interest except the services provided by the wife. There must be financial relationship between the offerer and the life assured, e.g. the services performed by the son without depending on his father will not constitute insurable interest in the father.

*Insurable interest must be valuable*

In business relationship, the value of insurance must be determined properly. Insurance is limited only upto the amount of insurable interest, measured in terms of money value.

*Insurable interest should be valid*

insurable interest should not be against public policy and should be recognized by law as such.

*The legal responsibility may be the basis of insurable interest*

Since the person will suffer financially up to the extent of responsibility, the proposer has insurable interest to that extent only.

*Insurable interest must be definite*

The insurable interest must be present definitely at the time of the proposal, not vague. Mere expectation of gain and support will not institute insurable interest.

*Legal consequence of insurable interest*

The insurable interest must be there to form a legal and valid insurance contract. It would be null and void without insurable interest.

## (III) LIFE INSURANCE IS BASED ON UTMOST GOOD FAITH

It is settled in law and is the practice in insurance business that the life insurance contract requires that the principle of utmost good faith should be conserved by both the parties, i.e., the insured and insurer. The principle of utmost good faith provides that both the parties, insured and insurer, must be of the same mind at the time of contract because only then the risk may be correctly assessed. Both the parties must make full and true disclosure of all material facts to each other.

As regards material facts, these facts are those pieces of information which may affect the decision of parties to enter or not to enter into life insurance contract. The principle of utmost good faith, therefore, means that the contracts which require absolute and utmost good faith on the part of both the parties, i.e. the insured and the insurer, concerned with life insurance contract.

There must be full and true disclosure of all material facts to the risk. Full and true disclosure refers to that there should be no concealment, misrepresentation, half disclosure and fraud of the subject matter to be insured.

### Which are the Material Facts?

In life insurance, material facts are: Name, address and

occupation of the insured person; date of birth, age, height and weight, etc.; facts about life and habits; family history; information about the health of offerer; and quantum and nature of income of proposer.

For the contract of life insurance, the person taking out a policy has to fill-up a proposal form. The insured must give all material facts known to him. Generally, a printed form is supplied to the insured to answer the questions contained by giving detailed information in respect of the above discussed facts. The proposer has to declare that he has furnished all information truly and correctly.

*Duty of both parties to the Insurance Contract*

Both the insured and the insurer are equally responsible to disclose all material facts. Since the decision is taken by the insurer on the basis of facts supplied by the insured, it is more of responsibility of the proposer to disclose the material facts.

*Legal Consequence of Utmost Faith*

In the absence of utmost good faith, the contract will be voidable at the option of the person who has suffered a loss due to non-disclosures of material information. The intentional non-disclosure amounts to fraud and renders the contract as void; unintentional non-disclosure is voidable at the option of the party, not at fault.

*Facts not Required to be Disclosed*

However, the following facts are not required to be disclosed by the insured:

Circumstances which are diminishing the risk; facts which are known or should reasonably be known to the insurer in his ordinary course of business; facts which are waived-off by the insurer; and facts of public knowledge.

## (IV) WARRANTIES

Warranties are the stipulations or conditions embodied in a policy either expressly or impliedly, which form the part and parcel of the main contract of life insurance.

A warranty is promise made by the insured to the insurer

that something shall or shall not be done or that a certain state of affairs does or does not exist.

In a contract of insurance, a common case of implied warranty is to disclose dangerous nature of goods to be insured. It is immaterial for what purpose a warranty is incorporated in the policy and whether it is material to the risk or not, but being included in the policy, it must be strictly complied with. If it is not so complied with, the insurer may be discharged from liability as from the date of the breach of warranty.

Warranties are an integral part of the contract. These are the bases of the contract between the insured and insurer. If any statement, whether material or non-material, is untrue, the contract shall be null and void and the premium paid by him may be forfeited. The statement of the insured shall form part of the policy and will be the basis of the contract. The warranties may be of the following kinds:

*(i) Informative Warranties*

In life insurance, the informative warranties are more important. The proposer is expected to disclose all the material facts to the best of his knowledge and belief.

*(ii) Promissory Warranties*

Warranties relating to the future may only be the statements about his expectation or intention; for example, the proposer promises that he will not take up any hazardous occupation and will inform the insurer if he does so.

*Breach of Warranty*

If there is any breach of warranty, the insurer is not bound to perform his part of the contract unless he chooses to ignore it. The effect of a breach of warranty is to render the contract voidable at the option of the other party provided there is no element of fraud. In case of fraudulent representation, the contract will be void.

## (V) PROXIMATE CAUSE

The efficient or effective cause which causes the loss is called proximate cause. It is the real, direct and actual cause of loss. If the cause of loss is insured, the insurer will pay, otherwise the insurance company will not indemnify the loss and deny claim.

In life insurance, the doctrine of proximate cause is not applicable because the insurer is bound to pay the amount of insurance whatever may be the reason of death. This principle is not of much importance in life insurance except in following cases:

*(i) War-Risk*

Where a policy on exclusion of war and aviation risk is issued, the efficient or direct cause of death is important because the insurer can waive its liability if death occurred, in this case, while the insured was engaged in operation of war and aviation. Only premium paid by the insured or surrender value accrued on the policy, whichever is higher, is payable, and the total policy amount is not payable.

*(ii) Suicide*

If the insured commits suicide within one year of the policy, or there was intention to commit suicide, then payment of policy would be restricted, only up to the interest of the third party in the policy provided the interest was expressed at least one month before the suicide.

*(iii) Accident Benefit*

A problem arises when an insured under an accident policy is killed or suffers an injury which has an immediate cause and also a remote cause. In an accident benefit policy, double of the policy amount is paid. So, the cause of death in this policy is more important.

## (VI) ASSIGNMENT AND NOMINATION

The life insurance policy can be assigned freely for a legal consideration or love and affection. The assignment shall be complete and effectual only on the execution of such endorsement either on the policy itself or by a separate deed. Notice for this intention must be given to the insurer who will acknowledge the assignment. Once the assignment is completed, it cannot be revoked by the assignor unless re-assignment is made by the assignee in favour of the assignor.

The holder of a life insurance policy may either at the time of effecting policy or at any subsequent time before the policy matures, nominate the person or persons to whom the money secured by the policy shall be paid in the event of his death. A nomination can be cancelled before maturity. When the policy matures, or if the nominee dies, the sum shall be paid to the policyholder or his legal representative.

## (VII) RETURN OF PREMIUM

Ordinarily, the premium once paid cannot be refunded. However, in the following cases, the premia paid are returnable:

### By Agreement in the Policy

The insured may pay full premium while effecting the insurance, but it may be agreed to return it wholly or partially on the happening of certain events.

### For Reason of Equity

Equity implies a condition when the insurer shall not receive the price of running a risk he runs. Thus, the contract does not come into effect in this case or it is held to be void *ab initio*.

## (VIII) OTHER FEATURES OF LIFE INSURANCE

Life insurance contract has the following additional features:

### (1) Alcatory Contract

Alcatory contract refers to contract that depends on chance. In ordinary contract, approximately equal value is exchanged by both the parties, but in life insurance contract, the full sum assured may be payable even if all premia are not paid. Thus, on the event of death, higher amount is payable.

### (2) Unilateral Contract

Life insurance contract is unilateral contract, because only the insurer makes an enforceable promise. The offerer had already performed his duty of payment of premium. If the first premium is paid, the insurer is bound to accept subsequent premium and to pay the amount of claim when it arises except in case of fraud.

**(3) Conditional Contract**

Life insurance contract is conditional contract because the insurer shall pay the assured sum only when the contract is continuing by payment of premium. In addition, the promise of insurer to pay the sum assured is also conditional upon the furnishing of satisfactory proof of death and other conditions mentioned in the policy.

**(4) Contract of Adhesion**

Contract of adhesion means that the terms of the contract are not arrived by mutual negotiations between the parties as in the case of ordinary contracts. The offerer is not in a position to bargain about the terms of contract because these terms are already determined. The only course open to the offerer is whether to accept or not a particular policy as a product which is a standard one for all alike.

**(5) Indemnity Contract is not Applied**

The indemnity contract is not applicable in case of life insurance contract because the value of loss at death cannot be ascertained. It is not possible to ascertain the time up to which the insured would have survived and it is also difficult to ascertain the amount of money to be earned by him during life-time.

**(6)** Doctrine of subrogation is also not applicable to life insurance contract.

# 8

# *Life Insurance Corporation of India: Organisational Set-up*

## INTRODUCTION

In June 1956, a Bill was passed in Parliament for establishing Life Insurance Corporation of India (LIC), which started functioning with effect from September 1, 1956. LIC is a body corporate having perpetual succession and a common seal with powers to acquire, hold and dispose of property and may sue and be sued in its own name.

## OBJECTIVES OF LIFE INSURANCE CORPORATION OF INDIA

The following are the important objectives of establishing LIC:

### To Widen the Scope of Insurance

The main objective of LIC is to spread life insurance awareness much more widely and in particular to the rural areas and to the socially and economically backward classes with a view to approaching all insurable persons in the country.

**To Provide Protection**

Another important objective of LIC is to provide adequate financial cover against death at a reasonable cost.

**Mobilizing the Savings for Development**

LIC also contributes towards maximizing mobilization of savings of public for further channelizing them into the economy by selling insurance products/cover-linked savings adequately attractive.

**To Act as Trustees**

It is also an important objective of LIC. LIC acts as trustee of the insured public in their individual and collective capacities.

**To Meet Insurance Needs**

LIC is established with a view to meeting the various life insurance needs of the community that would arise in the changing social and economic environment.

**To Provide Services to the Public**

Another objective of LIC is to involve all people working in the corporation to the best of their capability in protecting the interest of the insured public by providing efficient service with courtesy.

## ORGANIZATIONAL SET-UP OF LIC

### (I) The Set-up of LIC Involves

#### *(a) Committees*

Various committees of the corporation are constituted under the LIC Act and the regulations are framed by them. General superintendence and direction of the affaires of LIC is entrusted to an Executive committee. This committee exercises all powers over matters delegated to it by the Corporation. An investment committee is constituted for advising the Corporation in matters pertaining to investment of funds. It is composed of not more than 7 members and 3 are members of the Corporation and the others are persons having special knowledge and experience in financial matters. Other committees constituted by the Corporation for helping the corporation are:

Personnel Advisory Committee
Building Advisory Committee
Development Advisory Committee
Budget Advisory Committee

The Chairman of the Corporation is the *ex-officio* Chairman of all these Committees.

In the discharge of its functions, the Corporation, vested with powers under Section 21 of the LIC Act, shall be guided by such direction in matters of policy involving public interest as the Central Government may give it in writing.

### *(b) Central Office*

The Central Office of the LIC is located in Mumbai. The central office confines itself mainly to giving broad policy directions and decisions and co-ordinates the activities of various divisions.

### Functions of Central Office

(a) It has directional and executive responsibilities over a limited field.
(b) Investment policy and investing of funds in accordance with that policy are the sole responsibility of the Central Office.
(c) The formulation of underwriting standards, premium rate and underwriting of large proposals which are beyond the limits of the operating divisional offices, particularly, policies for large sums insured and policies on lives of sub-standard nature are also attended by the Central Office.
(d) Submission of statutory returns to the Government, standardization of procedure, forms, drawing-up of prospectus, premium rate, policy conditions and making arrangements with regard to reinsurance and other unspecified/residual responsibilities are undertaken by the Central Office.
(e) Inspection of the various offices and internal auditing of the various offices are also done by the Central Office.

### (c) Departments

The policy decisions are made by the Chairman of the Corporation with the help of the Executive Committee and various other Committees and they are assisted by the various departments of Central Office. The Central Office has the following departments:

Development; Publicity and Public Relations; Accounts; Investment; Secretarial and Personnel; Inspection; Internal Audit; Legal and Mortgages; Building; Foreign; Actuarial and Electronic Data Processing Department.

#### *(1) Field Organizational Formation*

The LIC has a large number of insurance agents for the procuration of Life Assurance business. These insurance agents are remunerated to way of commission on the premium received on policies sold by them. The LIC has a number of Development Officers, who were originally designated as inspectors or Field Officers, to asset the agents in the selling of life assurance, to train them up and to supervise their working. The Development Officers are full-time salaried employees of the Corporation and their functions are as under:

Appointment and training of agents in the selling of life insurance; giving guidance to the agents in rendering efficient after sales services to the policyholders; creating enthusiasm in the agents to procure more and more business; and keeping up the agents' interest when there is ebb in their business flow.

The work of the Development Officers and the Agents attached to a particular branch is supervised by the Branch Manager who is assisted in this work by an Assistant Branch Manager (Development) where the Branch controls a very large field organization. Generally, the Branch Manager is also assisted by an Assistant Branch Manager (Administration) in supervising the office administration of the branch.

### (d) Different Departments of LIC

#### *(1) Development Department*

Development Department deals with the planning of the development of new business, opening up of new offices, matters relating to development officers and agents who constitute the external wing of the organization. The agents have an important role in the development of insurance in the country. The following services are normally expected from the agents:

(a) Programmed selling, i.e. selling of right type of policies suitable to the needs of the prospective customers for the right amount.
(b) Proper completion of all requirements at the underwriting stage so as to minimize references back.
(c) Persuading the offerer to furnish age proof and effect nomination at the proposal stage itself so as to obviate likely difficulties that may arise later.
(d) Keeping in touch with the policyholders for ensuring regular payment of premia in time.
(e) Assistance to the policyholder for revival of the policy in case of default including giving revival quotations and getting all revival requirements completed.
(f) Assistance to the policyholders in matters of alteration of plans or sum assured necessitated on account of change in the needs of the policyholders.
(g) Assistance to the policyholders in claim settlement.

The Development Officers of the Corporation are to assist their agents in matters connected with procurement of new business and to discharge other relevant functions. The main functions of the Development Officers are as under:

(a) To develop and increase the procurement of new life insurance business in a planned way as far as may be practicable in the area allotted to him or in which he is allowed to work through agents placed under his supervision by the Corporation.
(b) To guide, supervise and direct the activities of all such agents.
(c) To recruit and train new agents so as to develop a stable agency force.
(d) To act generally in such a way as to activate the existing agents and motivate new agents.

(e) To provide all such services to the policyholders as will produce better policy servicing.
(f) To work in the area allotted to him by the Corporation as a representative of LIC.
(g) Any other types of duties as LIC may call upon him to do.

The Agents and Development Officers are an important wing of the corporation. The Development Officers are remunerated by means of regular salary and other allowances whereas the agents are remunerated for their services by way of commission payable on the amount of premia collected. Commission rates vary according to the plan and term of assurance.

On major popular policies of insurance offered by LIC, the commission payable on first year's premium is 25% of the premium, second year and third year's commission is $7^1/_2$% and commission on subsequent years premium is 5%. The higher rate of commission on the first year's premium is to compensate the agents for their extra effort which they have made in selling idea of insurance to prospects. All matters relating to Development Officers and Agents are handled or processed by the Development Department of the Central Offices and they are assisted by various operating offices.

*(2) Publicity and Public Relations Department*

Like all corporate entities, life insurance entities have Public Relations Department, manned by trained, qualified and extrovert personnel. The overall publicity arrangements and the maintenance of public relations are effected by this department.

*(3) Investment Department*

Premium money flows in like a stream every day. Money can not be kept idle. It has to be invested in permissible securities and stocks. This department is, therefore, concerned with the day-to-day management of various investments of the Corporation.

*(4) Accounts Department: Proper Accounting is Very Important in all Companies/Corporations*

The Accounts Department is to co-ordinate and

consolidate the accounts of various units of the Corporation. The accounts department is concerned with the preparation of the budgets of various operating offices and effecting budgetary control.

*(5) Secretarial and Personnel Department*

This department deals with all staff matters as well as establishment needs of various offices.

*(6) Legal Department*

This department has the responsibility to advise other departments on legal issues and looks after/follows-up the conduct of the litigations in various courts.

*(7) Building Department*

It has the responsibility of planning and executing the construction programmes (building construction) and the development of properties of corporation including their general maintenance.

*(8) Internal Audit Department*

Audit ensures correctness of accounts and other operations. Therefore, this department makes concurrent audit of the transactions of the corporation in the light of the administrative policy standards and procedures laid down.

*(9) Inspection Department*

Inspection provides on-the-spot guidance and observes whether all policies, procedures and healthy practices are being followed in all the operating units/offices. Inspection department is, therefore, responsible for the periodic inspections of the various offices.

*(10) Actuarial Department*

Costing and evaluation are very important aspects of insurance companies. Actuarial Department is, accordingly, in charge of the various actuarial aspects of insurance. These include the premium rates, terms and conditions of life insurance policies, etc.

*(11) Foreign Department*

This department handles all foreign business activities of corporation.

**(II) Organizational Structure of the Life Insurance Corporation of India**

Under the provision of LIC Act, the organizational set-up consists of a four-tier structure.

**Structure of LIC**

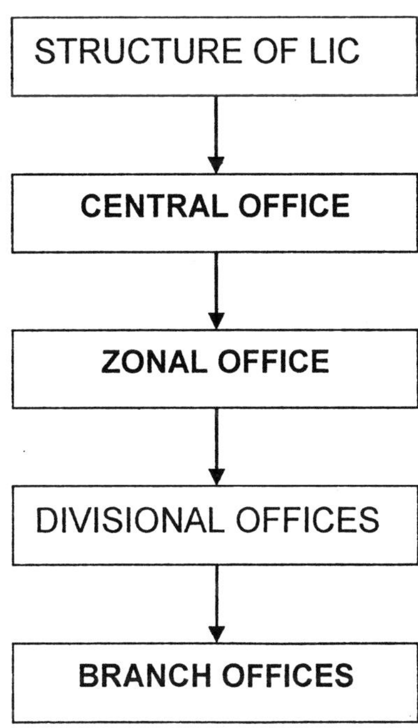


*(a) Central Office*

Central Office is at the top of organizational structure basically concerned with formulation of policies and corporation's planning for development of business and formulating corporate strategies to retain leading position in the insurance market.

*(b) Zonal Offices*

There are five zonal offices in the country:

Functionally, the zonal offices assist the central office in the matter of development, planning and review of business and supervision of divisional offices within their jurisdiction. The five zonal offices are situated in Delhi, Kanpur, Kolkata, Mumbai and Chennai.

These zonal offices have several divisional offices and branch offices under their jurisdiction, activities of which are mainly relating to the managerial function of co-ordination. They are accordingly concerned with the execution of the decisions arrived at by the Corporation from time to time.

**Functions of a Zonal Office**

(a) The functions of a zonal office consist of control over the entire development and field staff and execution of planning strategies for the business development of the zone.
(b) Giving pieces of advice on all personnel and legal matters, management of buildings belonging to the corporation, purchase of stationery, equipment and furniture, printing of literature and forms, etc. for the whole zone.
(c) Compiling of the accounts of the zone and giving general guidance for all divisional matters, particularly in the matter of accounting principles and procedures.
(d) Investigation of all doubtful claims arising in the zone.

*(c) Divisional Offices*

A Divisional Office is akin to a head office of an erstwhile insurer and is concerned with all activities of the insurer from procurement of new business to the settlement of claims. The Administrative Reforms Commission (ARC) submitted its report on Life Insurance Corporation's administration to the Government of India in December 1968. The government has decided that "Some of the decision-making powers of the central office and the zonal offices should be decentralized to Divisional Offices and powers of functionaries delegated to the lower levels. The role of the Zonal Office be drastically curtailed and steps should be taken to enable the Divisional Offices to function virtually as the head offices where decisions would terminate. Therefore, the zonal offices of the corporation are for the present in a stage of transferring most of the functions to the divisional offices. Government functioning is highly bureaucratic and delegation is hard to implement. Let us hope that one day, keeping in view the globalization process, free trade regime would be in place and at that time, LIC would surely be a privately owned organization.

## Departments of a Divisional Office of LIC

### *New Business Development Department*

This department handles all new proposals of life insurance from the stage of registration of proposal till issue of the policy.

### *Policyholders' Servicing Department*

It handles all policy servicing aspects right from the stage of issue of the policy till settlement of claim.

### *Accounts Department*

This department handles all accounting work including control on branch accounts, maintenance of bank accounts and accounting of premium collection and other money receipts and all payments.

### *Development Department*

Department of development handles all work in connection with field organization including maintenance of business statistics, appointment of agents and field officers, etc. It is like a planning department.

### *Personnel and Establishment Department*

This department handles all staff matters including maintenance of salary and leave records, inward mail and dispatch work, supply of stationery and furniture. It is staff (services) department.

*Group and Superannuating Schemes Department*

It is saddled with responsibility of processing and servicing group business.

*Machine and Adenoma Department*

It looks after purchase, maintenance, up-keep, replacement of machines, equipment and computers, etc.

*(d) Branch Offices*

There are branch offices under each divisional office of LIC. These offices are concerned with the execution of the decisions arrived at by the corporation from time to time. These offices do tactical planning to translate strategic planning into concrete business, keeping in view the grass-root realities.

In view of the ARC recommendations, at present, branch offices are also in the process of transition from merely business producing and selling wings of the organization to that of an office giving complete service to its policyholders within the branch in all matters from the inception of the policy till the settlement of claims. The major/special sections of branch office are new business development, the policyholders servicing, accounts and establishment.

**Functions of a Branch Office**

The functions of a branch office of LIC are as under:

*Registration of New Proposals*

The main function of a branch office is registration and scrutiny of new proposals, collection of premium under the new proposals and issue of receipts.

*Correspondence*

The branch office has to make correspondence with the proposers (prospects) and the agents in connection with the proposals.

*Settlement of Commission*

Settlement of commission on first premium instalment and payment of medical fees to doctors are the responsibilities of this section.

*Collection of Premium*

Another important function of a branch office is collection of premia under various policies and giving services to the local policyholders.

*Supervision*

A branch office supervises the working of agents and field officers attached to the branch.

*Disbursement*

Disbursement of loans on different policies is serviced by the branch.

In major cities, a number of branch offices known as city branch offices, have been established for procuring new business with aggressive marketing strategies.

Let us accept it as hard fact that the basic operating and servicing office is the branch office which has to be proactive in rendering top class service to the existing policyholders. It is undisputed fact that a satisfied customer is worth hundred new customers because he/she would function as voluntary ambassador for the LIC. Divisional Office is the controlling office and gives manifold support to branches, on its own or on being requisitioned by the branch offices.

# Insurance Legislation in India

A series of Acts were passed to regulate insurance business in India. The legislation was considered necessary as the insurance activities went on increasing with the growing awareness among the prospects for more reasons than one. The process started with the passage of Insurance Act, 1938.

## The Insurance Act, 1938

In 1934, the Government appointed S.C. Sen, a well-known solicitor, as Officer on Special Duty in the Department of Commerce to study and report on the amendments to insurance legislation. Sen propounded the British ideal of minimum statutory control with maximum publicity. With some modifications, the government set-up an informal Advisory Committee of leading insurance men, headed by N.N. Sircar, the then Law Member. This committee elicited views and suggestions from many stakeholders and submitted a bill to the Legislative Assembly in 1937. The bill stirred up intense public interest in the country; trade associations submitted memoranda, insurance associations pressed for amendments and a Lloyd's representative flew over from London to watch their interest. Over a thousand amendments were suggested from various quarters and at last the Insurance Act, 1938 was enacted.

However, soon the market started criticizing the Act for its drafting mistakes, contradictions and impractical clauses. Though it was widely conceded that the act wrote a fresh chapter into the history of Indian insurance by attempting to prevent the formation and continuation of mushroom companies, and by introducing sound insurance business practices. Some authors commented that it became the most controversial law among Indian statutes.

In quick response to the criticism, the government made two amendments to the Act in 1939. To remove certain difficulties in administration, the Act was again amended in 1940. The market situation that came up with World War II and the insurers' experience of working with the Act necessitated further changes, and further amendments were made in 1941, 1942, 1944, 1946 and 1948.

Despite the flaws, the 1938 Act gave the Indian market a regulatory foundation and among other things, provided for the constitution of a Department of Insurance, compulsory registration of insurance companies, provision for deposits, control on investments of funds, filing of returns on investments and financial condition, licensing of agents, control on commission, prohibition of rebates, filing of policy conditions and premium rates duly certified by an actuary (in the case of life business), periodical valuation of liabilities, and provision for policyholders' directors. The Act granted very wide powers to the Controller of Insurance in the matter of insurance regulation. The government visualized that the Controller of Insurance should be a person of extraordinary calibre, be actuarially qualified, having human considerations and broad outlook to administer law tactfully and even-handedly. The Indian insurance legislation was lauded by contemporary commentator as an excellent attempt to penalize the corrupt directors and executive officers, check wild cat schemes and scandals, and to stop acquisition of insurance companies by designing financiers.

The Insurance Act became the corner-stone of Indian insurance legislation and along with the insurance Rules formed under it, still remains the most comprehensive legislation on the subject.

### The Insurance Amendment Act, 1950

The introduction of this comprehensive legislation,

however, did not prevent the large-scale increase of new companies and the failures of existing companies. In response to the situation, in April 1945 a committee under the chairmanship of Sir Cowasji Jehangir was appointed to enquire into the undesirable developments in the management of the insurance companies and recommend suitable remedial measures. On the basis of this committee's recommendations, a bill was introduced. The bill was thrice referred to a Select Committee and thrice withdrawn on account of various reasons. Again, a committee under the chairmanship of S. Ranganathan was appointed to report on the working of the Indian Insurance Act and to give suggestions for further legislation. The Bill was redrafted, incorporating the suggestions of the committee and passed as the insurance Amendment Act, 1950.

The salient features of this Act are the requirement of minimum capital, stricter control on investment and submission of periodical returns on investments, ceiling on expenses of management and agency commission, and appointment of administrators for mismanaged companies. The amendment created a statutory Association called the General Insurance Council. The existing Insurance Associations at Bombay, Calcutta and Madras were converted into the Bombay, Calcutta and Madras Regional Councils under the General Insurance Council with powers to frame and enforce tariff rates and regulations. Another statutory body called the Tariff Committee was constituted under the General Insurance Council and vested with powers to control and regulate the rates, advantages, terms and conditions that may be offered by its members and associate members in respect of general insurance business. The Tariff Committee was an All India body controlling and exercising powers over all Regional Council. Although the actual rates were framed by the Rating Committees of Regional Councils, the Tariff Committee had the power to decide all major outstanding issues and, if necessary, override the Regional Councils.

### The Insurance Amendment Act, 1968

Even after the enactment of the amendment to the Insurance Act, the failure of companies did not stop. As per published reports, during the ten-year period from 1945 (when the Jehangir Committee was constituted) to 1954, 533 valuation reports of insurance companies were submitted to the Controller of Insurance. Of these, 86 valuations showed a deficit, which was not covered by the free paid-up capital. Of these, 25 insurers went into liquidation and another 25 insurers had to transfer their business to other companies. This situation created an increased focus on the social security angle of insurance and the hardships that the common people would suffer if insurance companies became bankrupt. In response to the situation, the Insurance Act of 1938 was again amended in 1968 in order to provide for better social control over general insurance business. This amendment is popularly referred to in insurance circles as the introduction of social control measures of 1968 or as Social control amendments.

The amendment provided for regulation of investments, minimum solvency margin regulations, payment of premium before commencement of risk, licensing of surveyors, empowered the Controller to carry out inspection, investigation and search, and seizure of books. These amendments, which came into force in June 1969, renamed the Tariff Committee of the General Insurance Council as the 'Tariff Advisory Committee' and established it as a body corporate with perpetual succession and made the Controller of Insurance as its Chairman.

### The General Insurance Business (Nationalization) Act, 1972 (GIBNA)

On January 19, 1956, the Central Government took over the 154 Indian Life Insurance Companies, 75 provident societies and 16 non-Indian insurance companies then operating in India. These were nationalized and the Life Insurance Corporation of India was formed on September 1, 1956 by the enactment of the Life Insurance Corporation of India Act, 1956. The persistent problem of insolvency of life insurers was possibly the most compelling reason leading to the nationalization of the life insurance business. Corresponding changes on the general insurance side were also being contemplated by the government.

On May 13, 1971, an ordinance was promulgated by the President of India to take over the management of the existing 107 general insurance companies by the Government of India. Vide the General Insurance Business (Nationalization) Act, 1972, the General Insurance Corporation of India (GIC) and its four nationalized subsidiaries were formed with effect from January 1, 1973 and all the existing 107 general insurance companies were merged with these four companies. The four Nationalized general insurance companies thus formed were The National Insurance Company Limited with its head office at Kolkatta, The New India Assurance Company Limited headquartered at Mumbai, the Oriental Insurance company with New Delhi as its head office, and the Untied India Insurance Company Limited with its head quarters at Chennai. A small segment comprising a few state government Insurance Departments insuring properties owned by the respective states had substantial financial interests, Crop Insurance Departments of State Governments, the Calcutta Hospital and Nursing Home Benefits Association Limited, Export Credit and Guarantee Corporation Limited, and the Deposit Insurance Corporation were expected from the scope of the take over. These insurance companies are referred to as exempted insurers in the market. The cumulative effect of all these successive developments was that the Indian general insurance industry was changed into a state monopoly from January 1, 1973. (As explained earlier, the life insurance industry had already become a state monopoly).

The general insurance market was thus left with four public sector insurers who sold the same products at the same rates, either under tariffs formed by the Tariff Advisory Committee or under market agreement entered among the four companies and competition was limited only to the quality of service. Nationalization was generally successful in generating more confidence in the insured, as contrast signed with government owned companies were perceived as backed by a sovereign assurance. The new public sector companies inherited a diversified portfolio, talented personnel and strategic business connections on which they could build on. Insurance penetration increased, ancillary services got organized and employment opportunities grew rather consistently for 15 to 20 years.

Nationalization, however, had its own share of weaknesses. Problems arose due to overstaffing, governmental interference in management, lack of freedom in decision-making, inability of the management of nurture feelings of company loyalty, as well as deficiencies in the system, which could neither provide enough motivation for meritorious employees nor effectively penalize employees for non-performance or lethargy. Professionalism started waning and market penetration stagnated. Growth in the balance sheet was largely limited to the country's inflation and the returns that companies could earn by investing their surplus funds were low. The report of the Advisory Group on Insurance Regulation (AGIR) of the Standing Committee on International Financial Stands and Codes set-up by the Reserve Bank of India describes the national market situation with one holding company and four subsidiaries as follows:

The "phased globalization of the Indian economy that started in the early nineties began having its impact on this monopolistic structure. Further, the liberalization of insurance markets was among the objectives of the Uruguay round negotiations being conducted under the auspices of GATT. These negotiations included trade in services, and insurance had been included in the context of financial services (Para 59 of UNCTAD Report, January 19, 1993).

**Machinery of the Insurance System**

The legal entity that assumes the risk is the insurer. An entity seeking to transfer risk (an individual, corporation, association of any type, etc.) becomes the insured party once risk is assumed by an insurer, (the insuring party) by means of a contract called as insurance policy. The fee paid by the insured to the insurer for assuming the risk is called the premium. Generally, an insurance contract includes, at a minimum, the following elements, the parties (the insurer, the insured, and the beneficiaries), the premium, the period of coverage, the particular loss event covered and the amount of coverage (i.e. the amount to be paid to the insured or beneficiary in the event of a loss). The policy also states the kind of loss events (perils) that it covers either as an active statement or by a set of exclusions (events not covered).

When insured parties experience a loss for a specified peril, the coverage entitles the policyholders to make a claim against the insurer for the covered amount of loss as specified by the policy. When an insurer makes a payment on the claim, the insured is said to be indemnified against the loss events covered in the policy. Insurance premiums from many insured are used to fund accounts reserved for later payment of claims, theoretically, for a relatively fewer claimants and for overhead costs. An insurer has to set aside and maintain adequate funds for anticipated losses (i.e. reserves) and for his expenses in running the establishment and servicing the insured. The remaining margin is an insurer's profit.

### *Agents*

Apart from the above, there are insurance agents who represent the insurer to the insured and procure the business on behalf of their principal. Agents are given a commission on the business that they bring in. Agents are sometimes referred to as insurance advisors (or counsellors).

### *Brokers*

Insurance Brokers form another component of the insurance system. As the agent represents the insurer to the insured, the broker represents his client, someone in need of insurance, to one or more insurance houses. An insurance broker shops around of the best insurance policy amongst many companies.

However, with insurance brokers, the fee is usually paid in the form of commission from the insurer that is selected, rather than directly from the client. There are also companies known as insurance consultants. Similar to an insurance broker, an insurance consultant also shops around for the best insurance policy amongst many companies. However, in this context, the customers cause these consultants to shop around for the best insurance policy amongst many companies.

Neither insurance consultants nor insurance brokers are insurance companies and no risks are transferred to them during insurance transactions.

### *Third Party Administrators*

Third party administrators are certain expert companies in particular field that are contracted by insurance companies to perform claims handling service for a group or category of clients. These companies often have special expertise that the insurance companies do not have.

*Co-insurance*

Cases do exist where the insurers do not want to keep (or retain) the entire risk with them. In such cases, the insurers agree to share the risk and the premium proportionately. This arrangement is referred to as co-insurance.

*Re-insurance*

In many cases, the insurers may feel that retaining a particular risk or group of risks could be too risky for them. In other words, they may not like over exposure to a particular risk or type of risks. Often they retain a part of the risk up to the level that they feel comfortable, and transfer the remaining to another insurer called reinsurer. Thus, reinsurers provide insurance to insurance companies. Reinsurance is a means by which an insurance company can protect itself against the risk of losses by transferring its risk to other entities.

To sum up, reinsurance companies are insurance companies that sell policies to other insurance companies, allowing them to reduce their risk and protect themselves from very large losses. The reinsurance market is dominated by a few very large companies with huge reserves. A reinsure may also be a direct writer of insurance risks as well.

Insurance surveyors and claims adjusters are terms used to describe someone who evaluates the damage caused to property of people when an insurance related accident occurs. In both the United Kingdom and the Republic of Ireland, the term Loss Adjuster is used. They verify the extent of loss, examine the loss *vis-à-vis* the coverage of the insurance policy, investigate liability for the damages caused, and assess the liability under the policy. These professionals handle property claims involving damage to buildings and structures, or liability claims involving personal injuries or third person property damage from liability situations, such as motor vehicle accidents, or damage to ships or cargo on board, as the case may be. Some are specialized in a particular type of claims, while some surveyors and adjusters handle multiple types of claims and are known as Multi-Line adjusters.

## How is Insurance Regulated?

Insurers are regulated in different countries through different systems and procedures. However, there are some fundamental philosophies that form the basis of most of the insurance regulatory regimes among various countries. Some of the fundamental philosophies are discussed in this section.

Insurance companies are broadly classified into two: (a) Life insurance companies that sell life insurance, annuities and pension products, and (b) Non-life or General Insurance companies that sell other types of insurance. The main reason for the distinction between the two types of companies is that life, annuity and pension business is long-term in nature, coverage for life assurance or a pension can cover risks over many decades. By contrast, non-life insurance usually covers a shorter period, such as one year. These companies typically insure automobiles, buildings, household items, business, travel risks, merchandise in transit, ships, airplanes, accident risks and the like.

Insurance regulation is distinctly different from regulation in other branches of finance or economics. By virtue of the contract between the insured and the insurer, the premium paid to the insurer stays with him in return for a promise of indemnification in the event of a loss. The insurer needs to act as per his promise only if the fortuitous event happens. Theoretically, this situation arises only for a small number of policies issued by the insurer. Statistically, as the number of policies increase, the proportion of the number of losses to the number of policies actually decreases.

The uniqueness of insurance necessitates that its regulations have to be laid down in an intricate manner. Regulations need to be rigid enough to prevent fraudulent fly-by-night operators, flexible enough to promote genuine business decisions, and delicate enough to foster creative ideas. In contrast to the *laissez faire* or 'let the people do as they choose' philosophy in many other area so business, concepts of responsible underwriting, clarity of contract terms, transparency of dealings, prudent investments and policyholders' protection have been matters of regulatory concern.

## Watch on Funds

The insurer thus has large amounts of public funds under

his control and a much larger amount of promises to keep. Because of this unique position insurance holds in the market and the desired social objectives the insurance mechanism must serve, regulation has not only been accepted but encouraged by the insurance business as well as by the customers.

**Ensuring Long-term Financial Solvency**

The insurers have to guarantee performance of a financial obligation in the event of certain contingencies that might affect the insured at various degrees of probability. When such situations arise, if an insurer fails to hold the safety net, the particular insured's trust is betrayed. The larger issue is that the feeling of comfort and confidence that the general public resposes in the insurance industry gets shattered. Financial solvency is the foundation of public confidence in the private insurance mechanism and historically has been the primary objective of regulation. Here, the insurance regulator uses macro-level controls, such as prescribing a high capital base for issuing licenses and ensuring healthy solvency margins so that only deep pocketed players enter the insurance market.

**Standardizing Insurance Products**

Customers of tangible goods and services can easily evaluate the product and promises made by sellers. However, for customers of insurance, evaluating an insurer's promises to perform certain obligations under certain specified future situations is not an easy task. In contrast to consumable commodities and many financial services, insurance products are not subject to easy evaluation by the customers at the purchase point. One often finds that many insurance products are purchased merely to fulfil conditions set by banks or other financing institutions when loans are sanctioned. Many of the contract conditions are sometimes not comprehensible to the common man. Here, the insurance regulator ensures a considerable degree of standardization of insurance products.

The degree of standardization of products varies from country to country, from rigidly controlled tariff markets, such as India, Taiwan, Thailand, Sri Lanka at one end of the spectrum to open markets with minimal controls, such as Singapore, United Kingdom and many States of USA at the other extreme where insurance products are by and large controlled by the market forces of demand and supply. Self-explanatory terms of standardization, such as 'Prior Approval', 'Modified Prior Approval', 'Flex Rating', 'File and Use', 'Use and File', 'State Prescribed', etc. are internationally used to denote the degree of control exercised by the regulator on insurance products.

### Preventing Fraud and Speculation by Insurers

Because of the fiduciary nature of the policyholder-insurer relationship and the resulting opportunity for fraud and financial speculation, complete freedom of entry of new insurance firms into the market is not desirable. The situation of a large amount of public money getting pooled up in a few hands for long periods allows the possibility of the insurers mismanaging public funds through imprudent speculative investments, risky money management decisions or even sheer complacency, unless the market is well regulated. On the other hand, unless regulations allow sufficient flexibility, the insurers will not be able to make prudent innovative decisions to ensure a healthy growth of the funds entrusted to their care and custody. The insurance regulator has to decide how much freedom the insurers should enjoy while managing public funds. Strict norms for investment, transparency in balance sheets, and audit of accounts are some methods that regulators employ for enforcing discipline in financial management.

### Creating a Level Playing Ground

Economists concur that intensive unregulated competition in marketing insurance products can produce inadequate rates and insolvency, sharp loss adjusting practices, abortive policy language, and possible tendencies towards monopolization, all of which are recognized to be against public interests. Here, the regulator has to create a level playing ground for all insurers. Ensuring an equitable and congenial environment for all business houses well entrenched in the market, government guaranteed insurers, multinational corporate houses, novice insurers and local tender feet insurers is a daunting task for a regulator, apart from attempts towards standardizing insurance products. Regulators try to ensure a level playing ground by drawing uniform norms for drawing balance sheets, valuation of assets, actuarial vetting of rates, etc. also, norms are laid down for ensuring policyholders' protection and fairness in dealings. Standards of ethics are insisted upon in advertising as well as in correctly conveying policy terms to the insured through trained agents. The regulator has to maintain uniform yardsticks of strictness with all insurers whether dealing with violations of regulations or grievances relating to deficiencies in services.

**Monitoring Re-insurance**

The insurers need to enter into different types of reinsurance contracts as part of their business. The regulator has to ensure that foreign exchange is not unduly drained off through reckless reinsurance programmes of the insurers. Objectives of regulation could include maximizing the country's capacity to retain its insurance business within, or ensuring that local companies do not carry too much of risk, disproportionate to their capacity. Regulations would ensure that the insurers secure the best possible reinsurance protection, get competitive rates for placing the reinsurance business and simplify the administration of business. Many regulators specify that the insurers shall cede such percentage of the sum insured on each policy for different classes of insurance written in the country to a national reinsurer or reinsures registered in the country.

Other concerns include the financial position of the reinsurers, the possibility of the reinsurers becoming insolvent when there is a chain of catastrophes, unequal reinsurance arrangements entered into by inexperienced insurance companies and the possibility that insurance companies use reinsurance contract only as a means of cash transfer abroad. Experts in the field argue that having very low reinsurance limits may result in excessive outflow of foreign exchange and thus, it has to be guarded against. On the contrary, high retention limits may result in erosion of the stability of a company in case of large or catastrophic claims. There are instances of general insurance companies in some developing countries ceding hundred per cent of their business to reinsurers (i.e. zero retention limit), or acting as 'fronting' companies of reinsurers. Such activities are not regarded healthy for the market.

**Pricing of Insurance Products**

Proper rate fixing or pricing of an insurance product is an area of concern for the regulator. Stories of rate cutting are not unheard of even in closed markets where only government companies transact insurance business. Under-pricing of insurance products is malady very common to the relatively free markets of insurance. Cutting of rates below the actual cost of the indemnity weakens the industry. In open competitions, insurance rates are often dependent on the bargaining strength of the insured than the features of the risk as such. Large buyers, therefore, may obtain their insurance too cheaply, as opposed to others who are not in a position to drive sharp bargain. Effective regulation is needed to ensure that insurance products are priced on sound technical reasons.

An insurance policy should be correctly priced for different reasons. While a high price would bring better profits to the insurer, the insured has to bear the brunt of it. Also, potential clients would shy away from the market, thereby limiting the insurers' scope of reaping the advantages of the law of large numbers. A price less than adequate to meet the risk should no doubt bring joy to policyholder at the sales office. However, lesser price would erode the insurers' bottom line and weaken their capacity to meet their obligations in the event of a loss. Historically, insurance law-makers have dreaded this situation. As per the findings of the Joint Committee of the Assembly and Senate of the State of New York as early as 1911, "wherever there has been a cutting of rates below the actual cost of the indemnity and the policyholder gets his insurance very cheaply, its effect on all companies is weakening. They observe that the mutual character of insurance is so strong that nothing that tends to give inferior protection can be for the public good". An insurer's pricing objectives depend on the overall objectives of the insurer and the state of the insurance market. These pricing objectives may be expressed in three main ways to achieve a specified rate of return on capital, to maximize profits, and to maintain or extend market share.

Regulators address the issue of product pricing based on certain operational principle depending upon the degree of regulation each country decides upon. The guidelines issued by the Motor Accidents Authority (MAA), the regulatory body of the

New South Wales State of Australia, for the preparation of the rate filing reports are given below as an example—

> "Premiums must be sufficient to pay all acquisition and policy administration costs, provide a sum of money to meet the best estimate of the cost of claims (including claims management expense), provide a profit margin representing an adequate return on capital invested and compensation for the risk, and provide for other matters a prudent insurer would make provision for" (Hart, Buchanan, and Howe).

Rates should ensure the survival of the insurance company, achieving optimum strategic positioning, providing quality and value for the service, contributing to the society's well-being, and optimizing the returns for a given type of risk. Insurance pricing methods can be divided into three major categories: (i) individual rating, (ii) class or manual rating, and (iii) modification rating, usually referred to as merit rating. Principal modification rating methods include schedule rating, experience rating, retrospective rating and premium discount plans, the terms of the insurance contract, the conditions under which losses are payable (the insurance cover), and the past experience of losses in the particular type of insurance are taken into reckoning while fixing rates.

**Data Repository and Risk Evaluation**

Regulators require insurers to maintain their own internal databases and to create national data warehouses so that the products can be priced scientifically based on statistical data. In places, like Japan, New South Wales of Australia and Massachusetts of USA, the concept of Reference Loss Cost Rate (RLCR) is followed. Here, the insurer compares his past loss experience in a particular segment of insurance with the corresponding overall past loss experience in a particular segment of insurance with the corresponding overall past loss experience of the industry from a national data warehouse. Internationally there are many accepted standards of pricing insurance products and reserving or making provisions for future payment of claims. Premiums are the main sources of income for the insurers from which all the insurer's expenditure has to be met. An insurer's expenditure includes his management expenses, such as rent, office maintenance, salaries, agency commissions, advertisement expense, taxes, etc. on one hand, and pure claims costs, assumed liabilities, incidental expenditure, such as surveyor's fees, legal expense, etc. on the other.

### Theory of Large Numbers

When a dice is repeated many times, the average outcome is the expected value. The premium that an insured would pay would be minuscule compared to the magnitude of the loss that the insurer is liable to pay in the event of a claim. However, historically, the actual number (frequency) of loss-making policies are very less in comparison to the number of policies issued, and the total quantum of losses payable (severity) is lesser than the total amount of premium received. Thus, in any given period, the losses of the few are borne by the majority of the policyholders who do not incur losses. Statistically, the insurers know that the probability of incurring losses actually decreases when the number of policies increases. This apparent paradox is referred in insurance parlance as the law or theory of large numbers.

### Reserving

Even in the case of yearly policies, the insurer's liabilities go beyond the close of the policy period. The amount of the liability for future claim payments can be very uncertain, particularly for long-term classes and cannot be measured precisely. An insurer's standards for creating reserves or reserving for his liabilities are most important for his security. These liabilities include the insurer's liability to meet payments on claims that have been reported to the insurer (reported claims), payment on claim that have already occurred but have not yet been reported to the insurer called as incurred but not reported (IBNR) claims, payment on claims that have not yet occurred but for which the premium has already been paid, other payments, such as super annotation, long service leave, holiday pay, and so on. These liabilities have to be assessed for creating sufficient reserves. In countries where procedural delays are inherent to the judicial system, liability claims can take many years for a court judgment. The award may consist the liability amount, interest, as well as costs of the claimant. It is important, therefore, for the insurer to estimate his anticipated liabilities accurately and create reserves for settling them. This process, known as reserving, is done using actuarial calculations in many developed markets.

**Present Day Trends in Insurance**

The insurance industry has grown down the years alongside the economy. Modern day economists consider insurance penetration as yardstick of economic development. Most of the developed and developing countries have been taking significant steps in both economic and insurance reforms over the last three decades. The reform process is an ongoing process.

Bodies such as World Trade Organization (WTO), World Bank, Asian Development Bank (ADB), Basel Committee on Banking Supervision (BCBS) and many other international bodies have taken active interest in addressing insurance-related problems at intentional forum. The International Association of Insurance Supervisors (IAIS) is a full time body working for the development of insurance through multi-pronged strategies. It has developed core insurance principles relevant to contemporary markets, promoted discussions on areas of common concern, augmented educational endeavors of developing countries, and provided a forum of interaction among the insurance supervisors and professionals all over the world.

**Summary of the Above Discussion**

The unit has provided an overview of insurance and the basic concept of insurance so that you can appreciate the importance of insurance in the society and the economy. A brief history of the evolution of insurance as a separate stream of knowledge over the years has been provided in this unit. The evolution of the Indian market has also been traced. The unit familiarizes you to the insurance mechanism and the players in the insurance field. It also touches upon some common terms in the insurance market. The principles of insurance will be discussed in detail in unit 2. Fundamental aspects of insurance regulation along with its purposes have been discussed. A brief mention of the present day trend in insurance has been given.

(1) Insurance is an arrangement, whereby many other people who also are susceptible to the same type of losses share the financial losses of a few.
(2) The insured and the insurer are the two parties of an insurance contract.
(3) A risk is the uncertainty part of any activity that cannot be reasonably foreseen to happen within a particular time or in a particular manner. In insurance, the chance or likelihood of a loss to occur is the risk covered.
(4) An objective risk is one that exists in nature and is commonly applicable for all persons or entities facing the same situation. Risks are subjective when it depends on the individual's perception as to how far an objective situation can apply in his particular case.
(5) Risk can be categorized as 'pure' when there is a chance of a loss without any chance of gain. In case there is a possibility of a gain from the loss, the risk is called a 'speculative' risk.
(6) Risk perception is the subjective Judgement that people make about the characteristics and severity of a risk.
(7) Physical hazards refer to certain physical conditions that create or increase the chance of loss from any peril. Moral hazards denote the dishonesty of the insured that can increase the probability of a claim. Morale hazards refer to an indifferent or callous attitude of the insured that increases or inflates the quantum of loss.
(8) Personal losses such as death and poor health, losses to one's material possession such as houses and vehicles, loss of expected income from one's business consequential to a property loss, and liabilities to third parties are examples of insurable loses.
(9) Chinese merchants travelling treacherous river rapids would redistribute their wares across many vessels to limit the loss due to any single vessel's

capsizing. Babylonians developed a system around 1750 BC, whereby if a merchant received a loan to fund his shipment, he would pay the lender an additional sum in exchange for the lender's guarantee to cancel the loan, should the shipment be stolen. In Rhodes, there was a system, whereby, merchants whose goods were being shipped together would pay a proportionally divided premium that would be used to reimburse any merchant whose goods were jettisoned during storm or sinkage.

(10) The Great Fire of London that devoured 13,200 houses and caused losses of about pound 2 million to insurers, created a new awareness about insurance and increased cooperation among insurers that resulted in the creation of the fire (insurance) offices in 1868 and popularized fire insurance.

(11) The insurance principles of a group lay down that the losses of a few had been appreciated in India from very ancient times. In ancient India, the concept of 'Yogakshema' or insurance is found in the Rig Veda. Manu Smriti speaks of a system of co-operation and Yajnavalkya mentions some transactions akin to insurance. The 'Joint Family System' practised in India is seen by many as a form of micro-insurance to take care of calamitous situation, including death and sickness within the extended family.

(12) In post-World War-I India, encouraged by the spirit of nationalism, businessmen in Bombay established five offices to meet the insurance needs of Indian trade. The new insurance companies received support from the growth of nationalism in India, and Mahatma Gandhi and Nehru spoke in favour of Indian insurance institutions. Later on, hundred of Indian businessmen signed a pledge to insure only with Indian offices. As a result, Indian insurers' share of total business written in India rose from a mere 11 per cent in 1928 to 22 per cent in 1935 and to 31 per cent in 1939, largely at the expense of foreign offices, while the total business itself had increased only by 5 per cent during that period.

(13) The Act granted very wide powers to the Controller of Insurance in the matter of insurance regulation. The government visualized that the Controller of insurance should be a person of extraordinary calibre, qualified, tactful and even-handed. Compulsory registration of insurance companies, control on investments of funds, licensing of agents, control on commission, prohibition of rebates, and filing of policy conditions and premium rates duly certified by an actuary (in the case of life business) were made compulsory. The Indian insurance legislation was lauded by contemporary commentators as an excellent attempt to penalize the corrupt directors and executive officers, check wild cat schemes, and to stop acquisition of insurance companies by designing financiers.

(14) The Insurance Act became the corner-stone of Indian insurance legislation and, along with the Insurance Rules formed under it, remains the most comprehensive legislation on the subject.

(15) The main changes as result of the amendment were as follows:
  (a) Requirement of minimum capital,
  (b) Stricter control on investments,
  (c) Submission of periodical returns on investments,
  (d) Ceiling on expense of management and agency commission,
  (e) Appointment of administrators for mismanaged companies, and
  (f) Creation of Statutory bodies: General Insurance Council and Tariff Committee to frame and enforce tariff rates and regulations.

(16) Sir Cowasji Jehangir, chairman of the original committee, and S. Ranganathan, Chairman of the review committee.

(17) The amendments provided for:
  (a) Regulation of investments,
  (b) Minimum solvency, margin regulations,
  (c) Payment of premium before commencement of risk,

(d) Licensing of surveyors, and powers to the controller to carry out inspection, investigation and search and seizure of books.

Tariff committee of the General Insurance Council was renamed as Tariff Advisory Committee and established as a body corporate with perpetual succession, and the Controller of Insurance was made its chairman.

(18) After enactment of GIBNA, the general insurance market was left with four public sector insurers which sold the same products at the same rates, either under tariffs framed by TAC or under market agreements, and competition was limited only to the quality of service. Nationalization improved the confidence of the insured, as contracts signed with government owned companies were perceived as backed by a sovereign assurance.

(19) The four nationalized general insurance companies formed under GIBNA were the National Insurance Company Limited, the New India Assurance Company Limited, the Oriental Insurance Company, and the United India Insurance Company Limited.

(20) The legal entity that assumes the risk is the insurer. The entity which transfers the risk is the insured party, the fee paid by the insured to the insurer for assuming the risk is called the premium and the evidence of the contract is the insurance policy.

(21) Insurance Agents represent the insurer to the insured and procure the business on behalf of their principal. Insurance Brokers represent their clients, someone in need of insurance, to one or more insurance houses and shops around for the best insurance policy amongst many companies. Insurance surveyors/ Claims Adjusters are those who evaluate the damage caused to property or people when an insurance related accident occurs.

(22) Insurance regulation is considered different from regulation in other branches for various reasons:

(a) The product is bought and premium paid is for the promise of indemnification in the event of a loss.

(b) The insurer needs to act as per his promise only if the fortuitous event happens, which may arise only for a small number of policies.

(c) Regulations need to prevent fraudulent fly by night operators and ensure that the companies are there with sufficient funds to pay the claims when a loss occurs.

In contrast to the *laissez faire* philosophy in other areas of business, policyholders' protection has been the matter of regulatory concern.

(23) In insurance, the premium paid to the insurer is in return for a promise of indemnification in the event of any loss (partial or full of the subject-matter). The uniqueness of insurance necessities its regulations to be cover under the following aspects:

**Watch on Funds:** The insurer thus has large amounts of public funds under his control and a much larger amount of promises to keep.

**Ensuring Long-term Financial Solvency:** The insurer has to perform a financial obligation in the event of a loss that might happen at various degrees of probability. Financial solvency of the insurer is the foundation of the insurance mechanism, and historical the primary objective of regulation.

**Standardizing Insurance Product:** While customers of tangible goods and services can easily evaluate the products and promises made by sellers, evaluating an insurer's promises to perform certain obligations under certain specified future situations is not easy for those concerned with insurance.

**Preventing Fraud and Speculation by Insurers:** As a large amount of public money gets pooled up in a few hands for long period, there is a possibility of insurers mismanaging public funds through imprudent speculative investments, making risky money management decisions or being complacent, unless the market is well regulated.

**Creating a Level Playing Ground for all insurers:** Intensive unregulated competition in marketing insurance products can produce inadequate rates, denial of claims and abortive policy language, which are against public interest. So, the regulator has to create a level playing ground for all insurers.

(24) Regulators have to regulate reinsurance. Insurers need to enter into different types of reinsurance contracts as part of their business. The regulator has to check whether foreign exchange is unduly drained-off through reckless reinsurance programmes. Reinsurance should be for maximizing the country's capacity to retain its insurance business within and ensuring that the local companies do not carry too much of risk, disproportionate to their capacity. Many regulators insist that a percentage of the sum insured written in the country shall be ceded to national reinsure(s) registered in the country.

Regulators should ensure that the insurers secure the best possible re-insurance protection and get competitive rates for placing their reinsurance business. They should prevent unhealthy practices such as ceding hundred per cent of their business to reinsurers (i.e. with zero retention limit), or acting as 'fronting' companies of reinsurers. Such activities are not regarded healthy for the market.

Upto the 19th Century, insurance was in its inceptional stage and, therefore, there was no need for any insurance legislation. In most cases, the Companies Act, 1883 was applicable to business concerns, banking and insurance companies. New Indian Insurance Companies and Provident Societies started at the time of national movement. But these were financially unsound. It was felt that the Companies Act, 1883 was inadequate to provide security for insurance purpose. Therefore, two Acts were passed in 1912, namely, Provident Societies Act V of 1912 and Indian Life Insurance Companies Act VI of 1912. These acts were in pursuit of the English Insurance Companies Act of 1909 with the only difference that the Indian Life Insurance Companies Act related to life insurance only and excluded the non-life insurance business from its fold. The Act put life insurance business on sound footing and created healthier atmosphere than it was before. This led to dissolution and merger of many Indian and non-Indian life insurance companies. But legislations in India were confined to life insurance only because there were very few general insurance companies and thus it did not call for any legislation to control their limited activities.

The above-mentioned two Acts were governing only life insurance. There was no control on general insurance because such business was not much developed. Besides this, the Acts had the following limitations.

### Defects in the Acts

The above mentioned Acts had the following limitations:

There were no regulations relating to investment of insurance companies' funds. The need for restriction on investments was felt in India because unenlightened public was not able to judge the financial position of a company and its activities were secret for the most part, enough to mislead the public, if it wanted to. As there was no restriction on investment in English Act, no restriction was, therefore, placed in India too.

The control and enquiry was slight. Non-compliance of rules and regulations was not strictly penalized.

The foreign companies were required to submit report of their total business both in India and outside India. But separate particulars regarding business done in India were not demanded and the absence of these made it impossible to get any idea of the cost of procuring business in India for foreign companies and there was also no scope of comparing their data with similar data of the Indian companies.

The Government actuaries were not vested with the power to order investigation into the affairs of a company even when it appeared that the company was insolvent. Under the power of exemption, several new companies were granted exemption from submitting report to the Government.

Any one could start life insurance business only with the sum of Rs. 25,000. It was too low an amount of capital to prevent the mushroom growth of insurance companies. Foreign insurers were not bound to deposit a certain sum of life insurance premium collection on policies issued in India. Thus, it was not sufficient amount to check the flotation of unhealthy concerns and it provided discrimination in India.

The above discussed defects were compelling that the old Acts should be replaced.

**Reasons for Replacement of Act of 1912**

The above compelled the replacement. Persistent demands were made by various important public bodies and Swadeshi movements in that regard. The public demanded that general insurance business should also be controlled. The insurance companies particularly Fire, Marine and Accident insurance companies developed very fast during 1914-18 due to the First World War. Therefore, it was essential to control such new companies and to provide them with some proper guidelines and regulations. The important underwriters and business units demanded that there should be a full-fledged Insurance Act. The persistent demand was that the foreign underwriters should also be governed by the Indian Legislation. Some guiding principles for starting new business or for completing the jobs were required.

Therefore, the Government placed a bill for essential amendment of the Act in 1924. The bill was containing a wide scope of insurance business. The bill reached the Legislative Assembly after thorough scrutiny and comments by different bodies.

During the time, an important thing happened miraculously about the enactments of insurance business in England. The Government of India thought it fit to watch the course of new legislation of insurance on insurance law in England. Clauson Committee was appointed under the chairmanship of Mr. A.C. Clauson to report the possible and required changes in the Legislation in England. Therefore, Government of India thought it wise to postpone the bill to include the recommendations of Clauson Committee. The Clauson Committee submitted its report in February, 1927, but no action was taken on its recommendations by the government of England.

In 1928, the Government of India passed a temporary legislation with the main object of collecting statistics regarding insurance matters so that the information collected would be of value when the time would come to pass a comprehensive Act. This Act was not very comprehensive. The Government of India wanted to wait for the English Legislation which was expected to be passed in 1929 or so and to base the law for India on the British model. But the legislation was not passed in Britain. The slow progress of events in Britain again revived the agitation for amendment of the law of insurance in India.

### Demand for Another Act

Demand for another Act was made because the Act of 1938 was not very wide and comprehensive. There was forceful and constant demand for a new law which could control the Indian and non-Indian insurance companies and could reduce the competition between these two types of companies. The government accepted the genuine demand and appointed one special officer for investigation. The special Officer appointed for the purpose of bringing about the required reform of legislation in 1925 was a well known Kolkata Solicitor. He was placed on special duty to report on the amendments necessary to modernize insurance legislation in India. His report was considered by the Advisory Committee appointed by the Government of India consisting of representatives of all branches of insurance. The Committee made several changes and the Government of India introduced the bill in the Legislative Assembly in 1937 and after much debate and several amendments/changes, it emerged in the form of the famous Insurance Act of 1938.

### Insurance Act of 1938

Insurance Act of 1938 is the most important legislation on insurance business in India. This Act was well balanced and the first comprehensive piece of legislation in India to govern both life and non-life branches of insurance. The Act provided for the prevention of the growth of mushroom companies, to enforce working on sound principles, prevent misappropriation of funds and protect the assets.

This Act came into force in July, 1938. Since 1938, there were six amendments made from time to time upto 1945. In 1945, it was deemed necessary to protect the interest of insurance companies. Therefore, in 1945, a Committee was constituted under the chairmanship of Sri Cowas Ji Jehangir to investigate into all types of misconduct of the insurance companies. This Committee submitted its report and recommended for amending many sections of the Act and to introduce new sections in the Act of 1938. On the basis of these recommendations, one amendment bill was drafted and sent to the Select Committee concerned and at last it was enacted on 18th April, 1950 by the Parliament. According to this Amendment Act, there are provisions relating to administration. Total right of control over Insurance companies was vested in the Central Government. Now, the Government controls the insurance business and, for that purpose, appointed the Controller of Insurance. Under the provisions of the Act, the insurance companies are required to follow the provisions of the Act, otherwise they can be penalized for violation of the Act. The Life Insurance business was nationalized in 1956 and certain provisions of the Act of 1938 were made applicable to Life Insurance Corporation of India. General Insurance Corporation of India Act was passed in 1972 to govern the business of general insurance which was also nationalized in 1972.

## Important Provisions of Insurance Act, 1938

The Salient features of Insurance Act, 1938 have been discussed under the following heads:

Wide Scope; Requirement as to Capital; Deposits; Registration; Submission of Returns; Prohibition on Rebate and Restriction on Commission; Licencing of Insurance Agents; Investments; Prohibition on Loan; Investigation; and Duties and Powers of Controller of Insurance.

These important provisions of Insurance Act, 1938 are disused as under:

### *(I) Wide Scope*

The Insurance Act, 1938 is wide and more comprehensive. It was well balanced and was the first comprehensive piece of insurance legislation in India covering both life and non-life branches of insurance.

#### *(A) Application*

The Insurance Act, 1938 applies to all types of insurance business, i.e. life, fire, marine, etc. done by companies incorporated in India or elsewhere. It also governs the provident companies, mutual offices and cooperative societies.

*(i) Definitions:* Section 2 of the Insurance Act, 1938 defines the various terms and words used in the Act. Some of the terms are discussed as under:

*Marine Insurance:* Section 2(13)A of the Insurance Act, 1938 defines marine insurance as, "Marine Insurance business means the business of effecting contracts of insurance upon vessels of any description, including cargoes, freights and other interests which are legally insured in or in relation to such vessels, cargoes, freight, goods, wares, merchandise or property of whatever description insured for any transit by land or water or both, and whether or not including warehouse risks or similar risks in addition to or as incidental to such transit and includes any other risks customarily included among the risks insured against in marine insurance policies".

*Life Insurance:* Section 2(II) of the Indian Insurance Act, 1938 defines Life as:

> "Life Insurance business is the business of effecting contracts upon human life".

*Fire insurance:* Section 2[(6)](a) of the Insurance Act, 1938 defines fire insurance as:

> "Fire insurance business means the business of effecting, otherwise than incidentally to some other classes of insurance business, contract in insurance against loss by or incidental to fire or other occurrence customarily included among the risks insured against in fire insurance policies".

*Miscellaneous Insurance Business:* Under Section 2(13)(b) of the Insurance Act, 1938:

> "Miscellaneous Insurance business means the business of effecting contracts of insurance which are not principally or wholly of any kind included in clauses (6)(a) and 13(a).

### *General Insurance Business*

Under Section 2(6)(b) of Insurance Act, 1938:

> "General insurance business means fire, marine or miscellaneous insurance business, whether carried on singly or in combination with one or more of them".

### *(B) Prohibition*

Section 2 lays down that only such organizations are allowed to carry on business of insurance in India which are—

Registered co-operative societies; or Public companies or registered under any foreign Act.

According to Section 2-C of the Act, there is prohibition on transactions of insurance business by certain persons.

"Save as hereinafter provided, no person shall, after the commencement of the Insurance Act, begin to carry on any class of insurance business in India and no insurer carrying on any class of insurance business in India shall after the expiry of one year, from such commencement, continue to carry on any such business unless he is—

A Public Limited Company or a society registered under the Cooperative Societies Act, 1912 or under any other law for any country outside India not being in the nature of a private company; a body corporate incorporated under the law of any country outside India not being in the nature of a private company.

Every notification issued under the sub-section shall be laid before parliament as soon as may be after it is issued.

### (2) Requirement as to Capital

*Under Section 6 of the Insurance Act*

It is notified and made compulsive that no insurer carrying on the business of life insurance, general insurance or re-insurance in India on or after the commencement of the Insurance Regulatory and Development Authority Act, 1999 shall be registered unless it has—

(a) A paid-up equity capital of rupees one hundred crores, in case of a person carrying on the business of life insurance or general insurance, or

(b) A paid-up equity capital of rupees two hundred crores, in case of a person carrying on exclusively the business as a re-insurance.

Provided that in determining the paid-up equity capital specified under clause (i) or clause (ii), the deposits to be made under section 7 and any preliminary expenses incurred in the formation and registration of the company shall be excluded.

Provided further that an insurer carrying on business of

life insurance, general insurance or re-insurance in India before the commencement of the Insurance Regulatory and Development Authority Act, 1999 and who is required to be registered under this act, shall have a paid-up equity capital in accordance with clause (i) and clause (ii), as the case may be, within six months of the commencement of that Act.

***(3) Deposits***

The Act provided for registration of all insurers and a substantial deposit with the Reserve Bank to prevent the growth of insurers of small financial resources or speculative concerns.

*According to Section 7 of the Insurance Act*

"Every insurer shall, in respect of the insurance business carried on by him in India, deposit and keep deposited with the Reserve Bank of India in one of the offices in India of the bank for and on behalf of the Central Government, the amount hereafter specified, either in cash or in approved securities, estimated at the market value of the securities on the day of deposit or partly in cash and partly in approved securities so estimated:

In case of Life Insurance Business, a sum equivalent to one percent of his total gross premium written in India in any financial year commencing after the 31st day of March 2000, not exceeding rupees ten crores.

In case of general insurance business, a sum equivalent to three percent of his total gross premium written in India, in any financial year commencing after the 31st day of March 2000, not exceeding rupees ten crores.

In the case of re-insurance business, a sum of rupees twenty crores, provided that, where the business done or to be done in marine insurance only and relates exclusively to country craft or its cargo or both, the amount to be deposited under this sub-section shall be one hundred thousand rupees only.

***(4) Registration***

Every insurer is required to obtain a certificate of registration from "The Controller of Insurance" in order to carry on insurance business in India. The Central Government has been empowered to exercise its full control over the insurance business in India by putting the condition of compulsory registration.

*Under Section 3 of the Insurance Act*

No person shall, after the commencement of this Act, begin to carry on any class of insurance business in India and no insurer carrying on any class of insurance business in India shall after the expiry of three months from the commencement of this Act, continue to carry on any such business, unless he has obtained from the Authority, a certificate of registration for the particular class of insurance business.

Provided that in the case of an insurer who was carrying on any class of insurance business in India at the commencement of this Act, failure to obtain a certificate of registration in accordance with the requirements of this sub-clause shall not operate to invalidate any contract of insurance entered into by him if before such date as may be fixed in this behalf by Central Government by notification in the official gazette, he has obtained that certificate.

*Application for Registration*

The applicant has to apply to the Controller of Insurance, in the prescribed form along with the following documents, namely:

> A certified copy of the Memorandum and Articles of Association; name, address and occupation of directors; a statement of the class or classes of insurance business done or to be done; principal place of business or domicile outside India; and a certified copy of the published prospectus; a receipt showing payment of fee as may be determined by the regulations which shall not exceed fifty thousand rupees for each class of business or as may be specified by the regulations made by the Authority; and such other document as may be specified by the regulations made by the Authority.

On receipt of application for registration and on making

such inquiries as the authority may deem it fit to make and is satisfied that:

(a) Financial condition and general character of management of the applicant are sound;
(b) The volume of business likely to be available to, and the capital structure and earning prospects of the applicant will be adequate; and
(c) The interest of the general public will be served.

The Authority may register the applicant as an insurer and grant him a certificate of registration. The Authority shall withhold registration or shall cancel a registration already made if any requirement is not satisfied.

*Cancellation of Registration*

The Authority (Controller of Insurance) shall cancel the registration of an insurer either wholly or in so far as it relates to a particular class of insurance business, as the case may be:

(a) If the insurer fails to comply with the provisions of section 7 or 8 of deposits;
(b) If the insurer is in liquidation or is adjudged an insolvent; or
(c) If the business has been transferred to any other insurer; or
(d) If the whole of the deposit made in respect of insurance business has been returned to the insurer under section 9; or
(e) When clause 9 of section 2 related to insurer's definition ceased or cancelled or suspended; or
(f) Defaults in complying with any rules; and
(g) Carries on any business other than insurance business or any other prescribed business.

*Renewal of Registration*

Generally, the certificate of registration issued by the Controller is valid for one year only and the insurer has to make application alongwith receipt of deposit fee with the RBI. Section 3 lays down that the application for renewal of registration must be made before 31 December of the relevant year. The application fee for renewal shall not be less than Rs. 500 in any case or ¼% of the gross premium, whichever is higher.

### *(5) Submission of Returns*

The Act provides for the creation of a post of Superintendent of Insurance and it was made obligatory on all companies to submit all the quinquennial returns (once in five years) in the prescribed form within a stated period. The Superintended has been given wide powers to reject all incomplete and inaccurate returns.

*Under Section 14 of the Insurance Act*

The audited accounts and balance sheet and actuarial report and abstract and four copies thereof shall be finished as return to the Controller in the case of the accounts and balance sheet and the actuarial report within six months and in the case of the abstract within nine months from the end of the period to which they refer. If the principal place is outside India, the period of submission may be extended by three months.

Of the four copies so furnished, one copy shall be signed in the case of a company by the chairman and two directors and by the principal officer of the company and, if the company has a managing director or managing agent, by that director or managing agent. In case of a firm, it will be signed by two partners of the firm. In case of any insurer being an individual, one by the insurer himself and one shall be singed by the auditor who made the audit or the actuary who made the valuation, as the case may be.

Where the insurer's principal place of business or domicile is outside India, he shall forward to the Controller of Insurance along with the documents, a certified statement showing the total assets and liabilities of the insurer at the close of the period covered by the said documents.

The insurer shall, within the time specified in sub-section (I) of Section 15, furnish to the Controller four certified copies in the English Language of every balance sheet, account abstract, report and statement supplied to the public authority and in addition thereto four certified copies in the English language of each of the following statements:

(a) A statement audited by an auditor or by a person duly qualified under the law of the insurer's country showing the assets held by the insurer in India at the date of any balance sheet so furnished,

(b) A separate account of receipts and payments and a revenue account for the period covered by any account so furnished,

(c) A separate abstract of the valuation report in respect of all business transacted in India in each class or sub-class of insurance business, and

(d) A declaration in the prescribed form stating that all amounts received by the insurer directly or indirectly whether from his head office or from any other source outside India have been shown in the revenue account.

### *(6) Restriction of Commission and Prohibition of Rebating*

(a) *Prohibition of payment by way of commission U/S 40(1)*: No person shall, after the expiry of six months from the commencement of this Act, pay or contract to pay any remuneration or reward whether by way of commission or otherwise for soliciting or procuring insurance business in India, to any person except an insurance agent or a principal, chief or special agent.

(b) No insurance agent shall be paid or contracted to be paid by way of commission or as remuneration in any form an amount exceeding, in the case of life insurance business, 40% of the first year's premium payable on any policy or policies effected through him and 5% of a renewal premium, payable on such a policy, or in the case of business of any other class, 15% of the premium.

(c) Provided that insurance company, in respect of life insurance business only, may pay during the first ten years of their business, to their insurance agents 55% of the first year's premium payable on any policy or policies effected through them and 6% of the renewal premium payable on such policies.

**Limitations of Expenditure on Commission**

*Under Section 40-A of the Insurance Act*

(1) No person shall pay or contract to pay to an insurance agent, and no insurance agent shall receive or contract to receive by way of commission or remuneration in any form in respect of any policy of life insurance issued in India by an insurer after the 31st day of December 1950, and effected through an insurance agent, an amount exceeding—

(a) Where the policy grants an immediate annuity or a deferred annuity in consideration of a single premium, or where only one premium is payable on the policy, 2% of that premium;

(b) Where the policy grants a deferred annuity in consideration of more than one premium $7^1/_2$% of the first year's premium, and 2% of each renewal premium payable on the policy.

(c) In any other case, 35% of the first year's premium, 7½% of the second and third year's renewal premium and thereafter 5% of each renewal premium payable on the policy.

Provided that in a case referred to in clause (c), an insurer, during the first 10 years of his business, may pay to an insurance agent, and an insurance agent may receive from such an insurer, 40% of the first year's premium payable on the policy.

(2) No person shall pay or contract to pay to a special agent, and no special agent shall receive or contract to receive by way of commission or as remuneration in any form, in respect of any policy of life insurance issued in India by an insurer in after the 31st day of December 1950 and effected through a special agent in an amount exceeding:

In any case referred to in clause (a) of sub-section (I) one-half percent of the premium;

In a case referred to in clause (b) of sub-section (I) two percent of the first year's premium payable on the policies, and

In a case referred to in clause (c) of sub-section (I) fifteen percent of first year's premium payable on the policies.

*(b) Prohibition of Rebates (Section 41)*

(1) No person shall allow or offer to allow either directly or indirectly as an inducement to any person to take out or renew or continue an insurance in respect of any kind of risk, relating to lives or property in India, any rebate of the whole or a part of the commission payable or any rebate of the premium shown on the policy, nor shall any person taking out or renewing or continuing a policy accept any rebate of the premium shown on the policy, nor shall any person taking out or renewing or continuing a policy accept any rebate except such rebate as may be allowed in accordance with the published prospectuses or tables of the insurer:

Provided that acceptance by an insurance agent of commission in connection with a policy of the insurance taken out by himself on his own life shall not be deemed to be acceptance of a rebate of premium within the meaning of this sub-section if at the time of such acceptance the insurance agent satisfies the prescribed conditions establishing that he is a bonafide insurance agent employed by the insurer.

(2) Any person making default in complying with the provisions of this section shall be punishable with fine, which may extend to Rs. 5000.

***(7) Licensing of Insurance Agents (Section 42) of the Insurance Act***

(1) The Authority or Controller or an officer authoresses by him in this behalf shall, in the prescribed manner and on payment of the prescribed fee, which shall not be more than two hundred and fifty (250) rupees, issue to any person making an application in the prescribed manner determined by the regulations, a licence to Act as an insurance agent for the purpose of soliciting or procuring insurance business provided that:

(a) In the case of an individual, he does not suffer from any of the following disqualifications:

(a) That the person is a minor;
(b) That he is found to be of unsound mind by a court of competent jurisdiction;
(c) That he has been found guilty of criminal misappropriation or criminal breach of trust, or

cheating or forgery or an abatement of or attempt to commit any such offence by a court of competent jurisdiction.

Provided that, where at least five years period has elapsed since the completion of sentence imposed on any person in respect of any such offence, the Authority (i.e. the Controller) shall ordinarily declare in respect of such person that his conviction shall cease to operate as a disqualification under their clause.

That in the course of any judicial proceeding relating to any policy of insurance or the winding-up of an insurance company or in the course of an investigation of the affairs of an insurer, it has been found that he has been guilty of or has knowingly participated in or connived at any fraud, dishonestly or misrepresentation against an insurer or an insured.

That he does not possess the requisite qualifications and practical training for a period not exceeding 12 months, as may be specified by the regulations made by the Controller in this behalf.

That he had not passed such examination as may be specified by the regulations made by the Controller in this behalf: Provided that a person who had been issued a licence under sub-section (I) of this section or sub-section (I) of section 64 UM shall not be required to possess the requisite qualification, practical training and pass such examination as required by clauses (v) and (vi), and

That he violates the code of conduct as may be specified by the regulations made by the Controller.

(ii) In case of a company or firm, any of its directors or partners does not suffer from any of the said disqualifications:

Provided further that any licence issued immediately before the commencement of the Insurance Regulatory and Development Authority Act, 1999 shall be deemed to have been issued in accordance with the regulations which provide for such licence.

(2) A licence issued under this section, after the commencement of the Insurance Regulatory and Development Authority Act, 1999, shall remain in force for a period of three years only from the date of issue, but shall, if the applicant does

not suffer from any of the disqualifications mentioned above and the application for renewal of the license reaches the issuing authority at least thirty days before the date on which the licence ceased to remain in force, the renewed for a period of three years at any one time on payment of the prescribed fee which shall not be more than two hundred and fifty rupees, and an additional fee of a prescribed amount, not exceeding one hundred rupees by way of penalty if the application for renewal of the licence does not reach the issuing authority at least thirty days before the date on which the licence ceased to remain in force.

### *(8) Investments*

Every insurer shall invest and at all times keep invested assets equivalent to not less than the sum of:

(a) The amount of his liabilities to holders of life insurance policies in India on account of matured claims, and

(b) The amount required to meet the liability on policies of life insurance maturing for payment in India, less–

  (i) The amount of premiums which have fallen due to the insurer on such policies but have not been paid and the days of grace for payment of which have not expired.

  (ii) Any amount due to the insurer for loans granted on and within the surrender value of policies of life insurance maturing for payment in India issued by him or by an insurer whose business he has acquired and in respect of which he has assumed liability.

  (iii) In the manner following, namely: twenty-five (25%) percent of the said sum in government securities or other approved securities and the balance in any of the approved investments specified in sub-section (I) of section 27(A) or, subject to the limitations, conditions and restrictions specified in sub-section (2) of that section, in any other investment.

*Under Section 27-A of the Insurance Act*

(1) No insurer shall invest or keep invested any part of his controlled fund otherwise than in any of the following approved investments, namely—

*Approved Securities:* Recognized securities, securities issued by Government, securities issued by Local Bodies, house building societies, securities, etc.

*Debentures or other securities of Municipality in a State:* Debentures of the companies secured against the fixed assets and on which interest has been paid for at least three years. Debentures issued by the local bodies, debentures of recognized housing construction society, debentures issued by co-operative societies.

*Preference shares:* Preference shares or guaranteed shares on which dividends at least @4% have already been paid over the last three years or shares issued by co-operatives, etc.

*First Mortgage:* Mortgage carrying first charge on any properties situated in India, which belong to any recognized housing construction society.

*Immovable property:* Acquisition of immovable properties in India and outside India where the company carries on an insurance business.

*Fixed Deposits in Banks:* The insurers can make investment of their funds through fixed deposits in a scheduled bank or in any co-operative society.

*Other Investments:* Any investment as notified in the official gazette by the central government from time to time.

Every insurer shall also submit to the Controller of Insurance a return in the prescribed form showing all the changes that have occurred in the investments aforesaid during each of the quarters in a year ending on the last day of March.

### *Restriction on Investments in other Securities*

(a) No investment in shares or debentures of a private company can be made.

(b) Not more than 2% of the authorised capital or total debentures of any investment company or banking company can be made and further not more than 10% of the total assets of the insurer can be invested.

(c) Not more than 10% of the total assets of Insurer

Company can be invested in shares or debentures of other companies, only up to 10% of such issuing company's share capital or debentures except in banking and investment companies.

(d) The insurance company cannot invest more than 10% of its assets in Fixed Deposits or Current Accounts with banking companies.

### *(9) Prohibition of Loan [(U/S 29(1)] of the Insurance Act*

No insurance company shall grant loans or temporary advances either on hypothecation of property or on personal security or otherwise, except loan on life policies issued by him within their surrender value, to any director, manager, managing agent, actuary, auditor, or officer of the insurance company, if the insurer is a company, or where the insurer is a firm, to any partner therein, or to any other company or firm in which any such director, manager, managing agent, actuary, officer or partner holds such position.

### *(10) Investigation (Under Section 33) of the Insurance Act*

The Authority may, at any time, by order in writing, direct any person (investigation authority) specified in the order to investigate the affairs of any insurance company and to report to the authority on any investigation made by him provided that the investigating authority may, whenever necessary, employ any auditor or actuary or both for the purpose of assisting him in any investigation under this section.

### *(11) Duties and Power of Controller of Insurance*

The Controller of Insurance, the supreme authority, possessing wider knowledge of insurance business and actuarial science, is appointed by the Central Government. He is responsible for as well as empowered to control and organize the working of insurance companies in India. His duties and powers as prescribed under various sections of the Insurance Act, may be outlined in two groups—General Duties and Powers, and Special Powers:

*(a) General Duties and Powers*

The General duties (functions) and powers of the Controller of Insurance are as follows:

(a) Registration and renewal of registration of insurance companies and issuing the certificate of registration and cancellation of registration, etc. (Section 3 and 3A).
(b) Power to check security deposits of the insurance companies and calling information regarding security deposits from the Reserve Bank of India (section 7).
(c) Power to receive periodically the annual accounts, reports and returns from the insurance companies.
(d) Power to issue licenses to the underwriters, indemnifiers and insurers, etc. (U/s 42 and 64 UM).
(e) Power to sanction the scheme of transfers, acquisition and amalgamation of the insurance business, (Section 36).
(f) Power to delegate authority to some subordinate authority.
(g) Power to solve the disputes of settlement of claims involving small amounts (Section 47A).

*(b) Special Powers*

*(i) Powers Relating to Returns:* Section 21 of the Insurance Act, 1938 lays down that if the Controller of Insurance finds, while investigating the affairs of an insurance business, that the returns submitted to him are not true and correct or are incomplete in any respect, he may—

(a) Call upon the insurer to furnish true and correct information or may instruct the insurer to complete the information already furnished.
(b) Examine any insurance official/authority with or without oath on any matter given in the report.
(c) Serve notice upon the insurance company so as to make available account books, returns and other documents, etc. in his office for inspection.

Generally, 30 days' time is allowed to correct or complete the information in the returns furnished in the office of Controller.

*(ii) Powers Regarding Appointment:* The following powers of the Controller of Insurance are relating to the appointment of higher officials in insurance companies:

*Section 34 (A):* For making the appointment of managing directors, full time directors, part time directors, managers and chief executives and their reappointments, the prior approval of Controller is necessary.

In the public interest or for protecting insurers' interest or for making the management more efficient, the Controller may remove any director or chief officer of any insurance company. The controller may remove such officials after serving proper notice in this regard and by providing a chance to be heard.

The controller may appoint additional directors for the period of three years in the best interest of general public or the insured or in the best interest of the insurance company. The maximum number of such additional directors may be 1/3 of the total strength but not more than 5 in any case.

*(iii) Powers to issue Directions:* The Controller may specifically issue any orders or directions to the insurance company, in case he/she deems fit, in the best interest of the general public, insured and in the best interest of the efficient management of the company itself.

### *(c) Other Rights/Powers*

The Insurance Act, 1938 (all provisions carried over to the 1999 Act) also prescribes the following important powers of the Controller of Insurance under the category of 'Other powers'.

Under Section 34E, the Controller may order to stop the business of insurance carried on by an insurance company.

Under Section 34-G, the Controller may order to make necessary alteration in re-insurance treaty.

The Controller may order to wind-up the operations of any foreign insurance company in India.

The Controller may delegate his powers to any of his deputies/officers to search any insurer's office and to impound the necessary documents if/as required for further investigations, etc.

The rules, provisions and prescribed rates, etc. as recommended by the Tariff Advisory Committee shall not be made into the regulations for the insurance business unless these are accepted by the Controller of Insurance.

He may examine on oath any agent and any insurance unit official and may demand necessary information, documents and account books, etc. relating to such persons. (Under Section 33-A): He is authorized to issue licenses to under-writers and loss indemnifiers and is also empowered to settle the disputes of settlement of claims of such organizations (U/s 64 UM).

# 10

# *Insurance Regulatory and Development Authority (IRDA)*

## INTRODUCTION

On the basis of the recommendations of Malhotra Committee, the Government of India constituted through resolution an Interim Insurance Regulatory Authority on 23rd January 1996. The relative Bill was introduced in the Parliament in 1996. The Bill was withdrawn and re-written as Insurance Regulatory and Development Authority Bill, 1999 and introduced again in 1999 alongwith three schedules containing amendments to the Insurance Act, 1938, Life Insurance Corporation of India Act, 1956 and General Insurance Corporation Act, 1972 and was passed as 'Insurance Regulatory and Development Authority Act, 1999'.

## PREAMBLE OF IRDA ACT

Preamble of IRDA Act, 1999 reads "an Act to provide for the establishment of an authority to protect the interest of holders of insurance policies, to regulate, promote and ensure orderly growth of the insurance industry and for matters connected therewith and incidental thereto".

The Act was enacted and it contains the following provisions:

*Statement of Objects and Reasons*: The insurance industry requires a high degree of regulation. The Insurance Act, 1938 provides for the institution of the Controller of Insurance to act as a strong and powerful supervisory and regulatory authority with powers to direct, advise, caution, prohibit, investigate, inspect, prosecute, search, seize, fine, amalgamate, authorize, register and liquidate insurance companies. However, after nationalization of the life insurance industry in 1956 and the general insurance industry in 1972, the role of the Controller of Insurance diminished in its significance over a period of time.

In April 1993, the Government of India set-up a high powered committee under the chairmanship of Sh. R.N. Malhotra, former Governor, Reserve Bank of India (RBI) to examine the structure of the insurance industry and recommend changes to make it more efficient and competitive, keeping in view the structural changes in other parts of the financial system of the economy. The Committee which submitted its report on the 7th January 1994 felt that the insurance regulatory apparatus should be activated even in the present set-up of nationalized insurance sector and recommended, *inter-alia,* the establishment of a strong and effective Insurance Regulatory Authority in the form of a statutory autonomous board on the lines of the Securities and Exchange Board of India (SEBI).

The recommendations of the committee were discussed at different forums including the Consultative Committee of the Parliament attached to the Ministry of Finance, management of Life Insurance Corporation, the General Insurance Corporation and its subsidiary companies, trade unions, chambers of commerce and consumer interest groups. The recommendation to set-up an autonomous insurance regulatory authority found wide support. In view of the general support received, the Government of India decided to bring in a legislation to establish an independent regulatory authority for the insurance industry. Since enacting legislation for creating the insurance regulatory authority was to take time, the then government constituted through a Government resolution an Interim Insurance Regulatory Authority pending the enactment of a comprehensive legislation. The Chairman, Insurance Regulatory Authority was notified as Controller of Insurance under the Insurance Act, 1938. The said interim insurance regulatory authority at present is discharging certain functions and exercising powers of the Controller.

In pursuance of the Budget Speech in July 1996, the then Government introduced on the 20th December, 1996, the Insurance Regulatory Authority Bill, 1996 for establishment of an authority to protect the interest of holders of insurance policies and to regulate, promote and ensure orderly growth of the insurance industry and for matters connected therewith or incidental thereto. The Bill was referred to the department's Standing committee of the Ministry of Finance. The Committee submitted its report on 9th May, 1997. However, the said bill incorporating therein the recommendations of the said Standing Committee was taken-up for consideration but could not be passed and the bill was withdrawn by the then government.

In order to provide better insurance coverage to our citizens and also to augment the flow of long-term resources for financing infrastructure, in the budget speech, 1998, the policy of the government was announced to open up the insurance sector and also to establish a Statutory Regulatory Authority. Accordingly, the Insurance Regulatory Authority Bill, 1998 was introduced in the Lok Sabha on the 15th December, 1998 providing for setting up a statutory insurance regulatory authority and containing three schedules incorporating amendments to the Insurance Act, 1938, the Life Insurance Corporation Act, 1956 and the General Insurance Business (Nationalization) Act, 1972. The Bill was referred to the Standing Committee on Finance on the 4th January, 1999 for examination and report. The Standing Committee, while recommending the Bill, suggested some amendments. These amendments were accepted by the government and amendments to the Bill were circulated on the 18th March, 1999. However, the Bill could not be taken up for consideration consequent on the dissolution of the Lok Sabha.

It was subsequently proposed to re-introduce a fresh Bill by incorporating the provisions of the Insurance Regulatory Authority Bill, 1998 and the amendments suggested by the Standing Committee on Finance. The Bill was titled Insurance Regulatory and Development Authority Bill on the basis of the recommendation of the Standing Committee. In the main text of the Bill, provisions were incorporated to give a statutory character to the interim Insurance Regulatory Authority and the three Schedules containing amendments to the Insurance Act, 1938, amendments to the Life Insurance Corporation Act, 1956 and the General Insurance Business (Nationalization) Act 1972.

The proposed Authority shall be body corporate, having perpetual succession and a common seal with power to acquire, hold and dispose of property and to contract. It consists of a chairperson and other members not exceeding nine in number, of whom not more than five shall serve full time, to be appointed by the Central Government from amongst persons of ability, integrity and standing who have knowledge or experience of life insurance, general insurance, actuarial science, finance, economics, law, accountancy, administration or any other discipline which, in the opinion of the Central Government, shall be useful to the Authority. The chairperson and other whole time members shall hold office for a term of 5 years or until the age of 65 years in the case of chairperson and 62 years in the case of other whole time members whichever is earlier and they shall be eligible for reappointment subject to age consideration. A part-time member shall hold office for a term not exceeding 5 years.

*Main Provisions of IRDA Act*: Section 14 of IRDA Act lays the duties, powers and functions of the authority. Powers and functions of the authority shall include the following:

(a) Issue to the applicant a certificate of registration, renew, review, modify, withdraw, suspend or cancel such registration.
(b) To protect the interest of policyholders in all matters concerning nomination of policy, assigning of policy, surrender value of policy, insurable interest, settlement of insurance claim, other terms and conditions of contract of insurance.
(c) Specifying requisite qualification and practical training for insurance intermediary and agents.
(d) Specifying code of conduct for surveyors and loss assessors
(e) Promoting efficiency in the conduct of insurance business.
(f) Promoting and regulating professional regulation connected with the insurance and re-insurance business.

(g) Specifying the form and manner in which books of accounts will be maintained and statement of accounts rendered by insurer and insurance intermediaries.

(h) Adjudication of disputes between insurers and intermediaries.

(i) Specifying the percentage of life insurance and general insurance business to be undertaken by the insurers in rural or social sectors, etc.

(j) Section 25 provides that Insurance Advisory Committee will be constituted and shall consist of not more than 25 members.

(k) Section 26 provides that authority may, in consultation with Insurance Advisory Committee, make regulations consistent with this Act and the rules made hereunder to carry out the purpose of this Act.

(l) Section 29 seeks amendment in certain provisions of Insurance Act, 1938 in the manner as set out in the First Schedule. The amendments to the Insurance Act are consequential in order to empower IRDA to effectively regulate, promote, and esure orderly growth of the insurance industry.

(m) Sections 30 and 31 seek to amend LIC Act, 1956 and GIC Act, 1972.

## CONTENTS OF THE ACT

### (1) Short title, extent and commencement as under:

This act may be called the Insurance Regulatory and Development Authority Act, 1999. It extends to the whole of India. It shall come into force on such date as the Central Government may, by notification in the official gazette, appoint. Provided that different dates as may be appointed for different provisions of this Act and any reference in any such provision to the commencement of this Act shall be construed as a reference to the coming in force of that provision.

### (2) Definitions of various Terms used in the Act

In this act, unless the context otherwise requires,

Appointee day shall mean the date on which the authority is established under sub-section (I) of Section 3. Authority will mean the Insurance Regulatory and Development Authority established under sub division (I) of Section 3. Chairperson will mean the Chairperson of the Authority. Fund will mean the Insurance Regulatory and Development Authority Fund constituted under sub-section (I) of Section 16. Interim Insurance Regulatory Authority will mean the Insurance Regulatory Authority set-up by the Central Government through resolution No. 17(2)/94-Ins-V, dated the 23rd January, 1996. Intermediary will mean insurance intermediary and those will include insurance brokers, reinsurance brokers, and insurance consultants, surveyors and loss assessors. Member will mean a whole-time or a part-time member of the Authority and includes the Chairperson. Notification will mean a notification published in the official gazette of the Government of India, Prescribed will mean prescribed by rules made under this Act, and Regulations mean the regulations made by the Authority.

Words and expressions used and not defined in this Act but define in the Insurance Act, 1938 or the Life Insurance Corporation Act, 1956 or the General Insurance Business (Nationalization) Act, 1972 shall have the same meaning, respectively, as assigned to them in those Acts.

### (3) Brief Profile of IRDA Act and its Functioning

**(a) Establishment and Incorporation of Insurance Authority**: With effect from such date as the Central Government may, by notification, appoint, there shall be established, for the purpose of this Act, an authority to be called 'The Insurance Regulatory and Development Authority'. The Authority shall be a body corporate by the name as foresaid having perpetual succession and a common seal with power, subject to the provisions of this Act, to acquire, hold and dispose of property, both movable and immovable, and to contract and shall, by the said name, sue or be sued. The head office of the authority shall be at such place as the Central Government may decide from time to time. The authority may establish offices at other places in India.

**(b) Composition of authority**: The authority shall consist of the following members, namely, Chairperson, not more than five whole-time members, and not more than four part-time members, to be appointed by the Central Government from amongst persons of ability, integrity and standing who have knowledge or experience in life insurance, general insurance, actuarial science, finance, economics, law, accountancy, administration or any discipline which would, in the opinion of the Central Government, be useful to the authority.

Provided that the Central Government shall, while appointing the Chairperson and the whole-time members, ensure that at least the persons having knowledge or experience in life insurance, general insurance, general business or actuarial science, are appointed.

**(c) Tenure of Office of chairperson and other members:** In IRDA, the chairperson and every other whole-time member shall hold office for a term of five years from the date on which he enters upon his office and shall be eligible for re-appointment provided that no person shall hold office as a Chairperson after he has attained the age of sixty-five (65) years. A part-time member shall hold office for a term not exceeding five years from the date on which he enters upon his office. Notwithstanding anything contained in sub-section (I) or sub-section (2), a member may relinquish his office by giving in writing to the Central Government a notice of not less than three months, or be removed from his office in accordance with the provisions of relevant section.

**(d) Removal of a member from office: In IRDA**: (1) The Central Government may remove any member who is, or at any time has been, adjudged as an insolvent or has become physically or mentally incapable of acting as a member, or has been convicted of any offence which, in the opinion of the central government, involves moral turpitude, or has acquired such financial or other interest as is likely to affect particularly his functions as a member, or has so abused his position as to render his continuation in office detrimental to the public interest.

(2) No such member shall be removed under clause (d) or clause (c) of section (1) unless he has been given a reasonable opportunity of being heard in the matter.

**(e) Salary and Allowances of Chairperson and Members:** The salary and allowances payable to and other terms and conditions of service, of the members other than part-time members, shall be such as may be prescribed. The part-time members shall receive such allowances as may be prescribed. The salary, allowances, and other conditions of service of a member shall not be varied to his disadvantage after appointment.

**(f) Restriction/Bar on future Employment of Members:** The Chairperson and the whole-time members shall not, for a period of two years from the date on which they cease to hold office as such, except with the previous approval of the central government, accept any employment either under the Central Government or under any State Government, or any appointment in any company in the insurance sector.

**(g) Administrative Powers of Chairperson:** The Chairperson shall have the powers of general superintendence and direction in respect of all administrative matters of the authority.

**(h) Meeting of Authority:** In IRDA,

The Authority shall meet at such times and place and shall observe such rules and procedures in regard to transactions of business at its meeting (including quorum at such meetings) as may be determined by the regulations. The Chairperson, or if for any reason, he is unable to attend a meeting of the authority, any other member chosen by the members present from amongst themselves at the meeting, shall preside at the meting.

All questions which come up before any meeting of the authority shall be decided by a majority of votes by the members present and voting, and in the absence of unanimity emerging, the person presiding shall have a second or casting vote.

The authority may make regulations for the transaction of business at its meetings.

**(i) Vacancies, etc. not to invalidate proceeding of authority:** No act or proceeding of the authority shall be invalid merely by reason of—

Any vacancy in, or any defect in the constitution of the authority, or any defect in the appointment of a person acting as a member of the authority, or any irregularity in the procedure of authority not affecting the merits of the case.

**(j) Officers and Employees of Authority:** In IRDA,

The authority may appoint officers and such other employees as it considers necessary for the efficient discharge of its functions under this Act.

The terms and other conditions of service of officers and other employees of the authority appointed under sub section (I) shall be governed by regulations made under this Act.

**(k) Transfer of Assets, liabilities, etc. of interim insurance regulatory authority:** On the appointed day—

All the assets and liabilities of interim insurance regulatory authority shall stand transferred to, and vested in the authority under this Act.

**Explanation:** The assets of the interim insurance regulatory authority shall be deemed to include all rights and powers, and all properties, whether movable or immovable, including, in particular, cash balance, deposits, all other interests and rights in or arising out of such properties as may be in the possession of the interim insurance regulatory authority and all books of accounts and other documents relating to the same, and liabilities shall be deemed to include all debts, liabilities and obligations of whatever kind,

(i) Without prejudice to the provision of clause (a), all debts, obligations and liabilities incurred, all contracts entered into or engaged to be done by, with or for the Authority.

(ii) All sums of money due to the interim insurance regulatory authority immediately before that day shall be deemed to be due to the authority, and

(iii) All suits and other legal proceedings instituted or which could have been instituted by or against the interim insurance regulatory authority immediately before that day may be continued or may be instituted by or against the authority.

**Duties, Powers and Functions of Authority in IRDA:** IRDA provides as under:

(a) Subject to the provisions of this act and any other law for the time being in force, the Authority shall have the duty to regulate, promote and ensure orderly growth of the insurance business and re-insurance business.

(b) Without prejudice to the generality of the provision contained in sub-section (I), the powers and functions of the authority shall include: issue to the applicant a certificate of registration, renewal as well as modify, withdraw, suspend or cancel such registration; protection of the interests of the policyholders in matters concerning assigning of policy nomination by policyholders, insurable interest, settlement of insurance claim, surrender value of policy and other terms and conditions of contract of insurance; specifying requisite qualifications, code of conduct and practical training for intermediary or insurance intermediaries and agents; specifying the code of conduct for surveyors and loss assessors; promoting efficiency in the conduct of insurance business; promoting and regulating professional organizations connected with the insurance and re-insurance business; prompting and regulating professional organizations connected with the insurance and re-insurance business; levying fees and other charges for carrying out the purposes of this Act; calling for information from, undertaking inspection of and conducting enquiries and investigations including audit of the insurers, intermediaries, insurance intermediaries and other organizations connected with the insurance business; control and regulation of the rates, advantages, terms and conditions that may be offered by insurers in respect of general insurance business not so controlled and regulated by the Tariff Advisory Committee under Section 44(u) of the Insurance Act, 1938 (4 of 1938). Other functions are as under:

Specifying the form and manner in which books of accounts shall be maintained and insurers and other insurance intermediaries shall render statements of accounts; regulating investment of funds by insurance companies; enforcing regulation regarding maintenance of margin of solvency; adjudicating upon disputes between insurers and intermediaries or insurance intermediaries; supervising the functioning of the Tariff Advisory Committee; specifying the percentage of premium income of the insurer to finance scheme for promoting and regulating professional organizations referred to in clause (vi); specifying the percentage of life insurance business to be undertaken by the insurer in the rural or social sector, and exercising such other powers as may be prescribed.

**(i) Grants by Central Government:** The Central Government may, after due appropriation made by parliament by law in this behalf, make to the authority grants of such sums of money, as the Government may think fit, for being utilized for the purpose of this Act.

**(i) Constitution of Funds**

(1) There shall be constituted a fund to be called "The

Insurance Regulatory and Development Authority Fund" and there shall be credited thereto:

> all government grants, fees and charges received by the authority; all such grants or moneys received by the authority from such other sources as may be decided upon by the central government; the percentage of prescribed premium income received from the insurers.

(2) The Fund shall be applied for meeting: The salaries, allowances and other remuneration payable to the members, officers and other employees of the authority, and the other expenses of the authority in connection with the discharge of its functions and for the purpose of this act.

**(ii) Accounts and Audit**

(1) The authority shall maintain proper accounts and other relevant records and prepare an annual statement of accounts in such form as may be prescribed by the Central Government in consultation with the Comptroller and Auditor General of India (CAG).

(2) The accounts of the Authority shall be audited by the Comptroller and Auditor General of India at such intervals as may be specified by him and any expenditure incurred in connection with such audit shall be payable by the Authority to the Comptroller and Auditor General.

(3) The Comptroller and Auditor General of India and any other person appointed by him in connection with such audit as the Comptroller and Auditor General generally has in connection with the audit of the government accounts and, in particular, shall have the right to demand the production of books of accounts, connected vouchers and other documents and papers and to inspect any of the offices of the authority.

(4) The accounts of the authority as certified by the Comptroller and Auditor General of India or any other person appointed by him in this behalf together with the audit report thereof shall be forwarded annually to the Central Government and that government shall cause the same to be laid before both houses of Parliament.

**(m) Power of Central Government to Issue Directions:** The Central Government is empowered to take action without prejudice to the foregoing provisions of this Act. The authority shall in exercise of its powers or the performance of its functions under this Act, be bound by such directions on questions of policy, other than those relating to technical and administrative matters, as the Central Government may give in writing to it from time to time.

Provided that the authority shall, as far a practicable, be given an opportunity to express its views before any direction is given under this sub-section. The decision of the Central Government, whether a question is one of policy or not, shall be final:

**(n) Power of Central Government to Supersede Authority**

(1) If at any time, the Central Government is of the opinion:

That, on account of circumstances beyond the control of the authority, it is unable to discharge the functions or perform the duties imposed on it by or under the provisions of this Act, or that the authority has persistently defaulted in complying with any direction given by the Central Government under this Act or in the discharge of the functions of performance of the duties imposed on it by or under the provision of this Act, and as a result of such default, the financial position of the authority or the administration of the authority has suffered, or that circumstances exist which render it necessary in the public interest to do so, the Central Government may, by notification and for reasons to be specified therein, supersede the Authority for such period, not exceeding six months, as may be specified in the notification and appoint a person to be the Controller of Insurance under section 2B of the Insurance Act, 1938 (4 of 1938), if not already done.

Provided that before issuing any such notification, the Central Government shall give a reasonable opportunity to the authority to make representations, if any, to the Central Government.

(2) Upon the publication of a notification under sub-section (I) superseding the authority:

The Chairperson and other members shall, as from the date of supersession, vacate their offices as such; all the powers, functions and duties which may by or under the provisions of this Act, be exercised or discharged by or on behalf of the authority shall, until the authority is reconstituted under sub-section (3), be exercised and discharged by the Controller of Insurance, and all properties owned or controlled by the Authority shall, until the Authority is reconstituted under subsection (3), vest in the Central Government.

(3) On or before the expiration of the period of supersession specified in the notification issued under Sub-section (1), the Central Government shall reconstitute the Authority by a fresh appointment of its Chairperson and other members and in such a case, any person who had vacated his office under clause (a) of sub-section (2) shall not be deemed to be disqualified for reappointment.

(4) The Central Government shall cause a copy of the notification issued under sub-section (1) and a full report on the action taken, to be laid before each house of Parliament at the earliest.

**(o) Furnishing of Returns, etc. to the Central Government**

The authority shall furnish to the Central Government at such time and in such form and manner as may be prescribed, or as the Central Government may direct to furnish such returns, statements and other particulars in regard to any proposed or existing programme for the promotion and development of the insurance business during the previous financial year.

Copies of the reports received under sub-section (2) shall be laid, as soon as may be after they are received, before each House of Parliament.

**(p) Chairperson, Members, Officers and other Employees of Authority to be Public Servants:** The Chairperson, members, officers and other employees of the Authority shall be deemed, when acting or purporting to act in pursuance of any of the provision of this Act, to be public servants within the meaning of section 21 of the Indian Penal Code (45 of 1860).

**(q) Protection of Action taken in Good Faith:** No suit, prosecution or other legal proceedings shall lie against the Central Government or any officer of the Central Government or any member, officer or other employee of the Authority for anything, which is done in good faith or intended to be done under this Act or the rules or regulations made thereunder:

Provided that nothing in this Act shall exempt any person from any suit or other proceedings, which might, apart from this Act, be brought against him/her.

**(r) Delegation of Powers**

The Authority may, by general or special order in writing, delegate to the Chairperson or any other member or officer of the authority subject to such conditions, if any, as may be specified in the order, such of its powers and functions under this Act as it may deem necessary.

The Authority may, by a general or special order in writing, also form Committees of the members and delegate to them the powers and functions of the authority as may be specified by the regulations.

**(s) Power to make Rules**

The Central Government may, by notification, make rules for carrying out the provision of this Act.

In particular, and without prejudice to the geniality of the foregoing power, such regulations may provide for all or any of the following matters, namely -

The salary and allowances payable to and other terms and conditions of service of the members, other than part-time numbers, under sub-section (1) of Section (7);

The allowances to be paid to the part-time members under sub-section (2) of Section 7;

Such other powers that may be exercised by the Authority under clause (XVII) of sub-section (2) of Section 14;

The form of annual statement of accounts to be maintained by the Authority under sub-section (1) of Section 17;

The form and the manner in which and the time within which returns and statements and particulars are to be furnished to the Central Government under sub-section (1) of Section 20.

The matters under sub-section (5) of Section 25 on which the Insurance Advisory Committee shall advise the authority, and

Any other matter which is required to be or may be, prescribed, or in respect of which provision is to be or may be made by rules.

**(t) Establishment of Insurance Advisory Committee**

The Authority may, by notification, establish with effect from such date as it may specify in such notification, a committee to be known as the Insurance Advisory Committee.

The Insurance Advisory Committee shall consist of not more than twenty-five members excluding *ex-officio* members to represent the interest of commerce, intermediaries, organizations engaged in safety and loss prevention, research bodies and employees' association in the insurance sector.

The chairperson and the members of the Authority shall be the *ex-officio* chairperson and *ex-officio* members of the Insurance Advisory Committee.

The object of the Insurance Advisory Committee shall be to advise the authority on matters relating to the making of the regulations under Section 26.

Without prejudice to the provisions of sub-section (4) the Insurance Advisory Committee may advise the authority on such other matters as may be prescribed.

**(u) Power to make Regulations**

The Authority may, in consultation with the Insurance Advisory Committee, by notification, make regulations consistent with this Act and the rules made thereunder to carry out the purposes of this Act.

In particular, and without prejudice to the generality of the foregoing power, such regulations may provide for all or any of the following matters, namely:

The time and places of meetings of the Authority and the procedure to be followed at such meetings including the quorum necessary for the transaction of business under sub-section (1) of section 10;

The transaction of business at its meeting under sub-section (4) of section 10;

The terms and other conditions of service of officers and other employees of the Authority under sub-section (2) of Section 12;

The powers and functions which may be delegated to Committees of the members under sub-section (2) of Section 23, and

Any other matter which is required to be, or may be, specified by regulations or in respect of which provision is to be or may be made by regulations.

**(v) Rules and Regulations to be laid before Parliament:** Every rule and regulation made under the Act shall be laid as soon as may be after it is made, before each House of Parliament, while it is in session, for a total period of thirty (30) days which may be comprised in one session or in two or more successive sessions, and if, before the expiry of the session immediately falling the session or the successive session aforesaid, both Houses agree in making any modification in the rule or regulation or both Houses agree that the rule or regulation should not be made, the rule or regulation shall thereafter have effect only in such modified from or be of no effect, as the case may be. However, any such modification or annulment shall be without prejudice to be valid if anything previously done under that rule or regulation.

**(w) Application of Other Laws not Barred:** The provisions of this Act shall be in addition to, and not in derogation of the provision of any other law for the time being in force:

**(x) Power to Remove Difficulties:**

If any difficulty arises in giving effect to the provisions of this Act, the Central Government may, by order published in the Official Gazette, make such provisions not inconsistent with the provisions of this Act as may appear to be necessary for removing the difficulty:

Provided that no order shall be made under this Section after the expiry of two years from the appointed day.

Every order made under this section shall be laid, as soon as may be, after it is made, before each house of Parliament.

### (4) Summary of the above Discussions

Insurance Regulatory and Development Authority (IRDA) has come to stay for the smooth management and control of insurance business in India. The performance of IRDA is being debated and appreciated both within and outside the nation. So far, IRDA has been trying very hard to streamline the business procedures in insurance sector with an utmost caution on the quality of service by both new and old players in the field.

The emergence of IRDA has been widely appreciated by the insurance experts, professionals, and insurance business players. However, the success of IRDA may be tested in the long-term when the insurance policies sold by the private business players get matured.

# 11

# *Privatisation of Insurance Sector*

## INTRODUCTION

It has been observed that the Public Sector Enterprises (PSEs) cannot perform their economic and business activities effectively and efficiently in any country. The public enterprises are not discharging their full responsibilities even in a socialist country. The total nationalization of business industry will lead to serfdom or anarchism. Democracy demands full freedom in all matters with people's choice, not forced. But, it is stark reality that it is difficult for every enterprise to compete in the market. The government has to restructure society and economy in such a manner that the poor, the unemployed can be profitably employed. Entrepreneurship has to be developed and all the educated persons have to set-up their ventures with the latest technology and under franchisee system or through ancilliarization in the industrial sector.

India has been planning for development using the Nehruvian-Mahalanobis economic model of mixed economy. Too much expectation from public enterprises will distort the economy and will ultimately lead towards wastage of precious and valuable scarce resources. Therefore, the government is going to recast the industrial policy considering the productivity and efficiency as criteria to continue particular units whether as public enterprises or private enterprises. It is a matter of satisfaction that the government has started taking pragmatic based criteria for the development of enterprises. The restriction on the use of full capacity by private enterprises is being removed to increase the output and productivity of the economy.

Time has come when the public enterprises will have to compete with the private enterprises. If the public enterprises are losing on the efficiency and productivity criteria, they should be closed down. If the private enterprises have more efficiency and higher productivity, those should be encouraged to increase production and output of the economy. It is universally agreed that the government cannot perform all the functions with equal efficiency. It should have nothing to do with business or industry as far as the ownership is concerned. Ownership should pass on to the private hands as the private sector has entrepreneurship. The regulatory role, promotional role, entrepreneurial role and planning role have not been fully performed by any government with the level of efficiency of the private sector. The government should concentrate more on regulatory and planning roles at the macro-level. The entrepreneurial role should be confined only to those areas where the private entrepreneurs are hesitant and cannot discharge their functions satisfactorily at national level. Non-profitable business activities like defense, transport, education, communication and other such types of activities concerning general welfare and national security should only be undertaken by the Government.

According to W.A. Levis:

> The nationalization of industry is not essential to planning. A government can do anything it wants to do by way of controlling industry without resorting to nationalization of ownership.

There should not be a state monopoly in the country in all fields. Competition is the backbone of an economy and it pushes up productivity. Therefore, competition should be encouraged to promote production and productivity in the economy. Competition may be between the public and private enterprises. The public enterprises should be preferred in some areas than private sector, and so, they should be permitted to continue to accelerate the growth of the economy. On the other hand, many public sector enterprises are wasting public money because of continuous losses or less than optimal production. Such enterprises should be handed over to the competent private entrepreneurs.

However, privatization may be done after analyzing the efficiency of the organizations and their role in the economy. Insurance industry along with other financial institutions has been constantly under pressure of privatization without going into the grass-root problems and their potential consequences. Many Committees and government agencies have been arguing in favour of privatization, denationalization and permitting foreign institutions to conduct insurance business in India.

### Privatization of Insurance Industry in India—Steps Taken by the Government to Privatize the Insurance Sector

In 1993, the government of India had set-up a high powered committee under the Chairmanship of R.N. Malhotra, former Governor of Reserve Bank of India, to examine the structure of the insurance industry and to recommend changes to make it more efficient and competitive, keeping in view the structural changes taking place in other parts of the financial system of the country.

### Purposes of Malhotra Committee

The following are the purposes of the Committee:

In terms of the objectives before the Malhotra Committee, it had surveyed, studied and analysed in its report the structure of insurance industry, to asses the strengths and weaknesses of insurance companies in terms of the objectives of creating efficient and viable insurance industry, to have a wide coverage of insurance services, to have a variety of insurance products with a high quality service component, and to develop an effective instrument for mobilization of financial resources for development. The report also contained the arguments and made recommendations for changing the structure of insurance industry, for changing the general policy framework, etc. The Committee had the task of making suggestions regarding the following:

(a) To make specific suggestions regarding Life Insurance Corporation of India (LIC) and General Insurance Corporation of India (GIC) with a view to improve their functioning.
(b) To make recommendations on regulations and supervision of the insurance sector in India.
(c) To make recommendations on the role and functions of surveyors, intermediaries like agents, etc. in the insurance sector.
(d) To make recommendations on any other matter which is relevant for development of the insurance industry in India.

**Malhotra Committee's Recommendations**

Let us be briefed about the recommendations of the Malhotra Committee. The Committee submitted its report in January 1994 recommending that private insurers be allowed to co-exist along with government companies like LIC and GIC. This recommendation had been supported by several factors, the most important being the need for wide insurance coverage in the economy. Major recommendations of Malhotra Committee are as follows:

(i) Raising the capital base of LIC and GIC upto Rs. 200 crores each, half to be retained by the government and rest sold to the public at large with suitable reservation for employees.
(ii) Private sector be granted permission to enter insurance industry with a minimum paid up capital of Rs. 100 crores.
(iii) Foreign insurance companies be allowed to enter by floating an Indian company preferably joint venture with Indian partners.
(iv) Steps to be taken to set-up a strong and effective insurance regulatory body in the form of statutory autonomous board on the lines of SEBI.
(v) Limited number of private companies to be allowed in the sector. But no firm be allowed to operate in both lines of insurance (Life and non-Life).
(vi) Tariff Advisory Committee (TAC) is to be delinked

from GIC to function as a separate statutory body under necessary supervision by the Insurance Regulatory Authority.

(vii) All the insurance companies be treated on equal footing and governed by the provisions of the Insurance Act. No special dispensation is to be given to government companies.

(viii) Setting up of a strong and effective regulatory body with independent source for financing before allowing private companies into this sector.

(ix) The committee suggested that settlements of claims were to be done within a specific time frame (without delay).

(x) The committee has made several recommendations on product pricing, vigilance, systems and procedures, improving customer service and use of technology.

(xi) It also made a number of recommendations to change the existing structures of the LIC and GIC.

(xii) The committee insisted that insurance companies should pay special attention to the rural insurance business (rural coverage).

## Impact of Privatization and Liberalization on Insurance Industry

The opening up of insurance sector for competition offers ample opportunities to both existing as well as new players to penetrate into untapped areas, sectors and sub-sectors and unexploited segments of population as presently both insurance density and penetration are at low level. Both indices being at very low level in the country, even compared to the countries with the same level of economic development and per capita income, are indicative of the vast potential of the growth of this sector in future.

The impact of privatization can be studied under three heads:

Opportunities; challenges or threats; and strategies.

### *(I) Opportunities*

The privatization of insurance industry will provide the following opportunities:

(1) *Untapped Market*: New comers in insurance industry

will get the advantage of untapped market. The untapped potential market for insurance products is quite large in spite of the efforts made by general insurance companies and LIC to extend their services throughout the country. But the choices available to the insuring public are inadequate in terms of services, products and prices. The Malhotra Committee estimated that in life insurance, 22% of the insurable population has been tapped so far. Premium per capita is only 2% in India. Premium percentage of GDP is 0.55% which is very less in comparison to the USA where premium per capita is equivalent of Rs. 1381 and premium as percentage of GDP is 4.80%. This huge gap from the global benchmark is itself indicative of huge untapped potential.

(2) *Mandatory Insurance*: In disaster prone areas, Government of India is going to make insurance mandatory. The interim report of the high powered committee set-up by the centre on disaster management has proposed mandatory insurance of life and property by people residing in a disaster prone area such as coastal belts, flood prone areas, sites near nuclear, chemical and hazardous industries and thickly populated areas.

(3) *More products Offered*: A state monopoly has little incentive to offer a wide range of products. It can be seen by a lack of certain products from LIC's portfolio and lack of extensive categorization in several GIC products such as health insurance. More competition in this business will spur firms to offer several new products and more complex and extensive risk categorization.

(4) *Growth of Economy*: With the allowing of holding of equity shares by foreign company either itself or through its subsidiary company or nominee, not exceeding 26% of paid-up capital of insurance company, various joint ventures between foreign investors and Indian partners will be operated resulting into supplementing domestic savings and economic progress of the nation.

(5) *Opportunity for Banks*: Banks, with their wide area

network with branches in all parts of the country, will have good opportunity to enter in insurance business or industry. Banks will succeed in this sector because they have data of customers, trained staff, a good network

(6) *Better Customer Services*: Privatization would result in better customer services and would help in improving the variety and price of insurance products. Competition will compel the players to bring new and innovative products, wider choice of prices and quality service to the policyholders (consumers).

*(II) Challenges*

Whether the insurer is old or new, private or public, expansion and extension of market will present multitude of challenges, as described hereunder:

(1) *New Insurers*: New insurers will have to invest a minimum capital of Rs. 100 crore. The normal gestation period is of five years. Hence, the new insurers will have to lock up their capital for at least five years before earning any profits. Besides, they will face problems of shortage of trained manpower for the insurance industry. The setting up of various offices and distribution network is a time-consuming process. Further, the new insurer-companies will have to compete with the established insurance companies like LIC and GIC, which have a corporate image and market presence for several years.

(2) *Expectations of the Consumers*: Today, LIC has more than 60 products and GIC has more than 180 products to offer in the insurance market. But most of them are outdated, as they are not suitable to the needs of the present-day consumers. Hence, all the insurance companies will have to offer innovative products to the consumers. The consumers are particularly expecting good pension plans, health insurance, term insurance, and investment products like unit linked insurance from the life insurance

companies. Similarly, the consumers expect innovative products from the general insurance for managing health care, property insurance, accident insurance and other products on an attractive terms and competitive premium. The consumers also expect reduction in the premium of the insurance products for another reason; that the mortality rate in India has come down three times in the last five years.

(3) *Premium on Customer Service*: The days of giving fixed insurance products are over. Now the customers need insurance solutions that match their needs or wants. The large-scale of operations, public sector bureaucratic and cumbersome procedures hamper nationalized insurers. Therefore, potential private entrants expect to score in the areas of customer service, speed and flexibility. It may mean better products and wider choice for the customers. For extending better service, insurance companies will have to build call centres to provide call-free telephone based sales and services. The call centres will provide product-related information, customers, accounts' information, queries and complaint handling. These call centres can be used for outbound sales and marketing companies.

(4) *Distribution Channel*: In the privatized insurance market, there will be multiple distribution channels which will include agents, brokers, corporate intermediaries, bank branches, affinity groups and direct marketing through tele-sales and internet. There will be competition among the channels also. Intense competitions will grow among the old and new insurers in the liberalized insurance market. There would be substantial shift in the distribution of insurance in India. Many of these changes are due to international trends. World wide insurance products move from pure service produces to pure commodity products. Then they could be sold through the medical shops, groceries, novelty stores, etc. Once the products gain awareness and popularity, then they can move to remote channels such as telephone or direct mail.

(5) *Consumer Education*: The existing level of consumes' education and awareness about insurance products is very low. Only 62% of the Indian population is educated and less than 10% are well educated. Even the educated are ignorant about the various products of insurance. Hence, it is necessary that all the insurance companies should undertake the executive plan and policy for education and awareness of consumers about insurance policies. The consumer organizations and media can also play very important role in education of the consumers. This will result in expansion and depth of the insurance market and will also enable the needy consumers to purchase appropriate policies. In fact, the private new comer insurers have already started putting a lot more emphasis on advertising and using creative tactics to educate the consumers.

(6) *Consumer Grievance Redressal Mechanism*: The insurance companies have to face an actuate problem of the redressal of grievances of consumers for deficiency in products and services. The IRDA has already appointed ombudsman for looking into the grievances of the policyholders and its judgment will be binding on insurers. In the competitive market, awareness level of consumers will increase and it will help consumers to fight for their legal right in case of deficiency in services. Therefore, the number of legal cases field by the consumers against the insurance companies is likely to increase substantially in future. This will be a challenge to the insurers.

(7) *New Product Innovations needed*: In India, only two products of LIC dominate with majority share out of 52 products. With more competition, good products will become an important differentiator among the various competing insurance products. A lot will depend on the kind of products that these outfits would launch. Initially, after launching simple products, the multinationals will shift to specialized

products, e.g. Royal Sundaram Alliance will launch a mix of personal and commercial insurance policies. This will cover fire, marine, motor, personal accident and health insurance. HDFC Standard Life will launch two core life insurance products and then another dozen of the same type.

(8) *Positioning of Insurance Products in the Market*: First of all, the biggest challenge for the insurance companies will be the change in the mindset of people, especially in regard to life insurance. Life insurance is seen more as a tax saving mechanism rather than safety net in case of death, in India, e.g. ICICI Prudential Life Insurance's Chief Marketing Officer, Saugata Gupta says that "Working on consumer attitude will be the greatest challenge". New types of products should be futuristic in outlook. To start with, low premium high cover policies should be introduced and better savings products at later stage.

(9) *Rural Area Exploitation the best Bet*: Life insurance business in India suffers from high premium and low returns. A normally competitive industry should be able to increase coverage, mobile large savings, and provide high returns. In terms of mobilizing savings in the form of insurance, India is ranked at 27th in the world. Now with the entry of numerous private companies in rural areas, it is expected that rural sector will be tapped as well. IRDA has made it mandatory for life insurance companies to sell 5% of their aggregated polices in the rural areas during the first year of operation and that to be progressively increased to 15% by the fifth year. But with gestation period being long and investment required being large, new entrants will feel very difficult to achieve it.

(10) *Information Technology the highly facilitating Factor*: Information technology has become an integral part of the insurance industry worldwide from general accounting to customer service, re-insurance, underwriting and risk management. These have integrated application and are decision-oriented. In

the Indian insurance industry, information technology is used as a reporting tool whereas, overseas, it is used more as a decision-making instrument. The policyholders would be able to check policy details from their balance to nominee schemes, the type of loans available and the amount in their investment accounts on-line and through Internet connectivity. The insurers' advisors can also check accounts of their customers as well as their own accounts.

*(III) Strategies*

The insurance players would be required to concentrate on the following main strategies to become more competitive and responsive to the needs of the societies:

(1) *Environmental Analysis*: The companies should concentrate on environmental change, its direction, magnitude and its short-term and long-term impact, formulating strategies to meet the challenges of high competition, preparing contingency plans and then designing action plans for effective implementation of formulated strategies.

(2) *Restructuring Organization will help*: The traditional hierarchy system is very slow in making decisions due to several levels of management involved, its procedural inflexibility and slow communication process/system. A manager in the privatized scenario is required to be an organizational specialist, country specialist and global specialist.

(3) *Speed, Cost Effectiveness and Innovations required*: The private insurance companies will have to make substantial investments in customer relationship management technologies. They will be required to have wide area network (WAN), connecting branches spread across wide geographical locations and work out modalities for facilitating premium payment through the Internet. LIC is setting up an interactive response system in more cities so that a policy holder need not travel to the office of company for

information. After all, the customer should have the choice of getting work done in the shortest possible time without having to visit the office of insurance companies.

(4) *Human Resources Development the key to business development and client servicing*: Human resource is important for any organization, more especially for organizations, activities of which revolve around special human interactions. The new private insurance companies need people with the right set of knowledge, skills and aptitude for insurance alongwith right type of products and services. The persons who are involved in selling the product and those who are doing the back office work need to equip themselves with newer skills and insights into every aspect of functioning of the company. They have a daunting task of exploiting potential in the industry and at the same time bring down risk level to the company for providing insurance coverage. They have to retain the existing customers for which they need to have better understanding of products and services by creating healthy internal environment with group harmony. Existing companies will have to frame their human resource policies to retain the competent personnel and motivate staff continuously since new companies entering insurance business will be eyeing them by offering lucrative salaries.

(5) *Efficiency in Distribution to be assured*: It is very important factor and may prove bottleneck to the new players. Insurance companies are making the products available through the ready distribution channels of banks, non-banking finance companies and housing companies. One has to be careful doing this, since creating distribution with distances does not automatically mean controlling them. There will be more places from where customer can purchase insurance polices with the starting of corporate agencies besides the consultants and agents currently selling these policies. Due to this, a new concept of

Bancassurance has emerged which is defined as a kind of service that the insurance companies use to offer their products through the distribution channels of banking industry. There is need to augment sources of revenues for survival. Bancassurance has promoted two big classes of financial institutions to combine their strengths and created a new means of marketing and servicing their products. Convergence of banking sector traditionally considered being more competitive and insurance sector having a vast untapped potential of growth has resulted into bancassurance.

(6) *Risk Management*: Insurance companies will have to bring new approach and sophistication in market research techniques, future portfolio expansion like all intermediaries in financial markets do.

(7) *Efficient Marketing Strategies*: Marketing strategies for insurance products in the emerging scenario could be understood in the following steps:

$R \rightarrow STP \rightarrow MM \rightarrow I \rightarrow C$

where

R = Market Research,
STP = Segmentation, Targeting, Positioning,
MM = Marketing Mix,
I = Implementation, and
C = Control.

The focus of emerging marketing strategies would centre on the prepositions like reduced costs, increased profitability, reduced time to market, improved customer intimacy, retained customers for life, establishing strong partnership. Formulation of a marketing strategy is more a process than an event. Environmental factors like macro-economic parameters, regulatory norms and theme, technology, infrastructure, legal set-up, competition by way of new entry, degree of globalization, etc. need to be scanned and considered in framing the likely scenarios. The competitive advantage of a company may stem from the many discrete activities in value chains. Each of these activities can contribute to a company's relative cost position or create a basis for differentiation.

(8) *Ethical Issues*: The governance problems in service industry like insurance have been raised time and again as well as risk management techniques. Companies will need to leverage this sophistication backed by information technology to select good risks and rate them. On the other hand, insurance companies invest the funds of policyholders and owned capital and accumulate surpluses and reserves. Companies try to earn the highest rate of return possible on investments consistent with risk objectives, because pre-eminence is related to investment performance. As the rate of return on investments increases, the insurance companies can lower the premiums they charge on new policies. Higher rate of return provides higher earnings on cash values and lesser the need for premium revenues. Premium rates are a competitive factor and high investment returns are crucial in maintaining and improving an insurance company's sales position. Strong investment performance supports growth in policy sales and sets aside the sense of helplessness among the employees and customers alike. Companies must realize this particularly in the emerging scenario of intense competition wherein customers will have a range of options for investments and insurance. At the same time, the regulators and companies will have to be cautious of customers who indulge in unethical practices by manipulating or hiding vital information in their dealings with companies and inflict losses, resulting in increase in cost of insurance. Ethics will have to be ensured in every activity of the company.

**Scenario of Insurance Industry in India as it obtains today**

Seventeen new players have entered the field of insurance, both life and non-life business, after opening up of insurance industry to private sector in India. Some of these are:

Tata AIG Life Insurance Company Ltd.
Birla Sunlife Insurance Company Ltd.
HDFC Standard Life Insurance Company Ltd.
Kotak Mahindra Old Mutual Life Insurance Company Ltd.
Reliance General Insurance Company Ltd.
ICICI Prudential Life Insurance Company Ltd.
Royal Sundaram Alliance Insurance Company Ltd.
Bajaj Auto Alliance Insurance Company Limited.
IFFCO Tokyo General Insurance Company Ltd.
ING Vysya Life Insurance Company (Pvt) Ltd. .
SBI Life Insurance Company Ltd.
Dabur CGNU Life Insurance Company Ltd.
Max New York Life Insurance Company Ltd.

SBI Life Insurance has lunched three products—Sanjeevan, Sukhjeevan and Young Sanjeevan and so far, it has sold more than 800 policies under its plans. Various insurance companies have tied up with banks to market their products, e.g. HDFC Standard Life has tied up with Indian bank and UCO Bank in the Eastern region. It has also entered into an MOU with Peerless Bank as the corporation's branches will help a rural reach for insurance company. Proposed joint venture Dabur CJU Life Insurance where Dabur group holds 74% and UK-based CJU life's 26% stake would be started with an equity capital of Rs. 110 crore. CGNU group being UK's largest insurer and one of the world's sixty largest insurers with assets worth $ 300 bn under its management and Dabur being India's leading FMCG Company, this venture may emerge as a leading player in insurance industry. Kotak Mahindra is likely to get approval for two more products, which include term insurance and equity linked policy in a bid to offer wider range of products.

In India, till now, only 20% of the insurable population is covered under insurance while the remaining population is yet to be insured. As the insurance sector has been opened up, the monopoly of government companies has broken and many new private players have entered into the insurance sector and thus the sector has become highly competitive, full of challenges. The insurance and the economic growth of the country mutually influence each other. As the economy grows, the standard of living of people also improves.

In fact, as the economy widens, the demand for insurance products emerges. A well developed insurance sector promotes economic growth by encouraging risk-taking. The average annual rate of growth of the country in the first three decades after independence was 3.5%. In the nineties, the average annual rate of growth of income has been 5.8% per annum. Life expectancy has also increased from 32 years in fifties to 61 years now. As life expectancy increases, there will be a need to take care of long retired life. So, the Indian life insurance market alongwith general insurance market is full of potential. The only need is to frame suitable strategies to tap the whole market in more efficient and effective manner.

# 12

# *Asset-Liability Management (ALM)*

## INTRODUCTION

Traditionally and previously banks were concerned only with increasing the size of their balance sheets. They were focusing on a few specific items of the balance sheet like deposits, credit to priority sector and reducing the size of NPAs – recovery of bad and doubtful loans and advances (Assets). After the introduction of prudential accounting norms, deregulation of interest rates, globalization and economic liberalization, Indian banks began facing serious problem of mismatch between their assets and liabilities due to volatility in the interest rates and foreign exchange rates. Emergence of new instruments, new players and new products at highly competitive rates in the market increased banks' risks. Now in a fairly deregulated environment, interest rates on all money market instruments are determined for most part, and often, by the market forces. All the banks are now allowed to determine own interest rates on domestic deposits and loans and advances over rupees 2 lacs.

The changes in interest rates affect the banks in two ways as under:

(1) Since assets (loans and advances) and liabilities (deposits and borrowings) are not realised

simultaneously, the mismatch affects the interest income.

(2) It affects the market value of assets like treasury bills, commercial paper and certificate of deposits, etc.

Therefore, it is no longer the case that banks shall be asset-driven and primarily concerned to find resources to finance lending. Rather banks are moving progressively to the stage of not only adjusting liabilities in accordance with potential assets but also adjusting assets in accordance with potential liabilities.

## MEANING OF ALM

The various types of risks faced by the banks can be managed through the management process known as Asset-Liability Management (ALM). Asset-Liability Management refers to the policy of the banks with regard to mix of assets and liabilities. In the context of RBI guidelines to the banks, 'asset-liability' management can be defined as a continuous process of planning, organizing and controlling asset/liability volume, maturities, yields and rates. In other words, asset-liability management can be defined as a function which involves planning, directing and controlling the flow, level, mix and rates on the bank assets and liabilities.

## OBJECTIVES OF ASSET-LIABILITY MANAGEMENT (ALM)

An Effective Asset-liability management of banks should encompass:

(a) Review of interest rate outlook.

(b) Fixation of interest product pricing of both assets and liabilities.

(c) Review of credit risk management and credit portfolio.

(d) Review of investment portfolio and risk management.

(e) Review of liquidity risk and management of liquidity risk.

(f) Review of policy of foreign exchange operations and risk management.

## BALANCE SHEET STRUCTURE: IMPLICATIONS FOR ASSET-LIABILITY MANAGEMENT (ALM)

The subject of assets (especially advances and investments) and liability (especially deposits and borrowings) management revolves around balance sheet. The ALM requires that assets and liabilities should be planned, organized and controlled so that profitability is managed and liquidity is managed.

The analysis of balance sheet of a bank reveals that among the liabilities, a significant portion comes from deposits (savings, term deposits and current account deposits) and among these deposits, term deposits bear a fixed rate of interest for a specified period but carry a risk of pre-mature encashment. The savings bank deposits have no maturity period. Borrowings (from RBI and other banks) are also among liabilities which carry interest at market rate but repayment is generally known.

The analysis of assets side reveals that the most significant portion of advances is linked to prime lending rate (PLR) which is a floating rate. Once the PLR changes, the rate on the loans and advances would change instantly without any time lag. An overwhelming majority of the investment portfolio is in the form of fixed rate government and other securities.

### BALANCE SHEET STRUCTURE

#### (A) Liabilities Side

*(a) Deposits*

*Savings Fund Accounts and Current Accounts:* The features of both the deposits are that there is no maturity date and the clients are free to deposit or withdraw any amount at any point of time.

*Term Deposits:* The term deposits may be in the form of cumulative term deposits, non-cumulative term deposits and recurring deposits. As regards liquidity, the client has the freedom to encash them at a pre-matured date if he needs money urgently. In case of recurring deposits, the instalment amount may not be paid in time.

In case, interest rates increase, the customers can decide in their favour.

*(b) Borrowing:* Terms of Borrowings are clear as regards liquidity and interest rates.

**(B) Assets Side**

*Investment:* The investment may be for medium and long-term and there is little flexibility for reshuffling. Major portion of investments carries fixed rate of interest.

*Advances:* The repayment of advances by customers is no doubt pre-determined but repayment still depends upon host of factors. Some part of cash credit and overdraft may not be availed of by the borrowing units leading to uncertainty in liquidity management.

## SCOPE OF ASSET- LIABILITY MANAGEMENT

Asset-liability management of a bank, earlier known as Treasury Management, is a part of overall risk management. Risk is defined as, "Risk is uncertainty as to the outcome of an event when two or more possibilities exist." The aim of asset- liability management is to manage risk exposures so that they are kept within the acceptable levels and at the same time help to generate income and maintain profitability. Efficient asset-liability management procedures should enable a bank to control and limit risks associated with maturity mismatching, interest rate gaps and foreign exchange exposure and so on. ALM addresses the following risks:

Liquidity Risk; Interest Rate Risk; and Market Risk.

**(I) Liquidity Risk**

Liquidity Risk refers to the ability of a concern to meet its commitment when due and to undertake new transactions if profitable. Liquidity risk can emanate in any of the following situations:

(a) Conversion of contingent liabilities into fund-based commitment.
(b) Non receipt of expected cash flows from recovery of loans.
(c) Increased availment of sanctioned limits.
(d) Disproportionate outflow of funds arising out of non-renewal/withdrawal of deposits.

Liquidity risk is categorised into two types:
(i) Trading Liquidity Risk, and (ii) Funding Liquidity Risk.

*Trading Liquidity Risk*

Trading liquidity risk arises as a result of liquidity of securities in the trading portfolio of the bank. Liquidity and return are negatively correlated. So higher returns can be expected by accepting an illiquid investment in the portfolio and should be monitored on frequent basis. In reality, one of the important considerations for the inclusion of investment in the trading portfolio is on the basis of its liquidity status. As the trading portfolio is short-term in nature with regulator-constrained maximum holding period of 90 days, it is better to include only those securities which are not only liquid at the time of creation but are expected to be liquid over the holding period of portfolio.

*Funding Liquidity Risk*

Funding liquidity risk arises as a result of mismatch between the timing of the cash flow of assets and liabilities, funding liquidity risk that arises due to mismatch is the outcome of difference in balance sheet strategies followed by different institutions in the same industry. It is possible that a few banks may suffer from shortage of liquidity while others may have excess funding liquidity.

**Measurement of Liquidity Risk**

There are two approaches to measure liquidity risk at balance sheet level. These are:

Liquidity Gap Analysis and Structural Balance Sheet Ratios.

*(1) Liquidity Gap Analysis*

The liquidity gap at a particular level of maturity is the difference between maturity of assets and maturing liabilities. When maturing liabilities exceed maturing assets, a negative gap is created and when maturing assets exceed maturing liabilities, a positive gap is created.

Reserve Bank of India, in its guidelines, has instructed the banks to classify maturing assets (cash inflows) and maturing liabilities (cash flows) in eight maturity periods (called tie buckets). The cash flows from assets and liabilities include both principal and interest cash flows.

The liability gap analysis is illustrated through an example of "Liquidity Gap Statement" of PRS Bank:

**Liquidity Gap Statement of PRS Bank as on 25-06-2012**

*(Rs. In Crores)*

| *Maturity* | *Assets* | *Liabilities* | *Gap* | *Cumulative Gap* |
|---|---|---|---|---|
| 01 day – 14 days | 2,000 | 2,300 | (300) | (300) |
| 15 days – 28 days | 3,000 | 3,600 | (600) | (900) |
| 29 days – 03 months | 4,000 | 5,000 | (1,000) | (1,900) |
| 3 months – 06 months | 4,000 | 5,600 | (1,600) | (3,500) |
| 6 months – 12 months | 2,000 | 2,000 | 0 | (3,500) |
| 1 year – 02 years | 3,000 | 2,600 | 400 | (3,100) |
| 2 years – 05 years | 6,000 | 4,000 | 2,000 | 1,100 |
| Over 5 years | 2,000 | 3,100 | (1,100) | 0 |

It can be observed from the above statement that the liability maturing over the next three months from 25-06-2012 exceed maturing assets by Rs. 1900 crores (cumulative gap). The total maturing liabilities at Rs.10,900 crores (2300 + 3600 + 5000) over the first three months require to be met by (a) fresh deposits, (b) renewal of deposits, (c) borrowings from other banks and RBI. At the end, the liquidity gap will always be nil because assets always equal to liabilities plus equity.

Banks generally do not and can not maintain 'NIL' gap in all maturities. The objective of this liquidity gap analysis is to determine the tolerable gap. These gaps are also called mis-matches. The RBI desires that the gap in the maturity buckets of 1-14 days and 15-28 days should be limited to 20% of the maturing liabilities of cash outflows in the respective maturity buckets.

With the information available in the liquidity gap statement, the banks can evolve prudential limits for the gaps according to their risk-taking capacities and as per guidelines/ norms fixed by the RBI from time to time.

### *Structural Balance Sheet Ratios*

The liquidity position of the banks can be assessed through structural balance sheet ratios.

Some of the ratios are discussed below:

### *Purchased Funds to Liquid Assets*

Purchased funds, for example, are call money borrowings including short-term refinance, etc. These funds should not constitute a significant portion of liquid assets. It is important and urgent to specify a tolerance limit for that purpose so that outflow of funds on account of purchased funds is controlled.

*Core Deposits to Core Assets:* Outstanding in loan books and the statutory reserves constituted core assets are considered for this ratio. The ratio of core deposits to core assets should be specified to maintain a stable liquid position.

*Call Borrowing to total Borrowing:* This ratio reflects the dependence of a bank on call borrowings to honour its commitments. Call borrowings are generally costly.

*Liquid Investments to Total Investments*: Liquid investments are convertible into cash at any time. More the liquidity lesser the profits, so the banks are to trade-off between liquidity and profitability.

*Liquid Assets to total Assets:* Extent of liquid assets available to meet outflows on account of deposits in normal/abnormal circumstances is shown by this ratio.

*Liquid Assets to Total Assets:* As banks deal in money, major part of money must be in the form of investment and liquid assets.

### *Liquidity Risk Management*

A rational idea that emerges after liquidity analysis is liquidity risk management. The issues which are relevant in managing liquidity risks are:

To keep constant watch over the fact whether the liquidity-asset mis-match (surplus or deficit), under consideration, is within tolerable limits as per the policy of the management of the bank. If yes, it is OK. If not, what should be various measures or strategies to be employed to ensure that the imbalance is within the tolerance limit.

Financial experts suggest that even if liquidity mismatch is within the tolerance range, the management should adhere to strategies which maximize benefits in a given market environment. However, keeping in mind the tolerance limits to be strictly followed, the management must be proactive rather than passive. Among the numerous strategies available are: trading portfolio, refinance facilities, market borrowing, wholesale deposits, securitization, loan sales, etc. Every strategy has to be evaluated in terms of cost and the intended benefit before implementation for managing the A-L mismatch.

### (2) Interest Rate Risk (IRR)

Interest affects all financial transactions. Banks' profits accrue from interest income more than non-interest income. The interest rate risk is the risk of decline of earnings owing to change in interest rates. The profitability of the bank is largely dependent on the interest spread (interest spread is the difference between interest earned and interest expended). A sizable chunk of banks' revenues and costs is indexed to interest rates. Since interest rates are unstable, so are the earrings.

The following kinds of risks will either individually or cumulatively result in interest rate risks:

*Rate Level Risk:* There is always a possibility of resetting interest rate levels either due to market forces or due to regulatory intervention. Suppose that RBI lowers Cash Reserve Ratio (CRR) by 2%, the result would be that the market would be flooded with excess liquidity which shall result in lowering interest rates.

*Pre-Payment Risk:* The decline in interest rates at times leads to pre-payment of loans. When interest rates are declining, customers who had taken loan at higher rates would like to substitute a cheaper debt or pre-pay the costly loan. The pre-paid cash in-flows will have to be re-deployed at a lower rate, which shall invariably affect profitability.

*Basic Risk:* It is quite possible to link liabilities and assets to two different bench-marks resulting in floating rate. Suppose that these two base rates do not move in tandem with each other, the net interest income either increases or decreases.

*Real Interest Rate Risk:* The level of inflation also plays a critical role in determining the real interest yield/cost.

*Volatility Risk:* The frequent changes in interest rates affect the business volume as well as pricing of the products. The effect or fluctuation in the short-term will have a greater impact on cash flows since the adjustment period is very short.

**Measurement of Interest Rate Risk**

There are three approaches available to measure interest rate risk; these are:

Earnings Approach; Interest Rate Gap analysis; and Economic Value Approach.

(1) *Earning Approach to IRR:* The earnings approaches which is an important top line performance indicator is expressed either as net interest income or net interest margin.

(a) *Net Interest Income (NII):* Net interest income is the excess of interest income over interest expenses. Mathematically NII is expressed as:

$$\text{NII} = \text{Interest Income} - \text{Interest Expenses}$$

Interest income includes interest income from advances plus interest income from investment.

*Note:* Interest for the purpose of interest income also includes dividend received from equity portfolio of mutual fund investments, etc.

Interest Expenses include: Interest paid on deposits plus interest paid on borrowings.

(b) *Net Interest Margin (NIM):* When NII is expressed in percentage on the basis of total assets or earning assets, it is called as NIM. Mathematically the formula is expressed as:

$$\text{Net Interest Margin} = \frac{\text{NII}}{\text{Earning Assets}} \times 100$$

$$\text{Or} \qquad = \frac{\text{NII}}{\text{Total Assets}} \times 100$$

(2) *Interest Rate Gap Analysis:* Interest rate gap analysis technique is similar to liquidity gap analysis technique. In interest rate gap analysis, the assets and liabilities are placed in the buckets on the basis of timing of change or expected change in interest rates on the assets and liabilities and not on the basis of cash inflows and outflows as in the case of statement of

liquidity gap. The RBI has prescribed a statement of interest rate sensitivity for regulatory reporting.

**Statement of Interest Rate Gap Analysis**

*(Amount in Crores Rs.)*

| *Time Buckets* | *Total Liabilities (A)* | *Total Assets (B)* | *Net Gap (C)* | *Cumulative Gap (D)* |
|---|---|---|---|---|
| 1 day–28 days | 4,198 | 4,324 | 126 | 126 |
| 29 days–3 months | 5,186 | 2,960 | (2,226) | (2,100) |
| 3 months–6 months | 21,860 | 21,302 | (558) | (2,658) |
| 6 months–12 months | 5,460 | 2,850 | (2,660) | (5,268) |
| 1 year–3 years | 13,202 | 5,972 | (7,230) | (12,496) |
| 3 years–5 years | 7,584 | 7,786 | 202 | 12,296 |
| Over 5 years | 2,344 | 24,756 | 22,412 | 10,116 |
| Non-sensitive | 20,684 | 11,210 | (9,474) | 642 |
| Total | 80,518 | 81,160 | 642 | - |

Total liabilities and total assets, i.e. columns A and B refer to rate sensitive assets and rate sensitive liabilities.

All the assets and all the liabilities are categorized into rate sensitive and rate non-sensitivity groups. Equity capital on the liabilities side and cash on the assets side are non-sensitive. Any change in interest rates would not have any impact on cash and equity. Equity in itself is not sensitive to interest rate changes; it is sensitive through other liabilities and assets.

The assets and liabilities are rate sensitive if—

The cash flows from them are on their maturity.

The cash flows represent an interim, or part principal repayment.

The interest rate applicable to the outstanding principal, changes contractually during the period under consideration.

The outstanding principal can be re-priced when some base rate or index changes.

Interest is payable on liabilities and interest is receivable on assets. If rate sensitive liabilities exceed assets, this will have negative effect on net interest income and *vice-versa*.

(3) *Economic Volume Approach*: The economic value approach takes into consideration the long-term impact of interest rate changes by covering the entire life of all rate sensitive assets and liabilities. Under this approach, the effect of interest rate changes are studied on an important variable called "Economic Value of Equity". Mathematically Economic Value of Equity is:

Economic Value of Equity = Economic Value of Assets –
Economic Value of Liabilities

It may be understood that the essence of the equation reflects the residuary nature of the claims of the equity shareholders who are the ultimate owners. The term economic value is preferred to the market value as number of assets and liabilities in the balance sheet of a bank do not have a ready market. Economic value of equity approach also removes the problem of different bases for valuation of items in the balance sheet. The balance sheet of a bank recognizes the changes in the value of few items while other assets and liabilities are reflected at historical cost despite the change in value. This approach is also superior to earnings approach. A higher accounting profit does not necessarily mean better performance unless the degree of risk attached to such profits is taken into consideration.

The economic value of equity approach is based on the present value of money which is the basic foundation of the subject of finance. The value of assets and liabilities is inversely related to the interest rates.

The interest rates of assets and liability influence the value as:

(a) When the rates of interest on assets and liabilities go up from the present level, the value of the assets would fall and *vice-versa*.
(b) When the value of assets increases or value of liabilities decreases, the economic value of equity increases and *vice-versa*.

**(3) Market Risk**

The Basel Committee on Banking Supervision (BCBS) in its

publication "amendment to Capital Accord to incorporate Market Risks", published in January 1996, has defined market risk as, "The risk of losses in and off balance sheet position arising from movements in market price".

Market risks can arise out of the following:

Interest rate risk; Equity position risk; Foreign exchange risk; and Commodities risk.

*Approaches to Measure Market Risk*

Measures for market risk are broadly categorized as under:

(1) Factor-based Measures.
(2) Volatility-based Measures.

(1) *Factor Sensitivity Measures*: Factor sensitivity measures assess the impact of change in the major factors on the market value of the portfolio. The most important factor sensitivity measure is the modified duration. Modified duration is the direct measure of sensitivity in value of a security or a portfolio of bonds for a change in interest rates. In duration method, the duration of an asset or liability is calculated as the weighted average maturity of the resultant cash flows, the weights being the present value of cash flows. Duration is less than the maturity of the coupon bond. Greater the duration of duration gap, higher is the interest rate risk exposure of the assets and liabilities.

One of the significant applications of the factor sensitivity measures is to use them for setting limits.

*Example*: A bank may set the maximum modified duration of its bond portfolio as (say) 8. This means that the price sensitivity that the bank is willing to accept in case of the bond portfolio is maximum 8% of the value of the portfolio for 1% change in interest rates. A loss more than 8% will not be tolerated by the bank. This limit is a caution to the trading manager in order to discourage them to earn higher commission (being percentage of trading profits) due to higher risk. There is higher risk if trading manager goes against the situation; it may lead to closure of banks as it has happened in case of Barings Bank of the U.K.

(2) *Volatility-based Measures*: Volatility-based measure, popularly known as value at risk (VAR), has gained a lot of

prominence. The most favourbale advantage of value at risk is its uniformity in measuring trading risk across various positions such as interest rates, equity, commodity and currency which is the weakest thing as far as factor sensitivity measures are concerned. As a result of uniformity of measurement, it is possible to aggregate risk across completely different positions (compare and contrast) among various positions to assess the relative riskiness.

The following example will make the VAR clearer:

Market value of Security: Rs. 400 crores
Confidence Level used for VAR computation 98%
Value at Risk = 10 crores
Holding period used for VAR computation 2 days
VAR = Rs. 10 crores

The example states that out of 400 crores of security Rs. 10 crores is value at risk. The maximum loss that bank will suffer on 2 trading days would not exceed Rs. 10 crores on 98% of the trading days (confidence level used for VAR computation is 98%). Only on 2% of the days, the loss would exceed the VAR of Rs. 10 crores. If we assume 200 trading days in a period, the above interpretation means that 196 trading days out of 200 days would have losses less than Rs. 10 crore. Only on 4 days out of 200 days, the losses would exceed the VAR computed.

*Methods for Computation of VAR*

There are three main methods for the computation of VAR:

*Historical Simulation:* Historical simulation which is based on historical/past data is non-parametric in nature. The main assumption of this method is that the past trends and volatilities in price would repeat in future also.

*Variance Co-variance VAR:* This is widely accepted and practised method at present. This method was popularized by the investment bank, J.P. Morgan, in the 90s. This method is parametric as it assumes that the prices follow normal distribution. This method is based on correlation, standard deviation, arithmetic mean and co-variance, etc. for the estimation of VAR.

*Monte Carlo VAR:* The term Monte Carlo is a technique of research operation. This approach is not based on the assumption of distribution of properties or assets' prices but involves empirical estimation and the statistical distribution from the prices which is then applied to simulate the prices leading to the estimation of VAR.

# 13

# *Premiums and Bonuses*

## WHAT IS PREMIUM?

(1) Premium is the consideration that the policyholder has to pay in order to secure the benefits offered by the insurance policy. It can be looked upon as the price of the insurance policy. It may be a one time payment. That is not common. Often, it has to be paid regularly over a period of time. A default in premium can endanger the continuance of the policy. If that happens, the policy will be treated as lapsed and the expected benefits will not be available. The consequences of default are specified in the policy conditions, which will be discussed in a later chapter.

(2) The calculation of premium is a highly complex technical process, involving actuarial and statistical principles. Only trained professionals can do it. Tables of premium rate for each plan of insurance are made available by insurance companies for the use of agents who have to quote the premium for a particular policy being offered to a prospect. This chapter is meant to make agent aware of the rationale behind the premium calculations.

### Risk, Net and Pure Premium

**Example**: In a village, there are 400 houses, each valued at Rs. 20,000. Every year, on the average, 4 houses get burnt, resulting into a total loss of Rs. 80,000. If all the 400 owners come together and contribute Rs. 200 each, the common fund would be Rs. 80,000. This is enough to pay Rs. 20,000 to each of the 4 owners whose houses got burnt. Thus, the risk of 4 owners is spread over 400 house owners of the village.

(3) In Chapters 5 and 6, examples were given to show how insurance works. The figure of Rs. 200 mentioned in Example 2 would be the cost of covering the risk of death of person at age 50 for one year. This cost is for insurance of Rs. 2000, which can be expressed also as Rs. 10 per thousand. Such cost to meet the risk of death for one year at a particular age is called the risk premium. The risk premium is based on the probabilities of death at various ages. Mortality tables prepared for use of insurance offices, contain data relating to such probabilities.

(4) The risk premium would be adequate to pay the claim, if all the policies were term assurance policies for one year. In the case of Endowment policies, claims have to be paid on survival after some years. Therefore, the actual premium collected would have to be more than the risk premium, to the extent of being able to pay the survival benefits, whenever falling due. Here also, the mortality tables would be used to estimate the number of persons who may survive the terms.

(5) The premium collected by insurers are not utilized every year for payment of claims. This is so for many reasons. One is that the real experience may not be exactly as indicated by the mortality tables. Second, the portion of the premium is meant to meet survival benefits. The balance premium remaining, with interest will be invested and will earn some interest. To the extent of the expected interest earnings, the premium charge can be reduced. The premium worked out after taking into account the interest, is called the net premium or pure premium.

**Loadings**

(6) The administrative expenses of the insurers have to be met out of the premiums paid by the policyholders. To this extent, the premium to be collected will be higher. Such additions to the pure premium are called 'loadings'.

(7) One of the loadings is due to administrative expenses. Loading may be made for other reasons as well. One of them would be for unexpected contingencies and fluctuations. A major

catastrophe like an earthquake or accident or riots or epidemic, can raise the number of deaths to a much higher level than normal. The risk premium based on mortality tables would be found to be inadequate to meet catastrophic claims. Insurers, therefore, as a matter of safety, provide for such contingencies and fluctuations, by 'loading' the premium suitably.

(8) Bonus has to be given to participating policyholders. Bonus is declared out of the surpluses determined after actuarial valuations. (The terms 'bonus' and 'valuation' are explained later in this chapter). Surplus in a way, reflects the profitability of the business or the quality of management of the business. Nevertheless, insurers load the premiums on account of bonus. In practice, the actual bonus declared would be higher than the loading. Otherwise, it would mean that the quality of the management of the business leaves much to be desired.

**Level Premiums**

(9) If it is expected that out of 10,000 persons at a specified age, one is likely to die within one year, the mortality rate at that age is said to be 0.01%. The risk premium chargeable for person at that age would be Rs. 0.10 per Rs. 1,000 sum assured. If a policy has a term of 20 years, the risk premium and therefore the premium charged would vary for each of the 20 years. Apart from being difficult to administer, the premium at later ages, towards the end of the policy term, would be very high. People would find this beyond their ability to pay. That means that they will be without the protection of insurance at times when they need it most. To offset this problem, insurers spread the risk premium on uniform basis, throughout the term of the policy. Thus, the premium remains constant for 20 years, such uniform premium is called level premium. This implies that the premium collected in the early years of the policy would be more than necessary for the risk, and less than necessary towards the later part of the policy.

(10) There is another reason for level premiums being charged. It is possible that many policyholders would find the higher premium payable towards the latter part of the policy, too burdensome, and drop-out. The persons who drop out are likely to be healthier than those who continue. This would be adverse selection. The remaining policyholders would not be the same

kind of population, as the mortality tables would assume. Thus the calculations of the insurer would go awry. The business cannot be done.

### Office Premium

(11) The premium figure arrived at after loading the net premium or pure premium, is called the office premium. They are now ready for use. The premium figures printed in the promotional literature and brochures are the office premiums.

(12) The actual premium to be charged in any one case would require further adjustments, depending on the practice of the insurer. For example, the administrative costs are more if the premium is paid every quarter or month, instead of once in a year. The number of renewal notices and receipts to be issued and consequential accounting entries would vary according to the mode. If the mode is yearly, the probability of default in the subsequent renewal premium to complete the year does not arise. The insurer can utilize this amount for the entire year and earn more interest than if the premium were paid in instalments. Therefore, the premium rates would have to be slightly increased or decreased depending on the preferred mode of payment.

(13) The increase or decrease may be in percentage terms like 'add or subtract' 2.5% or in simple numbers like 'add or subtract' Re 1.00. Practices of insurers very. Some provide for rebates for yearly modes and no adjustments for quarterly or monthly modes. Some provide increases for quarterly or monthly modes, but no adjustments for yearly modes. This depends on how the insurer concerned has worked out the office premiums.

(14) Similarly, there may be adjustments to be made depending on the Sum Assured (SA). If the policy is for a small SA, the administrative costs would, as a proportion of premium, be more than if the policy is of a large sum. So, many expenses like clerical costs, printing of policies, etc. are constant and do not vary according to the SA of the policy. Depending on the manner the loading is made, insurers will provide rebates for higher SA or extras for small SA.

### Extra Premiums

(15) Extra premium may be charged on any particular policy. This may happen because of the grant of some benefit in

addition to the basic benefits under the plan, like accident benefit or premium waiver benefit. Riders provide additional or supplementary benefits. Extra premium may become chargeable because of underwriting decisions. If the risk of the life to be insured is assessed as more than normal because of health or because of nature of jobs or habits, underwriters may charge extra premium. These are usually stated as say Rs. 2 per thousand, and will be added to the premium otherwise chargeable.

## Calculation of Age

(16) The premium to be charged will vary according to the age of the life assured. Premium rates for each plan of assurance are calculated for each age. If after the policy is issued, the age is found to be different from the age stated in the proposal, the premium mentioned in the policy will be changed from inception. Either the shortfall will be collected as arrears or the excess will be refunded. Insurers prefer to admit the age at the commencement of the policy.

(17) Age has to be determined as on the date of commencement of the policy. As the date of birthday of the life insured, and age has to be reckoned only in complete years, not months and days, three different methods are followed by insurers. These are age next birthday, age last birthday or age nearest birthday. If a person is born on 20th August 1986, the age next birthday on 10th July 2002 would be 26, the age last birthday would be 25 and the age nearest birthday would be 26.

## Premium Calculation

(18) The following illustrations are based on certain assumptions with regard to practices of insurers. These assumptions are specified at the appropriate places. While making calculations for any policy, the practices of that insurer must be conformed to.

### *Step-I*

Find out tabular premium, i.e. premium quoted in published premium rates of given age (nearer, next or last birthday as the case may be) for the relevant plan and term. This premium is per thousand sum assured. Assume that the figure is Rs. 45.60.

*Step-2*

Deduct adjustment for large sum assured, if applicable, Assuming that the insurer allows rebates as follows:

Rebate per thousand Sum Assured (SA)

| | |
|---|---|
| Rs. 25,000 – Rs. 49,999 | Re. 1 |
| Rs. 50,000 – Rs. 99,999 | Re. 1.50 |
| Rs. 1,00,000 and over | Rs. 2 |

If this is a policy for Rs. 75,000 SA, the premium would be Rs. 44.10 (45.60 less 1.50).

*Step-3*

Make adjustment for mode of payment of premium. Assuming that the insurer provides rebates of 1% for yearly mode and that the mode proposed in this case is yearly, the premium would decrease by 1% of 44.00 or Rs. 0.44, making the premium Rs. 43.66.

*Step-4*

Add extras assuming that the extras in this case are Rs. 1.50 per thousand for occupational hazard and Rs. 2 per thousand for supplementary benefits. The total addition is Rs. 3.50 making the total premium Rs. 47.16.

*Step-5*

Multiply by SA (Rs. 47.16 × 75) equals Rs. 3537.00.

*Note:* If the adjustment of 1% for mode is made before the adjustment for SA, the deduction would have been 0.46 instead of 0.44. The difference can be significant, if the insurance is for a large SA. Insurers would clarify how they want it to be done.

(19) The above calculation was made for yearly mode of premium. Therefore, the figure of 3537 is the premium to be charged. If however, the mode was quarterly, then the annual premium worked out by the above method, will have to be divided by 4 to determine the quarterly instalment premium

(20) In the calculation shown in the earlier paragraph, the final figure arrived at has no paise. If there are paise in the final

figure, they may be (i) ignored, or (ii) rounded off to the next higher integer, or (iii) rounded off to the nearest, integer, or (iv) rounded off to the nearest 50 paise or any other adjustment as the insurer may practise.

(21) A few examples are given below:

| | *Plan Term* | *SA* | *Age* | *Mode* | *Other Riders* |
|---|---|---|---|---|---|
| 1. | 14-30 | Rs. 25,000/- | 35 | Half yearly | DAB + EPDB |
| 2. | 5-35 | Rs. 50,000/- | 30 | Yearly | Health extra Rs. 3% |
| 3. | 75-20 | Rs. 30,000/- | 30 | Monthly (SSS) | DAB + EPDB |

*Note:* DAB stands for Double Accident Benefit and EPDB stands for Extended Permanent Disability Benefit.

| | |
|---|---|
| 1. Tabular Premium is | Rs. 36.55 |
| Less adjustment | |
| (a) for × SA | 1.00 |
| (b) For half yearly mode 1.5% | 0.55 |
| Balance (per thousand SA) | Rs. 35.00 |
| Balance × SA = 35 × 25 | Rs. 875.00 |
| Add DAB + EPDB | Rs. 25.00 |
| | Rs. 900.00 |
| Half yearly premium | Rs. 450.00 |

| | |
|---|---|
| 2. Tabular premium | Rs. 28.40 |
| Rebate for large SA | Rs. 1.50 |
| Adjustment for qtly. mode | Nil |
| Balance | Rs. 26.90 |
| Balance × SA, i.e. 26.90 × 50 | 1345.00 |
| Add: healthy extra Rs. 3 × 50 | 150.00 |
| | 1495.00 |
| Quarterly instalment premium | Rs. 373.75 |

| | |
|---|---|
| 3. Tabular premium | Rs. 66.80 |
| Less adjustment for SA | 1.00 |
| Adjustment for mode | Nil |
| Balance | Rs. 65.80 |

| | |
|---|---|
| Annual premium 65.80 × 30 | Rs. 1974 |
| Add : for DAB + EPDB | 60 |
| | Rs. 2034 |
| Monthly instalment premium (SSS) | |
| (divided by 12) | Rs. 169.05 |
| | Rs. 169.00 |

**Life Fund**

(22) In normal trading businesses, the excess of income over the expenses in any accounting year, would be considered as profit and will be distributed among the owners. This is not so in life insurances. First of all, the contract for which the premium is paid, does not come to an end at the end of the year. It is a long-term contract. The profit, if any, can be determined only after that contract comes to an end. The premiums are yet to be paid in full. The liability continues and the insurer has to keep aside the money to meet such liabilities.

(23) The practice of the level premium implies that a part of the premium collected in any year, is meant to cover the higher risks of the future years and has to be kept till such risks arise. In relation to endowment plans, the premium has a savings element, which has to be paid as claim at the end of the term.

(24) For all these reasons, the principles of prudent life insurance management require that all the income from the life insurance business (including the earnings from the investments) be kept aside in a life fund, earmarked exclusively to meet the liabilities under the life insurance policies. The laws in India also stipulate this requirement. The life fund can be utilized only to pay the claims and the expenses of running the business. The life fund represents the Reserve for life insurance policies.

**Actuarial Valuation**

(25) Premium is calculated taking into account likely future experiences in respect of mortality, interest and expenses. These are assumptions or expectations. The future experience may or may not conform to these expectations. If they conform, the premium charged could be considered adequate and the business can be said to be properly funded. However, if the experience is worse than the expectations (mortality is more or interest earnings are less or expenses are more), then the

premium would be found to be inadequate and the business could run into difficulties. The practice followed by all prudent insurers is that periodically, they check the validity of these assumptions to make sure that the business is on sound lines. The process of doing so is called an 'Actuarial Valuation'.

(26) The Insurance Act in India requires that actuarial valuations be done every year. Some years ago, the law required that the valuations be done once in three years. Even then, many companies used to do the valuations every year. Prudence requires that the checking be done as frequently as possible. Computers have made it possible to make the necessary calculations easily.

(27) In a valuation, the actuary estimates the liability of the insurer in respect of the business in its books. He then estimates the amount of premiums that are due to be received in future, as these will add to the funds to meet the liability. The difference between the two is the fund that the insurer must have to remain solvent. This is compared with the actual existing life fund. If the present life fund is more, the insurer is solvent. If the fund is less, the insurer is not solvent. The method of estimating the liability of the business and of the future premiums, is very technical and complex, involving actuarial principles. It has to be done by an actuary with recognized professional qualifications. This is one of the reasons why every life insurer has an actuary, either as a full time employee or as a consultant.

(28) The insurer is required to maintain separate funds in respect of non-participating policies and in respect of participating policies. Separate valuations will be made in respect of these two funds. If the valuation shows that the funds are more than the estimated liabilities, the insurer is said to have a surplus, which can be distributed in ways in which profit is distributed by companies. The entire amount may not be distributed. Some part may be kept back as reserves. However, the laws stipulate that in respect of the surplus in the fund for participating policies, not more that 10% of the surplus can be distributed to the shareholders. The rest will have to be distributed to the policyholders as bonus.

## Bonus

(29) The distribution of the valuation surplus to

policyholders is done through the declaration of 'Bonus'. Only policyholders who opt for 'Participating' or 'With profit' policies would be entitled to bonus. Other policyholders who have 'Non-participating' or 'Without Profit' policies would be paying a slightly lesser amount of premium for the same kind of insurance cover, because of the factor of 'bonus loading'.

(30) Bonus is declared in various ways. The most common method is the simple reversionary bonus. The amount of bonus, is added to the SA if the SA under the policy is Rs. 50,000, and the bonus declared is Rs. 60 per thousand SA or 6% of SA. The SA under the policy would become Rs. 53000 straightway. If a similar bonus is declared the subsequent year, the SA would become Rs. 56,000.

(31) In a 'compound reversionary' system, the bonus will be added to the existing SA including bonuses attached earlier. In other words, in the example citied above, after the second declaration, the SA will become Rs. 56,180.

(32) A variety of practices is followed with regard to bonus. Some make the vesting of bonus conditional on the policy continuing to be in force throughout. In other words, it will be payable only on a claim arising, but not if the policy is terminated earlier for other reasons. Sometimes, the bonus is made payable only on maturity. Sometimes, a higher bonus is declared for policies that have been in the books for a minimum number of years. Some insurers allow the bonus to be discounted and encashed immediately. Some insurers use the bonus to reduce the subsequent premiums.

(33) All policies do not contribute equally to the generation of surplus. In the early years of a policy, there would be very little margin in the premium, after meeting the costs. The contribution would depend on how the premium adds to the fund that would differ according to the plan, according to the age of the life insured or according to the term of the policy. The actuary makes an analysis of the elements that have generated the surplus in the fund and tries to declare bonuses in such ways that compensate policyholders, according to the contributions made by the different kinds of policies. The attempt to be fair, however, has limitations, because the policies have necessarily to be grouped, for practical reasons.

(34) Given below are details of the bonus declared by the

LIC after the valuation as on 31-3-2002. This would illustrate how different rates are announced in the attempt to be fair.

| *Term* | *Rate of Bonus per thousand SA per year* | |
|---|---|---|
| | *Endowments* | *Moneyback anticipated* |
| Less than 11 years | Rs. 49 | |
| 11-15 years | Rs. 58 | Rs. 48 |
| 16-20 years | Rs. 65 | Rs. 58 |
| More than 20 years | Rs. 71 | Rs. 65 |

Whole life policies were allotted simple reversionary bonus Rs. 100 per thousand SA.

(35) A one-time bonus called terminal bonus or final additional bonus was declared for policies which had been in force for 15 years. This was in addition to the usual bonus already declared.

(36) Bonus is usually declared on policies, which are in force on the date of valuation. For example, the bonus after the valuation as on 31-3-2003 will be declared sometime in September 2003 and will benefit holders of policies which were in force on 31-3-2003. Policies which become claims after 31-3-2003 before the next results are announced in September 2003, would not get the benefit of bonus, although they have the right to participate till the date of claim. In order to overcome such anomalies, actuaries usually declare 'Interim Bonuses' payable on such policies, which become claims between two valuations.

# 14

# *Underwriting*

## INTRODUCTION

(1) A proposal is an application for an insurance cover. When a proposal is received, the insurer will not agree to grant the cover automatically. The insurer will make a decision as to the admissibility of the proposer to the pool of policyholders. This is because of the insurer's role as a trustee. It has to ensure that every new entrant into the pool has similar exposure to the risk as the others. This process of verifying the level of risk in each new entrant is called 'selection' or 'underwriting'.

(2) The underwriting process is an important one in the life insurance office. If the risk is wrongly assessed. The premium charged would not be appropriate. A lower premium affects the solvency of the fund. The cost of the additional risk, not recovered from the proposer, would have to be borne by the rest of the policyholders. That is not fair to them. A decision to charge a premium higher than necessary would not be fair to the proposer, because of the principle of utmost good faith. The selection has implications of fairness to the insurer and to policyholders, individually and collectively.

(3) If the underwriter finds that the life proposed to be insured has no adverse features affecting mortality, it is considered as a normal or standard or first class life. The

premium charged would be as per tabular rates. Otherwise, the terms of acceptance of the proposal would be different. In some cases, the insurer may refuse (decline) to grant insurance. The process of underwriting is, therefore, very important.

(4) The factors affecting risk on the life of an individual are called hazards. Hazards may be (i) physical, (ii) occupational, or (iii) moral. Physical hazards are:

**Age:** As age increases, the probability of death increases. These probabilities are built into the mortality tables and thereby into the premium rates. The underwriter looks into he factor of age, mainly because of its relationship with other factors. For example, being overweight is a positive factor among young children while it may not be so among older persons. Younger person who are underweight need closer scrutiny than elders who are underweight. Certain risks increase with age. Certain other risks decrease with age.

**Sex:** Mortality of female lives are seen to be more than male lives at younger ages, among the poorer and uneducated section. One reason could be the lack of adequate care in maternity cases. Underwriting considerations are also different in female cases. This is discussed in more detail later in this chapter.

**Build:** Build including height, weight, and chest and abdomen measurements, may suggest tendencies towards cardiac and other ailments like diabetes or TB, underwriters view variations from standard weights with care.

**Physical Condition:** The medical examination of reflexes, blood pressure, pulse rates, urine, etc. provides data with regard to the condition of important systems of the body.

**Physical Impairments:** Blindness, deafness, etc. and other conditions, which are not illnesses or degenerative, are hazards affecting the probabilities of death.

**Personal History:** This is important as pointers to the health as well as the lifestyle of the person.

**Family History:** This is looked at to see whether there is any hereditary factor that makes the person susceptible to illnesses. Family history of early deaths, of cardiac illnesses or diabetes, could be significant.

(5) Occupational hazards arise out of one's job. The nature of the job or the place in which the job is done have effects on the worker. Contact with an inhalation of fumes, excessive

temperatures, etc. affect health and life spans. Those on flight duties on aircrafts run a greater risk of death by accident. Those working in chemical factories are likely victims of various respiratory diseases. Those working with high voltage electricity are susceptible to electrocution and burns. The safety factor is important in heavy engineering factories, working at heights, working with high speed machines, and so on. Studies have identified occupations with various hazards and also tried to quantify the excess hazards, so that the underwriters can determine the appropriate extra premium.

(6) Moral hazards refers to the intentions of the proposer. If the proposal is being made because there is a genuine need for insurance, there is no moral hazard. If the intention is to seek undue advantage through the insurance policy, there is some moral hazards. The undue advantage may be to get a lower premium or to make some quick monetary gains. This has to be judged largely from circumstantial evidence like lifestyles, income as compared to premium payable, reputation for integrity, and so on.

(7) Moral Hazard is not measurable. There is no test to establish it. It is a matter of opinion. If moral hazard is suspected, no amount of extra premium will be appropriate. Underwriters would hesitate to accept such proposals at any cost. But they would like to be fairly certain before deciding so.

(8) In the following situations, moral hazards can be suspected:

- The proposer is old, has not been insured so far and the proposal is for a large amount.
- The proposal is for an amount much larger than what the income would justify.
- A large amount of insurance is proposed on the life of a family member while earning members are not insured or are insured for relatively small amounts.

**Financial Underwriting**

(9) One of the indicators of moral hazard is the size of the insurance proposed compared to the income. The extent of insurable interest of a person in his own life is unlimited. It is not limited to his current levels of income, because it is assumed that

these levels can go up any time. There is nothing that prevents a petrol pump attendant becoming the biggest industrialist of the country or those sleeping on the footpaths becoming rich film starts. Yet, the premium on the insurance policy has to be paid regularly. If it is being paid from current income, then the source of the premium needs to be checked. If someone else is paying for it, there could be issues of insurable interest and also gamble. The need for insurance has to be related to current situations and not to a desirable situation of the future. The underwriter has to be satisfied on these counts, making a judgement on these financial aspects is called financial underwriting. Thumb rules like 'Insurance not more than 10 years' income' are guidelines, but may not do justice in all cases.

### Data for Underwriting

(10) The underwriter makes his decision on the basis of the following:

The statements made by the proposer in the proposal form, which are assumed to be correct (principle of utmost good faith), providing data about himself and the person to be insured, habits and family history—

- Report of the medical examination.
- Report of the agent or other officials.

(11) In the case of large SAs, the underwriter may ask for additional medial reports (special examination) or from senior officials (for moral hazards), a matter of routine. The officials are expected to make enquiries about the life to be insured and the family, their occupations or businesses, their income levels and lifestyles, etc. proof may also be sought to substantiate the reports. A report from the agent is a must in all cases. The report of the agent may be sufficient, if he is experienced enough.

### Assessing the Risk

(12) After examining the data available, the underwriter will make a decision about the level of risk in the particular case. The underwriter need not be an actuary, but would be capable of interpreting data in the proposal papers, in terms of risk. He may avail of the assistance of doctors, who have been associated with

life insurance companies and have specialized knowledge about the effect of medical conditions on mortality. Insurers, normally, have such doctors, called medical referees, on their panels. In the case of very high SAs the insurer may even refer the case to the specialists in the panel of the reinsures.

(13) The assessment of risk is mainly a matter of individual judgment. However, it is necessary to ensure uniformity in decisions, which may be taken by local officers at various levels and offices, the reinsurers would also like to make sure that the decisions are not *ad hoc* or whimsical. Therefore, some insurers have developed guidelines on how to identify and interpret data, which is significant to risk. One such methods is the numerical rating system. Under this method, standards are laid down for each factor, like weight for different ages and heights. Variations are given values, indicating the level of significance. These values are then grouped and tabulated showing the extra mortality. And the appropriate extra premium. A variation of up to say, 20% may be considered normal or standard or first class. More than 20% up to 25% may be categorized as Class I, 35% to 50% as Class II and so on. The underwriter has only to calculate the variations and work out the extra premium for each case, depending on which class the life to be insured, falls. Most of the cases would be decided on this basis. The few, which do not fall clearly into these classes, will be referred to the experts for a decision.

(14) On the basis of the assessment of the risk, the underwriter will decide on the acceptance of the proposal. The decision may be one of the following:

- Accept as proposed at OR (Ordinary Rates), which means that the life is assessed Standard and the tabular rates can be offered.
- Accept with extra of (amount to be specified) per thousand SA. This means that the premium to be charged is increased by the amount of extra specified.
- Accept with a lien (to be specified). This means that the life is not assessed as standard, but the risk is expected to wear off and does not justify an increase in premium. Instead, the SA would be reduced to the extent of the lien, if the death happens within the next few years, not the full term. It could be constant

or could be decreasing (50% in first year, 40% in the second year and so on becoming 0% in the sixth year).

- Accept with modified terms, this means that the insurance would not be given for the plan and term proposed. A different plan or different term or a reduced SA or a combination of these would be suggested as an alternative. (The risk of insurance varies, from plan to plan. The risk is more in a whole life plan than in an Endowment plan. The risk in an ordinary Endowment plan is more than in a Double Endowment plan or an Endowment plan with Limited payments. A shorter term has less risk than a longer one).
- Accept with (specified) clause, which would be a clause excluding specific risk. Examples are 'First Pregnancy' or 'Flights as a pilot'.
- Postpone for a specified period, i.e. the proposal will be reconsidered after the specified period is over with a fresh medial report.
- Decline, which means that the risk is too heavy to be insured.

The Regulations issued by the IRDA require that the decision on a proposal must be conveyed to the proposer within 15 days.

**Non-Medical Underwriting**

(15) Insurers have found that, after medial examination, more than 90% proposals are accepted as proposed at O.R. Further, medical examinations from qualified doctors were not easy in all places. Even in urban areas, the prospects had to go to and wait at the doctor's clinic. The medical examination for insurance was not the doctor's first priority. Therefore, over the years, the LIC had underwritten proposals, without any medical examination relying entirely on the personal statements and declarations made by the prosper.

(16) Non-medical underwriting is limited to younger ages less than 45 years old. There is a limit on SA as well, which, over the years, had been raised up to Rs. 1 lakh. The limit is higher

for those in employment in reputed organisations with leave records, medical check-up at entry, etc. The limit is as high as Rs. 5 lakh in the case of Commissioned Officers in the Armed Forces and Rs. 4 lakhs for employees of Government. These limits are not sacrosanct. The conditions for non-medical insurance are decided by insurers from time to time, depending on their experience.

### Female Lives

(17) Insurers have been cautious about granting insurance on female lives. This was because of high pregnancy related deaths, particularly in remote areas. There was also a history of frauds. The practices have changed during the last fifty years. Working women and educated women are treated on par with men. Some women who do not have any earned income are considered, provided their husbands are adequately insured. Women in purdah (veil) are not considered. These are not rigid rules or principles. Every insurer will have its own experiences and practices. Some insurers allow lower premium rates for working women.

### Underwriting by Agents

(18) In an earlier chapter, it was mentioned that the agent has to inform the insurer about the factors that after the risk of the subject matter of insurance. The agent has to make sure of this by submitting an unambiguous report and also by ensuring that the proposal papers do not conceal any information. The agent's report is a source of data for the underwriter in the office. This is an obligation that the agent owes to the insurer. This is also an obligation that the agent owes to the insured. Otherwise, in the event of an early claim, the insurer might allege that certain important factors had been concealed and deny the claim. The claimant may allege that the fault was that of the agent.

### Recent Trends

(19) The underwriting standards for life insurance are constantly under review. Institutes and re-insurers study the experiences of insurers world over. Over the years, the advances in medical sciences have led to better insights into diseases and their causes. Dreaded diseases of the past are now manageable.

Diabetes and polio are examples. Some disease like small pox have disappeared. New diseases, like AIDS have surfaced. New strains of old viruses are surfacing. Insurers exchange data for mutual benefit. Persons who would not have been insured some forty years ago are now insurable.

(20) Insurers have also begun to take note of habits that affect health like smoking and drinking. The benefit of lower premium is given to those who do not smoke. Proposers may be tempted to understate their smoking and drinking habits, in order to obtain the benefits of the lower premium. They run the risk of being guilty of 'Suppression of material fats' and facing the consequences.

# 15

# *Group Insurance*

## INTRODUCTION

(1) Group insurance is a plan of insurance, which provides cover to a large number of individuals under a single policy called the "master policy". The individuals covered under the master policy are not parties to the contract. The contrast will be between the insurers and a body that represents the group of individuals covered. This body maybe the employer, who is interested in obtaining benefits for his employees, through insurance. The body may be an association of individuals through whom the collective interest of the individuals are safeguarded, like a trade or professional association. A bank or financier can make arrangements through a group policy to protect his interests against default securing because of the death of the debtors.

(2) In India, the development of group insurance has taken place since the early 1960s. Before that, the group insurance business was very little. Originally, group insurance was confined to employer and employee groups only. Since then, the scheme has been extended to cover different groups, provided they are identifiable by homogenous (common) attributes, like professions, membership of a cooperative society, etc. The number of persons covered by group insurance policies is

increasing at a faster rate than the individual policies. Now insurers find that they can reach larger number of people easily through group insurance.

(3) Group insurance schemes are used by the Government, as instruments of social welfare. Social security is a concern of Governments in all countries. But the dimensions of social security vary considerably. In some advanced countries, the entire living expenses of elderly persons are borne by the state as a social measure. In some countries, medial care is free. In some countries, benefits paid by the State during unemployment are more than the salaries of the employed. Social welfare measures are generally administered by the Governments out of funds generated through levies and taxations.

(4) The costs of administering these schemes have been increasing over the years and Governments have found it expedient to use insurance companies to pursue these objectives. Insurers are seen as the natural instruments to take over these functions, because life insurance business has a powerful social dimension.

(5) In India, the operations relating to social welfare are comparatively at an elementary level. The group insurance schemes of the LIC provide insurance cover of small amounts like Rs. 5000 or so to the poorer sections of society like landless agricultural labourers, handloom workers, rickshaw pullers, village artisans, etc.

(6) As stated earlier, group insurance is a plan of insurance, which provides cover to a large number of individuals under a single policy called the "master policy". The insurance contract is with the body that represents the individuals, the employer or the association. Because the contract is with the body, that body is the policyholder. The individuals are the beneficiaries. The amount and terms of insurance are negotiated by the policyholder and not by the individual beneficiaries. The benefits will be determined on bases that apply uniformly to all the individuals.

(7) The premium will be paid to the insurer by the policyholder, who may, or may not, collect the same from the individuals concerned. If the individuals contribute to the premium, that may be either full or partial. In many employer schemes, the entire premium is paid by the employer. Sometimes,

employees are made to contribute part of the cost. If the premium is colleted from the individuals concerned by an employer, the premium may be deducted from their salaries. That does not make this is policy under the salary savings schemes, because of two basic differences. One is that the ownership of the policy is that of the employer and not the employee. Secondly, the extent of cover and the terms are determined by the employers and not by the individuals.

(8) As many persons are covered under one single contrast, the administrative costs are low. Because the coverage is not at the choice of the individual concerned, the chance of an adverse selection is low. Therefore, the rules of medical examination are more liberal in the case of group insurance policies.

**Essential Features of Group Insurance Schemes**

(9) The most important requirements is that the group must not have been formed for the purpose of taking advantage of this scheme. The group must have some other bonding. Entry into or exit from the group must be for reason other than the availability of cover under the scheme. Also, there must a minimum number of members in the group. Twenty-five would be considered adequate. In many cases, the members would be in hundreds.

(10) The individual beneficiary will not choose the amount of insurance cover. The amount will be determined on criteria, which are applied uniformly to all the members of the group. For example, the cover may depend on age or years of membership or income (in the case of employees) or rank. If the criterion is of age or rank, then all individuals of the same age or rank will get the same cover. If the criterion is of income, depending on output, may be a suitable criterion, when the group consists of says farmers or beedi workers or milkmen supplying milk to a dairy.

(11) The inclusion of members in the scheme also is a matter on which the members will have no choice. Everybody fulfiling specified criteria, will have to compulsorily join the group. Usually, when the scheme is being introduced for the first time, the exiting members will be given a choice of joining or not joining the scheme. The choice, to be made within a specified period, will be final. In other words, if a member opts not to join, he cannot change his mind later. These are methods to avoid adverse selection.

(12) Individual lives are not separately assessed for risks. The underwriting or selection is of the group as a whole. The health, morals or habits of any particular individual are not scrutinized.

(13) The premium under a group insurance policy will change from year to year. This is so because the number of persons covered would change because of exit (deaths retirements, resignation) and new entrants. The amount of cover will also vary because of changes in age, income, rank, etc. of existing members.

(14) The premium may also change according to the mortality experience of the group. If the experience is better than originally expected, the benefit of the favourable experience would be passed on to the policyholder, by way of reduction of premium. This system is called profit sharing.

(15) One of the earliest schemes is the One Year Renewable Group Term Insurance Scheme. Under this, the members are covered for specific amounts, payable on their death. This is the simplest and the cheapest of the schemes. This is particularly helpful to relatives of employees, who die young and find that the amounts due under gratuity and Provident Fund Scheme are not adequate. This is also helpful to cover the liabilities of borrowers under mortgage or hire purchase agreements. The amount of cover can be related to the outstanding loans.

(16) Group Savings Linked Insurance Schemes are offered to employers for the benefit of the employees. Contributions from the employees are made up of two elements. Part of it is used as the premium for term insurance cover of the agreed amount. The balance is created to a savings scheme.

(17) Group Gratuity Schemes are also offered to employers and are related to the gratuity of employees. Gratuity is paid to employees who retire or die after long years of service. Since 1972, payment of gratuity has been made compulsory by the Payment of Gratuity Act. The amount of gratuity is linked to the number of years of service and the salary drawn during the last a few years.

(18) The Group Gratuity Scheme provides two advantages. Firstly, it can guarantee a certain amount of gratuity, which would be more than what the rules provide, particularly for those who die young and with relatively lesser service. The second advantage is that it makes it easier to fund the gratuity liability

of the employer. Actuarial advice is available from the insurer about the adequacy of the funds.

(19) In the absence of the arrangement of the group scheme with an insurer, the employer had three ways to pay gratuity. He could pay as and when the gratuity fell due out of his current revenues. This is not prudent business practice, because the amounts of gratuity payable can vary considerably from year to year depending on the demographic profile of the employees, causing fluctuations in profits and also possibilities of delays or even defaults in gratuity payments.

(20) Secondly, he could create an internal reserve for gratuity liabilities, this is better than the earlier method as the liability is being evened out. The risk here is that, if the management is not strict and disciplined, the reserved funds may be utilized for current requirements. Thirdly, he could set-up a gratuity fund as before and create a trust to administer the funds. The difference between this and the group gratuity scheme with an insurer is that, in the latter (a) the trustees hand over the funds to the insurer who will have better capabilities for managing the funds and also (b) there will be an insurance cover to provide additional funds for those who die young.

(21) Group Superannuating Schemes are also offered to employers and are related to the payment of pensions to employees. Pensions are increasingly becoming the preferred retirement benefit, mainly because of the increasing longevity of people. Lump sum benefits like Provident Fund and Gratuity maybe inadequate to last the longer life span. Therefore, employers offer pension benefits. The group Superannuation Schemes offered by insurers are intended to help employers administer the pension funds.

(22) The employer can manage the pension liabilities in different ways, like the gratuity liabilities. The group scheme offered by insurers has the advantage of easier administration and availability of actuarial and investment expertise. Further, it is possible to arrange for better benefits for those who die young.

(23) The scheme can be managed in two ways. One way is to fix the contribution from the employer, generally as a percentage of salary. The benefit available to the employees would be equal to what this contribution can buy. The alternative is that the benefit to be given to the employees is fixed and the appropriate contribution is collected.

**Special Schemes**

(24) The Employees' Deposit Linked Insurance (EDLI) scheme is applicable to all establishments and undertakings contributing towards provident fund under the Employees' Provident Fund and Miscellaneous Provisions Act, 1952, with effect from 1-8-1976, unless exempted under section 17(2A). It is linked to his balance in the provident fund account, subject to a maximum of Rs. 35,000. The Act empowers the Central Provident Fund Commissioner to exempt an employer from EDLI, if he opts for a group insurance scheme of LIC, which is more beneficial to the employees. The cover ranges from Rs. 11,000 to Rs. 37,000. The premium depends on the average age, occupations of members and the size of the group. The LIC's scheme has the advantage of low premium in many cases and the easy settlement of claims, compared to the Provident Fund.

(25) Group Insurance is a convenient medium for Government to pursue its social security goals. For example, the LIC has introduced the Landless Agricultural Labourers' Group Insurance Scheme (LALGI) on behalf of the Government. It provides term insurance protection to the extent of Rs. 2000 each to families of landless agricultural labourers, who do not own land and do not have any inheritable rights to agricultural land. The entire cost (premium) is borne by the Government.

**Group Leave Encashment Scheme (GLES)**

(26) As per the amendments to the Companies Act, made in 1988, and the accounting standards, employers have to fund the liability in respect of the leave encashment facility. The LIC's scheme enables such funding (including medial leave encashment). In addition, the scheme provides for a sum assured ranging from Rs. 5,000 to Rs. 25,000 payable to the families of employees who die while in service.

**Retrenchment Schemes**

(27) Studies show that the pensions paid by the Central and State Governments have increased from about Rs. 12,000 cores in 1996 to about Rs. 46,000 cores in 2002. Apart from the increase in wage rates and inflation, a major contributor factor for such exponential increase is the increasing life spans. The average expectation of life has gone up from 53 in 1980 to 63 in

2000. Employees, including Government, find it difficult to bear the increasing financial burden of retired employees.

(28) Employers who have to pay pensions purchase annuities from a life insurer as and when they have to release the pension. After purchase, the annuities will be paid by the insurers directly to the pensioners. The benefits can be tailored to meet the requirements of the employer and the pensioners. The purchase price would be decided by the employer, according to its policies and terms of employment. For a given purchase price, there could be various options as to how the annuity could be dispersed. The variations, as in annuities, would be when to begin and when it should end. It could end on the pensioner's death or continue as long as the spouse is alive or be for not less than a specified period. These could be left to the preference of the pensioner.

(29) Voluntary Retirement Schemes are very common these days. Employees receive substantial amounts from the employers. Group insurance schemes can help to channel such funs to steady and assured flows of income.

### Health Insurance

(30) Health insurance is, according to the laws in India, part of non-life business. Therefore, life insurers will not be catering to the insurance needs relating to sickness, except to a limited extent as riders to individual life insurance policies. It cannot become the subject matter of a group insurance policy. However, if the law changes in conformity with the provisions in other countries, life insurers will find a very big scope for a new line of business, both in individual and group policies.

### Agent's Role

(31) As mentioned earlier, group insurance has developed in India since the 1960s. The number of lives covered through group insurance policies is not much lower than the individual policies. The scope for this business is very vast. It is a very practicable method to extend the benefits of insurance to the masses. Corporate can benefit from the insurer's expertise, the agent who is conversant with the principles underlying group insurance might be able to innovate new ideas and develop schemes not tried so far.

# 16

# *Insurance for Rural and Social Sectors*

## LEGAL PROVISIONS

(1) Vide paragraph 19 of the First Schedule of the Insurance Regulatory and Development Authority Act, 1999, insurers have to undertake such percentage of life insurance business and general insurance business in the rural or social sector, as may be specified in the Official Gazetteer, by the Authority, in this behalf.

*32B. Insurance business in rural or social sector*: Every insurer shall, after the commencement of the Insurance Regulatory and Development Authority Act, 1999, undertake such percentages of lie insurance business and general insurance business in the rural or social sector, as may be specified, in the official gazetteer, by the Authority, in this behalf.

*32C. Obligation of insurer in respect of rural or unorganized sector and backward classes*: Every insurer shall, after the commencement of the insurance Regulatory and Development Authority Act, 1999, discharge the obligations specified under section 32B to provide life insurance or general insurance policies to the persons residing in the rural sector, workers in the unorganized or informal sector or for economically vulnerable or backward classes of the society and other categories of persons as may be specified by Regulations made by the Authority and such insurance policies shall include insurance for crops.

(2) The regulations made by the IRDA, in terms of these provisions, were notified in the official gazette on 19-7-2000. They were amended in October 2002 and notified in the Official Gazette dated 16-10-2002. Under these regulations:

- The rural sector has been defined as a place in which, as per the latest census, the population is less than 5000, the density of population is less than 400 per square kilometer and more than 25% of the male working population are engaged in agricultural pursuits. (Agricultural pursuits are defined as cultivation, agricultural labour, work in livestocks, forestry, fishing, hunting, plantation, orchards, and allied activities).
- The social sector is defined as including the unorganized sector, the informal sector, the economically vulnerable or backward classes and other categories of persons, both in rural and urban areas.
- The unorganized sector is defined as including self-employed workers such as agricultural labour, bidi workers, brick kiln workers, carpenters, cobblers, construction workers, fishermen, hamals, handicraft artisans, handloom and khadi workers, lady tailors, leather and tannery workers, papad-makers, powerloom workers, physically handicapped self-employed persons, primary milk producers, rickshaw pullers, safai karmacharis, salt growers, sericulture workers, sugarcane cutters, tendu leaf colletors, toddy tappers, vegetable vendors, washerwomen, working women in hills or such other categories of persons.
- The informal sector is defined as the small scale, self-employed workers typically at a lower level of organization and technology, with the primary objective of generating employment and income with heterogeneous activities like retail trade, transport, repair and maintenance, construction, personal and

domestic services, and manufacturing with the work being mostly labour-intensive, having often unwritten and informal employer-employee relationship.

(3) People below the poverty line are included in the expression economically vulnerable or backward classes. The expression other categories of person includes person with disability as defined in the personal and disabilities (equal opportunities, protection of rights and full participation) Act, 1995, and who may not be gainfully employed and also includes guardians who need insurance to protect spastic person with disability.

(4) These sections of society are normally neglected by insurers. They are difficult to reach and the scope for insurance is limited. But, they need insurance more than the other segments. Insurers who begin to transact life insurance business in the year 2000 or later, are required by these regulations to write, in the rural sector.

- At least 5% of the total policies written direct, in the first financial year, going up to—
- 9% in the second financial year,
- 12% in the third financial year,
- 14% in the fourth financial year, and
- 16% in the fifth financial year.

(5) With regard to the social sector, the obligations are laid down as:

- 5000 lives in the first financial year,
- 7500 lives in the second financial year,
- 10,000 lives in the third financial year,
- 15,000 lives in the fourth financial year, and
- 20,000 lives in the fifth financial year.

(6) It has also been provided that in the first year, if the period of operation is less than twelve months, the obligation of lives in the social sector, could be proportionately less. It is also provided that the IRDA may normally revise the obligations once in five years.

(7) With regard to existing insurers, the regulations provide that obligations would be decided by the IRDA after consultation, but the quantum would not be less than what had been recorded for the year ended 31-3-2002.

(8) The insurers would develop appropriate policies to comply with the obligations under the Act. The extent of the compliance will depend on the vigour with which the agents will carry forward the efforts in these sectors. Reports at the end of the year 2001-02 are that all the insurers have exceeded the limits laid down by the IRDA.

**Rural Sector**

(9) There are more than 5 lakh villages in India with a total population of nearly 75 crores. This represents a vast potential. But nearly 25% of them are below the poverty line compared to only about 7% in the urban areas, they are scattered and not continuous as in the urban areas. Therefore, to contact people, one has to travel long distances, along roads that are not well constructed. Only 60% of the villages are connected by all weather roads. There may not be convenient places for visitors to stay or to eat food. Agents may find it more profitable to spend their efforts in the urban areas. That is why there would be tendencies to avoid the rural market, unless compelled by the law or by the IRDA through Regulations.

(10) Apart from the large numbers in the rural areas, there are also indicators that show increasing prosperity in the rural areas, nearly 1.5 crore households in the rural areas are considered to have an annual income of Rs. 50,000 or above. More than 3500 branches of commercial banks operate in the rural areas, apart from the banks (RRBs) exclusively concerned with agricultural development. The consumption of various consumer items like biscuits, chocolates, soaps, detergents, washing powders, toothpastes, motorcycles, TV sets, radios, pressure cookers, etc. are more in the rural areas than in the urban areas. The FMCG producers find that the rural markets will be the main areas for the growth in future.

(11) The LIC's business from the rural areas had been increasing steadily. In 1997-98, the business was more than 53% in number of policies and more than 42% in sum assured. This is apart from the business covered under group schemes in the

social sector. The awareness about life insurance is not as low as it used to be some thirty years ago. The LIC had been doing intensive publicity through the mobile vans and other traditional as well as non-traditional media. The radio and television broadcasts reach almost every village through community sets.

(12) Despite the long distances and the inconvenient infrastructure for travel and staying, the effort may be rewarding. The rural folks are simple people, but not ignorant of worldly matters. If an agent can win their trust, selling insurance would be an easy proposition. He can be almost sure that no other agent would be able to make an entry into that village. But the agent will have to take care that the interest of the prospects are not jeopardized in any manner whatsoever. Policies may not be of big amounts, but the numbers would be large. The impact of these policies, particularly when the claims are paid, would be much more valuable than in the urban areas. The story of insurance would travel far.

### Social Sector

(13) In the earlier paragraphs, reference was made to the obligations of the insurers in the special sector, the benefits of life insurance are needed most by people in this sector, as they are relatively poor and have very little savings, if at all. Any loss of income through early death would make the surviving family poorer than before. The conditions would be worse if the deceased had not repaid loans, taken for the purpose of his work for personal requriements.

(14) Soon after nationalization of life insurance, this need was recognized and efforts were made to introduce what was called 'mass' insurance. The concept was to cover very large number of poor people in one scheme. The difference between such plans under the social sector and group insurance policies is that the former are not policies taken voluntarily by any employer or organization or association, but are part of the schemes of the government being implemented through the business of life insurance.

(15) Till early 2000, there were social security group insurance schemes (SSGIS) separately for recognized occupations; 24 occupations had been approved and as at the end of 1999, these schemes covered nearly 50 lakh persons for a

total sum assured of nearly Rs. 1750 crore. This averaged out to nearly Rs. 3500 per head. In fact, the SA differed from scheme to scheme. The benefit on death by accident was Rs. 25,000. The premium for the cover was paid by the state or from the social security fund set-up by the LIC in 1988-89, for this purpose.

(16) There was also the Rural Group Life Insurance Scheme (RGLIS), where under persons aged between 20 and 50 years were covered for sums of Rs. 5000 payable on death before the age of 60. The scheme was administered through elected panchayats.

(17) A new scheme was launched in July 2000, called the Janashree Bima Yojana. It was meant to cover all the rural and urban poor who were aged between 18 and 60 years and were bread winners of the family. The persons to be covered are recommended by a nodal agency, which is a statutory body or voluntary organization recognized for this purpose. It acts as the sole point of contact for the insurer, giving data about its members, collecting premia and making the claims as and when they arise. The sum assured under this scheme is Rs. 20,000 (Rs. 50,000 in the case of death by accident). The minimum number in the group has to be 250. Half the premium is paid by the social security fund and the other half by the members or the nodal agency or the State Government.

(18) The beneficiaries of the Integrated Rural Development Programme (IRDA), are covered by the Swaranjayanti Gram Swarojgar Yojana. A separate fund has been set-up by Government of India for funding the scheme. The scheme is administered through district rural development agency (DRDA) coming under Zila Parishad. All the person between 18 and 60 years and receiving subsidy/financial assistance/loan under IRDP after 1-4-1988 are eligible to join the scheme. The premium is fully borne by the Government of India. The insurance cover is provided for a period of 5 years from the date of disbursement of subsidy/financial assistance/loan. In the event of death before age 60, a sum assured of Rs. 5000 becomes payable to the nominee. In case of death due to accident, an amount of Rs. 10,000 becomes payable.

(19) Details of the Landless Agricultural Labourers Group Insurance Scheme (LALGI) have been given in earlier chapter. This scheme provides insurance cover of Rs. 2000 without accident benefit.

(20) The Krishi Shramik Suraksha Yojana, introduced in 2001, provides periodical lump-sum survival benefits and pension to agricultural workers. The member has to pay Rs. 90 at the beginning of every quarter and double the amount is contributed from the social security fund. Agricultural workers between 18 and 50 years of age are covered. On death before age 60, and SA of Rs. 20,000, along with accumulated amount with interest, is payable to the nominee. In case of death by accident, the insurance cover is for Rs. 50,000. PDB benefits are provided. On the life assured surviving 60 years, if the period of contribution is 10 years or more, a lump-sum will be paid, depending on his contribution. A minimum pension of Rs. 100 per month will be paid during his lifetime.

(21) The Shiksha Sahayog Yojana, also introduced in 2001, is designed to provide, at an additional cost, an educational allowance of Rs. 300 per quarter to students studying in classes 9 to 12, whose parents are below the poverty line (BPL) and are members of Janashree Bima Yojana. The payments will be made out of the social security fund of the Government through the educational institutions concerned.

# 17

# *Life Insurance Marketing*

## INTRODUCTION

(1) The purpose of all business is to create and retain customers. Without customers, there can be no business. Customers do not come on their own. They have to become aware of the availability of the goods or services on offer. Awareness is not enough. It must be convenient to access the offer. The cost must be seen to be reasonable for the benefit offered. An excellent product does not guarantee that sales will happen, unless people interested in that product come to know about it and find that the effort to get it is not too taxing. They will continue as customers when they are satisfied with what they have got. Business, therefore, has to inform the likely customers through media that reach them, make the goods and services available at convenient outlets and ensure that the customers experience satisfaction while using them. Marketing is the activity that comprises of all these. It focuses on the customers.

(2) The marketer asks questions like what do people buy, why do they buy (what are the needs), when and where do they buy, how do they buy, how much are they prepared to pay, what are their preferences and priorities, what do they look for while buying, what are their concerns, etc. The products, and the distributions, are then designed in ways that try to match these

requirements. Studies over the years have developed ideas and concept that help marketers become more effective in their functions.

(3) Marketing concepts relevant to tangible products like motor cars, refrigerators and cosmetics are not entirely applicable to the service businesses, like hotels, finance, health care, credit cards or travel. Every service is different. The needs of their customers are different. The ways of producing the services are different. Every service is catering to a different kind of need and is different in the internal dynamics of making the service available. Those entering a disco parlour are totally different from those entering a casualty department of a hospital. The two places cannot have the same ambience. Even in insurance, life is different from general, this chapter deals with some of the important concepts relating to marketing of life insurance, keeping in mind the responsibilities and functions of agent.

### The Distribution Channel

(4) A distribution channel is the route by which the product (or offer) prepared by the producer reaches the ultimate consumer (or buyer). The distribution channel bridges the distance between the producer (point of manufacture) and the consumer (point of sale). In the case of goods, the product manufactured in the factory passes through wholesalers, stockist and retailers, before it reaches the consumer. In the case of life insurance, the agent is the primary component of the distribution channel. He is the equivalent of the retailers. The supervisor of agents, by whatever name called, is an important part, because it is he who, by creating and training agents, makes the channel effective. New agents widen the channel.

(5) Equally important would be the other intermediaries, like brokers and insurance consultants. Some life insurers are trying to eliminate intermediaries to save costs. Directly accessing to eliminate intermediaries to save cost. Direct selling is one such attempt. This is increasing in foreign countries. In India, people by the large, know about life insurance, but still have lot of wrong notions about it. Personal contacts by agents may continue to be necessary for quite some time.

(6) Another method being attempted is the use of the extensive network of branches of banks. The customers of both

banks and life insurers are practically from the same segments of population. Through the same contact, the prospects can be helped to arrange for both bank deposits and life insurance. There would be saving in infrastructure costs and overheads. New insurers find this an easy way to access vast areas. It may be possible to develop composite products having the elements of both life insurance and banking. These trends have to develop.

**Sold Not Bought**

(7) Life insurance is not bought by anybody. General insurance is often bought because there are compulsions under the law (motor vehicles) or from the financiers asking for insurance as collateral security. In the case of life insurance, there is very little compulsion. The tendency is to defer the decision. The possibility of death is either ignored or not considered imminent. The requirements of today take priority over the requirements of tomorrow. Even if not absolutely essential, the requriemetns of today seem to be more compelling. Tomorrow never comes.

(8) Superstitious beliefs and cultural or religious backgrounds often interfere with the process of considering the usefulness of life insurance. There is also a tendency to leave everything to fate. There are notions about life insurance not being a good investment (yields are low, the money after 20 years is worth much less) and so on. By the time someone realizes himself the need for life insurance, the chances are that he may not be in the best of health and the insurer may have doubts about the insurability. Life insurance has to be had when in the best of health. Otherwise, the insecurer will refuse to grant the insurance cover. In this complex milieu, people need to be persuaded that there is need to be concerned about the future and that life insurance is a necessity, not an option. Insurance has to be sold.

(9) The person, who is met by an agent at his normal place of work or residence, is a better risk than the one who comes to the office and asks for insurance. The agent, who is the primary underwriter, can study and report on the circumstances and motivations of the former. The latter is likely to be a case of moral hazard and must be looked at more carefully.

## The Customer

(10) The service of life insurance happens at the time of claims when people will experience how the promises are being kept. Until then, it is a hope a promise, the significance of which is vague. The customer in life insurance is not only the person who bought the policy, but also the person who is making the claim. He is the one experiencing the service. This difference is not only in death claim cases. Even in the case of a maturity claim, where the claimant is the same as the policyholder or life insured, the two mind sets are different. At the start, at the buying stage, the mind set is one of anxiety and fear at the possibility of death and welfare of the family. At the end, there could be satisfaction that nothing untoward had happened, but also there could be disappointment that the moneys could have been utilized elsewhere better.

(11) Claimants of the death benefits are persons different from the ones who had taken out the policy and perhaps know little about the circumstances and conditions under which the policy was taken or had been looked after. They may not be familiar with their entitlements under the policy, they are also troubled people, coming to terms with the loss of an important member of the family. The insurer will be asking for information and documents of various kinds to decide on the admissibility of the claim. There could be discrepancies in the records of the insurers. Anybody from the insurance company, who helps the claimant in finding the right information and in completing the formalities, will be providing great satisfaction. If the agent who sold the policy is not available for any reason, the office can depute another person or another agent.

## Strengthening Relationships

(12) The agent is the main intermediary between the customers and the insures. The customer agent link is stronger than the agent-company link (this tends to be impersonal), which in turn is stronger than the customer company link. Customer loyalty to the insurer depends on how strong the agent's link with the customer is. A death claim provides a tremendous opportunity to strengthen this link.

(13) The agent is expected to keep in constant touch with his policyholders to become aware of the changes in his situation

including marriages, death of relatives, release of mortgages. Anyone of them may necessitate some changes like title to policy moneys or more insurance. The contact conveys a message that the agent cares for the policyholder and the family. An agent who is seen only at the time the policy was being bought, is likely to be perceived as selfish, not concerned about the policyholder's interest and therefore, not believed. The agent's who has no concern for policyholder could also be interpreted as not genuine and therefore, his promises are not very dependable.

(14) A study made by the Insurance Institute of India in 1987, by interviewing 2510 policyholders in 26 cities, had the following observations:

- Agents do not maintain regular contact with policyholders, although they are seen as available whenever necessary.
- 50% said that if they had any work to be done, they would go to the office directly rather than get in touch with the agent.
- Agents are perceived as knowledgeable, but also as concerned more with their own benefits than those of policyholders.

These observations reflect badly on the agents.

**Functions of an Agent**

(15) The agent's main function is to solicit and procure life insurance business for the insurer which has appointed him for that purpose. At the same time, he is trusted by the prospect to advise him suitably keeping his circumstances and needs in mind. He is thus in the unique role of a person trusted by both parties to the transaction. His functions would include—

- Understand the prospects needs and persuade him to buy a plan of life insurance that suits his interest best.
- Complete the formalities (paper work, medial examination) necessary to get the policy expeditiously.
- Keep in touch to ensure that changing circumstances are reflected in the arrangements relating to premium

payments, nomination and other necessary alternations.

- Facilitate quick settlement of claims.
- Be totally honest with both the prospect and the insurers.

(16) The Regulations framed by the IRDA lay down a code of conduct, which incorporates some of these concepts. The code says, *inter-alia,* that the agent shall:

- Identify himself and the insurance company of which he is an agent.
- Disclose the licence to the prospect on demand.
- Explain all available options to the prospect.
- Recommend a suitable plan taking into account the needs of the prospect.
- Disclose the scales of commission, if asked for by the prospect.
- Explain the nature and importance of the information required in the proposal form.
- Impress upon the prospect the need to disclose all information.
- Make all enquiries about the prospect.
- Inform the insurer about any material facts, including habits that could adversely affect the underwriting decision.
- Convey to the prospect about the acceptance or rejection of the proposal.
- Render necessary assistance to policyholder or claimants or beneficiaries in complying with requirements asked for by the insurer.
- Advise policyholder to effect nomination.
- Make every attempt to ensure remittance of premiums by the policyholders within the stipulated time, by giving notice orally and in writing.
- Not to induce prospects to submit wrong information.
- Not to interfere with the proposals introduced by other insurance agents.
- Not demand or receive from beneficiary, share of proceeds under an insurance contract.

- Not cause the termination of an existing policy with a view to effect a new proposal.

**Advantages**

(17) Life insurance is rarely bought as a response to advertisements. Advertisements are effective.

- As reminders to intimate change of address, pay premium, make nomination, etc.
- As information on bonus declaration, reveal special schemes, concessions, new plans, etc.
- To build corporate image as financially strong, as responsible social citizen, etc.

(18) The Regulations framed by the IRDA have made some stipulations about advertisements by insurers as well as by intermediaries like agents. These stipulations apply to all messages in the print and electronic media, hoardings, internet, leaflets, business cards, etc. that urge others to buy life insurance. These stipulations, *inter-alia*, state that:

- Claims made about the benefits should not be beyond the ability of the policy to deliver.
- Benefits described should match policy provisions.
- Words or phrases should not be used in such a way as to hide or minimize the cost of hazards.
- Important exclusion, limitation and conditions of the contract should be disclosed sufficiently.
- Information should not be misleading.
- Illustrations about future benefits or assumptions should not be unrealistic or unrealizable in the light of current performance.
- Benefits that are not guaranteed should not be referred to in ways that they are not noticed.
- There should be no implication of sponsorship, affiliation or approval that does not exist.
- These should not be any unfair or incomplete comparisons with products of competitors.

(19) Those who have received policy moneys on the death

of the life insured, are the best endorsement for a life insurer. They are the ones who have experienced what life insurance means and know what it can do differently from other financial arrangements. They know how it feels when a previously determined amount comes in at a time when the future looks bleak with debtors threatening to foreclose mortgages and attach property. Satisfied claimants are powerful and effective as word of mouth media. Their stories persuade strongly. In all services, the word of mouth is the most effective endorsement. In insurance it is particularly so. The word of mouth is an endorsement, not only for the need for life insurance, but also for the insurer and the agent in particular.

### Keeping Customers Happy

(20) A customer is satisfied when the product meets his needs. In life insurance, this happens at the time of the claim, which is a long way-off. It is important to keep him happy during this period, to avoid what is called 'Cognitive Dissonance'. This arises because of doubts about the decision to buy. In the case of life insurance, such doubts may easily arise because others (friends and agents) will talk about better alternative plans, better insurers, and so on. The only way to counter these possibilities is to be in touch with the prospect and reassure him at every possible opportunity that the purchase he made was not a mistake. In other words, the agent will be effectively repeating the sales talk, overcoming objections, till the benefits are seen through claims.

(21) Studies how that people are happy when they are recognized and respected and not taken for granted. Recognition happens when one's feelings, requirements, etc. are understood and not ignored. Agents can do a lot in terms of recognizing people. One way is to be available whenever the prospect or the policyholder asks a point for clarification. These may happen during the policy term itself, when a change in job or place may raise doubts as to the effects on the policy. Another way is to avoid denying the validity of his thoughts. There is nothing more meaning than to be discredited for one's idea. This is important while handling objections during a sale. Recognition is high when the thoughts of the other person are anticipated and attended to.

(22) Two other factors which make customers happy are Responsiveness (willingness to help) and Ease of Access. On both counts, agents can do much more than what the insurer's office can do. It is difficult for an office to be warm and personalized when dealing with anybody. The agent can. Some agents do not let the policyholders go to the office at all. They get everything done. Such agents are reinforcing the impression that the agent is trustworthy and can be depended upon to fulfil his promises. The image of the insurer remains high.

# 18

# *Role of an Insurance Agent*

## INTRODUCTION

(1) An insurance agent is defined in the Insurance Act. He requires a licence to be able to function as an agent. He is remunerated by way of commission on the premium paid under policies procured through his efforts. Insurers designate agents differently like consultants, advisors and so on. The designations do not matter. He is the main component of the distribution channel for the life insurance business.

(2) A life insurance agent would be required to solicit and procure new life insurance business, in a manner that is consistent with the interests of the policyholders and of the insurance company. For this purpose, he would have to do the following:

- Contact prospects for life insurance, study their needs and persuade them to buy.
- Complete all related formalities, including filling up proposal forms, collecting premium, arranging medical examination, collecting proofs (of age or income), reports and other information required by the underwriter.

(3) After having sold a new insurance policy, the agent has to ensure that the policy continues, without a lapse, till it becomes a claim. The conservation of the policy is in the interest of all the three persons concerned, the insurers, the policyholder and the agent. For this purpose, he has to:

- Keep in touch with the policyholder to make sure that renewal premiums are paid in time.
- Ensure that nominations are made or changed according to changing circumstances.
- Assist in settlement of the claim, by helping the claimants to complete the necessary formalities and requirements.

(4) The other function is to be of assistance to the policyholder in case he needs a loan under the policy or wants to make an assignment. These services strengthen the relationship between the agent and the policyholder.

**Prerequisties for Success**

(5) In order that he may perform all these tasks well, the agent has to be familiar with:

- The benefits under the various plans of insurance offered by his insurers.
- The office procedures for various matters including the forms and documents. The main documents have been listed out in an earlier chapter. The forms and procedures will vary between one insurer and another.

(6) As stated earlier, the insurance agent is an agent of the prospect as well. He is looked upon as a knowledgeable person, who can be trusted to give the right advice. To be able to match these expectations, the agent must be familiar with the benefits and advantages of other financial instruments suitable for savings and investments and also the laws, particularly on taxation mattes, relevant to these instruments. The variety of instruments available for an individual, is very vast and it is difficult for anyone to master the details of all of them. Some agents, who do not have the necessary knowledge, give answers

on the basis of guess work or hearsay. Others admit that they do not know enough and promise to come back after checking out the details. The latter are respected and trusted more.

(7) The important legal provisions relating to the business of life insurance are explained in a subsequent chapter. The tax implications of life insurance transactions are also explained in a subsequent chapter.

**Selling Insurance**

(8) The first requirement is to have a continually expanding list of prospects, persons who can be approached for insurance. These are names of people within reach, obtained from acquaintances, newspaper reports, directories, contact at parties meetings, seminars, etc. These names have to be qualified, which means that some preliminary work should be done to collect details about them. These details may indicate whether it may be worth approaching them for insurance. The work of 'qualifying' is done to ensure that the prospect is not apparently unfit for insurance like being sick, or with great moral hazard.

(9) Those in the qualified prospect list have to be met. A sale results when the salesman takes the prospect through well defined steps. The steps are not separate and clear-cut but blend into one integrated process. The steps are:

- Pre-approach
- Approach
- Interview
- Objections
- Close

**Pre-Approach**

(10) Pre-approach means preparing to approach the prospect. This requires forming some idea as to how the interview could be fixed and proceed, for which you require basic information regarding his income, his habits, his concerns, his interests, his saving capacity, his family position, etc. These facts can be had from a variety of sources, and you may even have to time make a personal call on the man himself, and get from him to the facts you need to persuade him in taking decision. If such a call is made, the proposal for insurance is not made at that

stage, although in some circumstances, a pre-approach call may develop further and end with the proposal and the cheque.

(11) The information collected during pre-approach will provide a reasonable idea of the prospects, financial position and his needs and concerns, and help to make a tentative recommendation of a plan. If you make the sale first in your mind, you will find it easy to make the sale to the prospect.

(12) It is advisable to write down the proposal. The advantages of a written proposal are:

- Details are not missed by either the agent or the prospect.
- The impression is more lasting.
- The prospect can go back to earlier data on his own.
- The prospect can understand, at his own pace.
- It is easy to stop at any point, clarify questions and continue further without losing the trend.

**Approach**

(13) When you knock at the prospect's door and are face to face with him, the dynamic phase of sales beings. You should make known to the prospect, at the very earliest, that you are calling on him for life insurance. There is no need to hesitate on this or to feel apologetic. The agent has to believe that he is calling on the prospect to render him the vulnerable service of ensuring financial security for him and his family.

(14) The agent should open the talk by explaining the purpose of his call in such a way so as to arouse enough interest. Otherwise, he may not pay attention to the proposal. In most of the cases, the situation may arise where the prospect will come out with a 'No', the agent should not be in hurry to convert the 'No' into 'Yes'. The purpose of the approach stage is not to sell insurance, but to sell an interview, which gives him the opportunity to talk about what he wants the prospect to think about.

**Interview**

(15) The interview should first of all, make the prospect listen. This happens if the agent refers to things which interest him, his needs, or things that matter to him, without making it

appear like patronizing or flattering. Any hint that the prospect's decision of the past (relating to insurance or investment) were not appropriate or need to be changed, will have the opposite effect. The proposal being made by the agent should be seen as beneficial and complimentary to the existing arrangement.

(16) The agent should follow some simple rules like the ones mentioned below:

- Do not talk more than necessary.
- Ask questions, and make the prospect talk, make it interactive.
- Create doubts and get him to ask questions for clarification.
- Listen to the prospect's point of view carefully. Do not interrupt, contradict or argue. People feel good when they are listened to and then they listen better.
- Make your talk interesting. Tell a true story of how life insurance has helped families in various situations and how families have suffered without it. Make the story have a personal appeal. Use names of his children or relatives. That will make the story more appealing.
- Use pictorial aids, graphics, and written presentations. If you have a lap top, use Power Point presentation.
- Let the prospect write down the figures of his needs, of his liabilities, of benefits of the insurance plan and of the premium. This ensures concentrated attention.
- Let your advice be in the best interest of the prospect, not your interest.

(17) Successful agents prepare their presentations carefully every time. They rehearse in their minds the way the interview should proceed. This ensures that they do not fumble for ideas or the right words. The ideas, too, come in the most natural and logical sequence. Lastly, a prepared sales talk conveys more enthusiasm and conviction than a talk without preparation. A well prepared approach ensures a favourable interview.

**Objections**

(18) Prospects will raise objections, one after another. Objections are a part of every sale. If prospects did not object, there would be no need for salesmen. People would buy on their own. Also, if the prospect remained silent, you will not know how his mind is working. The objection is his way of referring to the further information that he needs.

(19) The entire selling process is, therefore, interspersed with objections. At the stage of approach itself, the prospect may say 'I do not believe in life insurance', 'I do not need life insurance', and the like. Such objections are not against life insurance but rather against the agent whom he wants to put-off gracefully, or signs of indecision, or of a fear of being forced into buying.

(20) Then, there are objections during the interview, like, "I pay more than what I get back", it is advantageous only if I die. Meet me after six month. Such objections, which come up during the main discussion are real objections. However, their intention is not to put you off. It is quite the contrary. The prospect wants you to convince him. He wants you to give him detailed information that will remove his fear and doubts and to back-up his latent or unstated desire to buy. Every objection tells you about the prospect's thinking and gives you an opportunity to remove his mental block. Indeed, a prospect, who puts forward an objection, is actually asking you to give him one more reason to buy. A true agent should therefore welcome objections.

(21) Then there are objections raised at the closing stage, such as, "I will think it over", I will consult my father. See me next month when I get my confirmation/increment/promotion, etc. These objections reveal an inability to take a major decision.

(22) Objections cannot be treated in a summary manner. The answers must be complete and convincing to the prospect. He needs help to make the decision to buy. His doubts or difficulties need to be removed or clarified. The agent, while answering the objections, should never get into an argument. The "yes ...... but" method is the most effective. You agree (say, yes) in principle with what the prospect says under circumstances assumed by him, but, you say, "the actual circumstance are different" and then convey you point. The prospect is bound to be receptive to such an open 'give and take' in discussion. For

example, you may say, "Mr. Prospect, I agree that conditions are hard and people have difficulty in saving, but imagine how much more difficult it will be if your family has to carry on without you". The secret of successful selling is to make the prospect feel that he has taken the decision you only help him in the process by answering his objections. Agents should remember that an objection is a "blessing in disguise". It is also a stepping stone to a sale.

### Closing

(23) The 'close' has to be sensed in time, because very few prospects will, of heir own accord, say, 'I will insure'. The agent sensing the close takes the prospect's positive decision for granted by asking for his implied (not direct) consent, "will you pay the premium by cash or cheque"?, "do you have your school certificate at hand now or can you give it tomorrow"? (affirmative choice). A positive answer to any of these questions is an indication to go ahead. If the interview does not end with a close and is put-off to another tie, the interview will have to be gone through all over again.

(24) In selling life insurance, an appeal to the heart of the prospect is more useful than an appeal to the head, life insurance is both for the prime reason of protecting the loved ones, affording a good start in life to the children, duty to aged parents, or perhaps a desire for self-preservation in old age. So, a sale can be accomplished only when an appeal is made to one of the motives, an appeal to sentiments of love, of affection and of concern. The agent need not be an expert in psychology to do this.

### Service

(25) The prospect becomes a policyholder with the sale of a life insurance policy. The agent's relationship with the policyholder, thereafter, depends on the service that he renders. Service assumes more importance in life insurance, because unlike other savings or investment plans, a contract of life insurance is a long-term commitment. People are often too late. If the premium is not paid, the policy become a useless piece of paper. The agent's attention to service (including monitoring premium payments, nominations, revivals, if they become necessary, help in settling claims, etc.) will ensure that the insurance policy does not suffer from such neglect.

(26) Every servicing call gives an opportunity to the agent to review the insurance programme. The insurance already sold may become inadequate because of changes in the policyholder's financial position or family. Perhaps, he may need more insurance or he may suggest insurance of his relatives and friends, service benefits the policyholder. But it benefits the agent more by conveying messages about his liability and trustworthiness. This is his competitive advantage over other agents, of the same insurer and of other insurers.

**Ethical Behaviour**

(27) Of late, serious concerns are voiced about the properties in business, because, increasingly, there are reports of improper behaviour. Some of the world's biggest companies have been found to have cheated through false accounts and dishonest audit certification. The funds of banks have been misused by their managements to bolster the greed of some friends. Officials have used their authority to promote personal benefits. Courts of justice have failed to render justice. Increasingly, people who are trusted by the community to perform their tasks are seen to have betrayed the trust. Personal aggrandizement and greed prevails.

(28) The insurance agent is in a position of trust. On his assurance, the policyholder entrust their small savings to an insurer, trusting it to look after these funds and look after their dependants in later years. Issues of property and ethics are extremely important in this business of insurance.

(29) Unethical behaviors happen when the benefit of self are considered more important than of the other. The code of ethics spelt out by the IRDA in the Agents Regulations, and referred to earlier, is directed towards ethical behaviour while it is important to know every clause in the code of conduct to ensure that there is no violation of the code, compliance would be automatic if the agent always kept the interest of the prospect in mind. Things go wrong when the agent becomes concerned with the commission that he will earn from the policy, rather than the benefits to the prospect.

(30) The LIMRA, which is the premier international organization on matters concerning life insurance marketing, has found that ethics in life insurance selling consists mainly of putting the interest of the prospect/policyholder first. The

research studies show that such an approach helps the agent through:

- Improved business and earnings.
- Business remaining in the books longer, without lapsation.
- Stronger relationships with the clients.
- More referrals and word of mouth recommendations.

(31) Some agents think that they are doing the prospect a good turn, when they do not reveal some vital information in the proposal form, for fear of the underwriter raising awkward queries. In fact, they are doing harm to the prospect, because if there happens to be an early claim, who can guarantee that this will not happen, the claim may be repudiated. The loser at that time is the prospect's family. The commission collected by the agent is not affected. The loser is also the creditability of the entire life insurance industry, both agent and the insurers. Stories will circulate that insurers do not pay claims, the truth will not be known.

(32) Some of characteristics of good ethical behaviour are:

- Placing the best interest of the client above one's own direct or indirect benefits.
- Holding in the strictest confidence and considering as privileged, all business and personal information pertaining to the client's affairs.
- Making full and adequate disclosure of all fact so to enable clients make informed decisions.

(33) There could be a likelihood of ethics being compromised in the following situations.

- Having to choose between two plans, one giving much less commission than the other.
- Temptation to recommend discontinuance of an existing policy and taking out a new one.
- Becoming aware of circumstances, that if known to the insurer, could adversely affect the interest of the client or the beneficiaries of the claim.

# Personal Development through Insurance Business

## SCOPE

(1) This topic deals with the development of an agent who is an individual, not a company or firm. In the case of latter, this topic would be relevant for the director or partners or any other employee who may be performing the functions of meeting prospects, persuading them, etc.

(2) Personal development would result in enhancing one's capabilities to function as an agent. This would be measured partly by the business that is done and the commission that is earned. It is also to be measured in terms of the reputation that the person enjoys in the market. Agents can be spoken of well, as a person who knows, who can be trusted to look after the customer's interest, who will not mislead, who is nice to deal with, and so on. It is such reputations that help one to collect more and more references from satisfied policyholders and thus expand one's circle of contacts.

### Product Knowledge

(3) The primary requirement is to become quite conversant with the product that one sells. In other words, product

knowledge is important, product knowledge does not end with knowing the broad terms and conditions of the various plans of insurance. One has to be aware of the possible drawbacks in the policy, the tax implications, the fit with the clients' needs, the extent to which the client has to take precautions so that the benefits may not be lost, and so on. The agent must have knowledge of all the products offered by the insurer for whom he works, and not merely of the few which are most frequently sold.

**Customer Orientation**

(4) An agent is a professional, in the sense that there is a body of specialized knowledge that has to be studied and mastered. He is also a businessman. As a professional, he has to keep his client's interest in mind and not his personal gains from a transaction. As a businessman, he is concerned with the money that he makes from the transaction. The experience of highly successful agent is that if the client's interests are taken care of and they are satisfied, one's business tends to grow steadily. There is no conflict between the two, both go hand in hand.

(5) Customers are entitled to full information from those who provide services. This requirement, the right to information, is enshrined in the Consumer Protection Act. The law is only stating a principle which every successful salesman practises. In the case of life insurance, the person representing the insurer and having the responsibility to inform the consumer, is the agent. Before the agent can inform the consumer, he has to be informed himself. That is why it is repeatedly pointed out that product knowledge is important.

**Business Target**

(6) As a businessman, he has to have some goals with regard to revenue. The revenue, which is in the nature of commission on premium, deepens on the sales one makes. The number of sales depends on the number of contacts one makes. There is a relationship between the number of calls one makes and the number of closures that result. The proportions keep improving as one gains experience. The number of calls can therefore, be the target and the rest will follow. The calls may be on new person; from a growing list of prospects, the calls may also be service calls on existing clients for renewals or for

checking on the changes in status (marriage, children, new job, new premises, new businesses and so on) that may suggest either more business or change in the terms of the existing policies.

**Personal Growth**

(7) Agent may have personal goals, like wanting to rise in the hierarchy of the company. Some companies do provide opportunities for agents to accept higher responsibilities. One might like to become a senior agent, helping newcomer in the field. Some senior agents make it a point to attend seminars, workshops and conferences. They meet other in the profession. The benefit is mutual. They receive as well as give, as experiences differ and are unique. Professional agent set aside both funds as well as time for such purposes. The pay-off is high, although not immediately visible.

**Records and Review**

(8) Every individual has to manage himself well. Salesmanship, which the agent will master in course of time, is different from management. One does not have to be appointed as a manager in a company to learn management. Management is nothing more than using one's resources well, in order to achieve the desired results. This implies that one has to always look at whether one is getting or not getting what one is trying to get (goals) and also whether one is utilizing one's resources properly.

(9) A good manager continuously finds ways to improve the utilization of his resources. The resources include skills, knowledge, materials, money and time. If one is able to get at one's goal with lesser expenditure of resources, there is improvement. If the distances travelled per call reduce, as a result of better scheduling of the movement, there is improvement. If there is a reduction in the number of hours on calls required to complete a sale, there is improvement. Like this, a number of inputs can be monitored and ways found to improve both efficiency and effectiveness. To be able to do so, one has to maintain a record of one's activities and analyze the same periodically. The maintenance of detailed records is, therefore, the first step to good management of oneself.

**Time Management**

(10) One of the resources of any professional is 'Time'. Time is an input in work. The time taken to do anything is an indicator of the skill of the doer. Novices take more time than an expert to do the same job. One of the indicators of the professional development of an agent would be the time he takes to do various activities as an agent, to get an appointment, to explain a point, to conclude a sale. Time is necessary also for personal development, to read books and journals, to do physical exercises, to unwind and relax, to attend spiritual discourses, to reflect on one's behaviour to introspect.

(11) There are many things to do and time is required to do them. Many people say that they do find time to do what they know is important, but has not been done. Many people are so busy at work that they do not have enough time to spend with the family. Many people manage to find time for everything, including relaxing. The time available is the same for everybody, 24 hours a day. How well do we assign the available time? This question can be answered only by each person himself.

(12) We can attempt to achieve increasingly better use of time. This means that we can try to do more in the same or in lesser time. To attempt this, we need to know how we are spending our time. The only way to know is to keep a record of our activities on an hourly basis and review it periodically. We might discover that the time spent on various activities do not correspond to the importance of those activities. We may have to cut the time spent on some activities to find time to do something that we want to do but did not for want to time. The record of time spent on activities is the tool to manage time better.

(13) Some of the ways in which people waste time are:

- Having to do a job again because it was done wrongly. Correcting mistake in a job wrongly done takes more time than doing it right the first time. This is so in arithmetic and in cooking.
- After embarking on a job, we find that the available information is either not adequate or not relevant and the job has to wait till that information is obtained.
- Searching for things that have been misplaced or not kept in their proper place.

- Indecisiveness, inability to make up one's mind and keeping on changing one's plan.
- Attempts to be perfect. This leads to doing and redoing. It is not necessary to be perfect.
- Improper prioritization (important work gets neglected and has to be rushed through).

**Target Market**

(14) A good agent has to be clear about the market he is working in. For an insurance agent, the whole world is a potential market. but no one agent can insure that whole world. While the whole world is the total potential market, it is in fact several markets with distinctly different needs and characteristics. The very rich have different needs compared to the middle class salary earners. The young have different needs compared to the elderly. Working women with dependents have different needs compared to housewives. Thus, when the total market is viewed in terms of needs, it will break-up into a number of smaller segments.

(15) The target markets/segments may be identified in terms of geographical location (residence or office), age, occupation, religion, social status, income levels, family size, or business size, nature of business, technology, products, etc. Each segment has to be approached in a different way, agents tend to engage in specific segments of the market. One big advantage in doing so, is that the agent acquires knowledge in depth of that segment and is also known within that segment. Referrals become easier.

(16) The segment in which an agent operates is called his target market/segment. An agent may have more than one target segment. One agent may be working only within one department of government, like the police department or one big company with a salary savings scheme. Because he finds that the earnings from this source are adequate and it takes almost all his time servicing the policyholders. One agent was known to work only among the hardware merchants in a city, handling both life and non-life business of those traders. Although there were jewellers also in the same neighborhood. Another successful agent's target was the tea stalls in the city. An agent with an infrastructure of an office and a few employees may be in a position to cater to a

larger segment or more than one segment. It is prudent to make careful choices, depending on one's capability. The lure for additional business, should not lead one to ignore the very important aspect of servicing of the business.

(17) Ageing adults is an expanding market. Many of the existing customers would become part of this segment of the market soon. By proving information relating to pension plans to existing policyholders, the market of the ageing adult can be developed. The immense market potential for pensions could be tapped effectively if the customers profile is properly in focus.

**Trustworthiness**

(18) An agent sells himself before he sells his product. This may be true in many cases but is particularly true in the case of life insurance, because of the very intangible nature of the product as well as the long-term commitment. The customer buys mainly because he believes the statements and promise made by the agent. He believes them as if they are promises made on behalf of the insurance company. He is buying the promise. Whether he bought the right thing or not, will be known only in the future, when the promises are to be redeemed. That is the time of the claim. If an agent has to succeed professionally, he has to continue to enjoy the trust of the policyholder. This alone will lead to repeat business and to referrals.

**Long-term Relationships**

(19) An agent has to strive towards building long-term relationship with the policyholders. Many techniques can be suggested, but all of them depend on one simple principle. The other person has to feel important and not slighted. He has to feel that his concerns are uppermost in the agent's mind. The essential requirement is sensitivity to the other person's feeling and genuine concern for his needs. If there is no genuine concern, the relationship cannot become strong.

(20) The following may help to build relationships:

- Courteous behaviour, which comes from genuine (not pretended) friends' lines and respect.
- An attitude that seeks to help.
- Avoiding the slightest hint that the customers is ignorant or is at fault.

- Trying to understand the customer. The slogan the customer is always right does not mean that his contention or behaviour is always right. It means that, always, there is a justification for his behaviour or contention. If that is understood, it helps a lot to keep him satisfied.
- Listening to what the customer says. People feel good when they are listened to. Listen to the substance, not the words or manners. If he is angry, ignore the anger and 'listen', or pay attention, to the cause of the anger. There can be no empathy and no help without listening.

**Motivation**

(21) An agent is an independent professional. He cannot wait for someone else to come along and persuade him to action. Others will demand that he perform. He has to feel the urge and drive to perform. Otherwise, he will not do. When a person feels the urge and derive to do, he said to be motivated.

(22) All action is goal-oriented. This means that whatever anyone does is for a purpose, to attain something that will satisfy his needs and give him satisfaction. Thus, motivation to do is related to the doer's needs and satisfaction. Motivation to do includes motivation not to do. The need to relax makes one become inactive at work.

(23) Why should an agent want to perform? Why should he be motivated? What are his needs to be fulfilled? None of these answers would be the same for all agents. Even the need for money may not be the first need for all agents. The need for money will lead one to complete more and more business. Some agents may want to be counted among the top agents of the branch or the insurer or the entire country. That may also lead them to do more and more business. Some may want to be known as the most knowledgeable. That will lead them to invest time and money in learning, attending lecturers and seminars, etc. that same motivation may also lead some to help and train newcomers into the profession, to write books and articles based on one's experience. Some may want to build long-term relationships with the customers. That will lead them to find justifications to call on the customers as frequently as possible.

Some agents may want to be known as financial consultants providing total financial services to their clients. This may lead them to link up, through networks or otherwise, with stock brokers, security analysts and tax experts, offering mutual funds, new issues, portfolio management, etc.

(24) Motivations can be varied. The effort to learn and do well may come also from a motivation to avoid being among the non-performers. Some agents are driven by the need to be of help to the community, on matters not directly connected to insurance. That motivation may lead to a lot of insurance business coming his way because of the high esteem in which he is held by the community in which he operates.

### Morale

(25) A customer buys because he trusts the agent and his promises. It implies that the behaviour of the agent has to be one that exudes confidence and positive thoughts about the insurance company and its offerings. This is possible only if the agent feels good about his profession and his business.

(26) If he does not feel good, his disappointments and frustrations will be sensed in his voice and manners and that will harm the process of sales. Feeling good or not good about one's work is a question of morale or enthusiasm about work. If an agent is convinced that he is in a noble profession that looks after the welfare of people and their families as nothing else can do, he cannot but feel good about his work. To keep upto his morale, he has only to say to himself that his is a job that brings cheer to others at a time, when a whole lot of circumstances have conspired to take away that cheer. An eminently successful life insurance agent had said that his commitment do the job became firm, when one of his policyholders died young and he saw that the widow was surrounded by people—erstwhile friends—demanding payment of outstanding bills and mortgages. He was the only one offering to pay her. How can such an experience of joy in the widow's face, be anything but uplifting?

(27) Apart from the nature of the business of insurance, the agent must also feel confident that he is in a position to render effective service to his policyholders. It is possible that sometimes something may go wrong in the insurance office. The agent is in a position to make sure that the effects of that error do not reach

the policyholder. Good agents with adequate records can insulate their policyholders from the office, so that they experience only the positive aspects about the service and claim settlement procedures. Customer satisfaction and agent's morale will both be high as a consequence.

**Communication Skills**

(28) Communication is normally understood to refer to the information that one has to send to another, through words or symbols or pictures, in writing or verbally. Because of its importance in commercial and private life, the process of communication has been studied and written about extensively.

(29) Communication happens when meanings are made. When the meaning intended by the sender is the same as the meaning made by the receiver, there is perfect and complete communication. If the two meanings are not identical, there is said to be a communication gap or misunderstanding. Meanings are made even when nothing is said. A friend remaining silent can mean that he is worried about something. To a mother working in the kitchen, prolonged silence can cause anxiety about the whereabouts of the little child.

(30) An agent's main tool at work is his communication skills. He has to explain and to persuade. Any misunderstanding might become evident only much later. It will then be attributed to the failure of the agent to inform, alleging even deliberate chatting or suppression of material facts. Good effective agents make written presentation about their recommendations for insurance, pointing out both benefits and pitfalls. The written matter is explained during the sales interview. A further explanation will take place when the policy is delivered to the policyholder. At this time, the agent will make the policyholder go through the important clauses and conditions of the policy, highlighting the implications of the same.

(31) The seven C's of good written communication are:

- *Completeness*: stating all essential facts, anticipating and answering all possible doubts.
- *Courtesy*: pleasantly worded, meant to gain goodwill, requesting instead of commanding.
- *Consideration*: keeping in mind the reader's interest and level of understanding.

- *Clarity*: using simple familiar words, short sentences. Avoiding technical jorgon and uncommon abbreviations.
- *Conciseness*: avoiding superfluous and redundant expression.
- *Concreteness*: avoiding complicated imagery and saying directly, leaving no room for imagination.
- *Correctness*: particularly with numbers, dates, and references.

**Persuassive Skills**

(32) Persuasion is important in all selling. It is more difficult in insurance selling. What is being sold is a concept, an idea. There is nothing tangible, which could be shown as a sample. The idea has to be examined by the prospect in his mind, on the basis of words, figures, stories and mental pictures created by the insurance agent. He has to be convinced on the basis of his own logic and beliefs. It cannot be forced. The insurance agent has to influence the thinking process of the prospect, without being able to see it or share it.

(33) The principles to follow are the same as in counseling, where the person being counselled has to think for himself and decide whether any change in behaviour is called for. They are also the same when negotiators try to persuade hijackers to behave differently. The principles are:

- The decision has to be made by the prospect. He cannot be ordered about.
- The prospect cannot even be rushed. He will think at his own pace.
- The prospect's feelings, doubts and anxieties have to be acknowledged and taken seriously. They cannot be ignored or discounted.
- To facilitate the prospect's thinking, open-ended questions help. Such questions do not have any definite answers and compel one to reason out.
- The more the prospect talks, the more the agent understands how his mind is working.
- Do not interrupt the prospect.

- Do not challenge the prospect's assumptions and hypothesis. Help him find out the errors theirin. Open-ended questions help.
- Welcome his objections, because they indicate the thought process.
- Never make him defensive. He will become so, if he gets a feeling that his stance reposition or ideas are being considered invalid.
- Do not say that he is wrong. Adopt the 'yes-but' technique.

**Analytical Ability**

(34) The insurance policy being sold to the prospect must meet his requriemetns. It would be wrong to assume that popular standard plans of insurance would meet everybody's needs. In some situations, only a multipurpose policy will be appropriate, not an endowment plan. Such variations are more marked in the case of non-life plans. The methods of storage and the nature of the goods stores, the quality of constructions and the materials used therein all make differences to the nature of the risk as well as to the insurance needs. The prospect will not be able to highlight the relevant facts. He may not even know what is relevant. Only the agent can know what is relevant for the insurance coverage and the premium to be charged. A casual approach on the part of the agent may lead to an oversight of detail, which may later be interpreted as suppression of material facts, nullifying the cover taken.

(35) An agent must be able to analyze the various needs of the prospect and find the best plan to meet those needs. No assumptions can be made, a check list on the points to verify will be useful. It is like the pilot of an aircraft who does not depend on his memory or expertise, but goes through a check list before taking off and before landing, to ensure that every single system is correctly set for the maneuver. He cannot risk an oversight or accident. An oversight while planning insurance is as serious as an error in piloting aircraft. The omission can make the insurance plan non-functional.

**Behaviour with Others**

(36) Agents have to depend on the employees of the

company to be able to render satisfactory service to their policyholders. Employees are generally helpful, but not always. The difference in behaviour may be due to their intrinsic nature and attitudes. Some of them may not be customer-oriented. Sometimes, systems and procedures are inflexible and the employees may not be in a position to do what is being asked of them. In such situation, it does not help to blame the employees concerned.

(37) Very often though, the unhelpful attitude is caused by the behaviour of the agent or the policyholder himself, not understanding the difficulties of the employees and accusing them of being indifferent. Rigid stances begin. Cooperation becomes difficult. Some agents are known to throw their weight around, as if the employee concerned not only 'must' do what is being asked for, but do it immediately. That is humiliating.

(38) The principles governing influencing and persuasion, stated earlier, will come in handy to get the support and the cooperation of the employees. If their points of view are understood, some practical solutions may emerge to get over the difficulties. One simple method, which works often, is to explain the problem to them and ask them for help. Some may refuse saying that they are not concerned with your problems. Many are likely to be more cooperative.

(39) Behaviour with fellow agents is also very important to avoid misunderstanding and also interference in business dealings. Professionals do not interfere with the clients of the other professional. This is professional etiquette. Agents are professionals. They are also expected to maintain such proprieties. For example, if agent 'A' knows that a particular client is good enough for some big business and is being contacted by another agent 'B', he should not try to contact that client and try to procure the business. Some agents do so by telling the client that the advice being given by B is not in the interest of the client and so on. There are instance of one agent buy him through another and taking out a new policy. Temptations may be offered by way of sharing of the agent's commission. These are unprofessional behaviors. A doctor does not tempt patients by offering them concessions. Lawyers who stand outside courts, soliciting business are not looked upon as professionals.

(40) Interfering with another business and offering rebates to prospects are referred to in the Regulations and the Insurance Act as punishable offences. The agent's action should be guided, not by the threat of punishment under the law, but by his value system, that distinguishes between what is right and what is wrong.

# Consumer Protection Act, 1986 (COPRA)

(1) In the past several decades, there had been a movement to safeguard the interest of the customer. This has become known as consumerism and had developed as a reaction to business ignoring the rights of consumers and exploiting them. Issues of safety were raised, particularly in the case of motor cars. The following four consumer rights have been accepted as basic:

(A) The right to safety
(B) The right to be informed
(C) The right to choose
(D) The right to be heard (redress)

(2) Under this Act, a consumer, as an individual or along with other individuals, or through a consumer organization, can approach the various forums prescribed under the Act for redress, in case he is not satisfied with the gods or service provided. He has to allege a defect in the goods or service. A defect or deficiency is a fault, imperfection, shortcoming or inadequacy in the quality, nature or manner of performance, which is required to be maintained by or under any law or in pursuance of a contract or undertaking in relation to that service.

(3) In order to attend to complaints under this act, consumer dispute redressal forums are to be established in each District and for each state. The forum at the district level will hear complaints upto the value of Rs. 20,00,000 and the forum at the State level will hear complaints upto the value of Rs. 1 crore. As per provision for the constitution of a national Commission, which will attend to matters beyond the jurisdiction of the state forums and also appeals agents the decisions of a state forum, is in place.

(4) The COPRA applies to the insurance business as well. Policyholders have the right to seek redress against unfair practices or unsatisfactory service from insurers and from agents. The majority of disputes relating to insurance arise out of repudiation and delays in claims. On all these matters, agents can help a great deal to mitigate the complaint or grievance. A written presentation is a sure method of ensuring that the correct information is given. Delays in office procedures can be avoided through the agent's personal intervention. Such delays occur often due to non-compliance with requirements or ambiguity in title. If due care is taken at the time of proposal and all material information supplied, there cannot be a repudiation of a claim.

**Ombusman**

(5) In exercise of the powers conferred by sub-section (1) of Section 114 of the Insurance Act, the Central Government has framed rules known as Redressal of Public Grievances Rules, 1998, whereby Ombudsmen are appointed. Ombudsmen are appointed. Ombudsmen are appointed by the Governing body of the Insurance Council. Their function is to resolve complaints in respect of deputes between policyholder and insurers in cost effective, efficient and impartial manner.

(6) The complaints to the ombudsman may relate to (a) partial or total repudiation of claim, (b) any dispute regarding premium paid or payable in terms of the policy, (c) any dispute on the legal construction of the policy relating to claims, (d) delay in settlement of claims, and (e) non-issue of any insurance document to customers after receipt of premium.

(7) The Ombudsman shall act as counsel and mediator in matters within its terms of reference. It is not a judicial authority. It has no right to summon witnesses. It has to make its decision

on the basis of documents submitted to it. The complainant and the insurer are allowed to make personal submission. But lawyers are not permitted to argue the case.

(8) Complaints to the ombudsman lie only when the insure had reject the complaints or no reply is received within one month of the complaint or the reply is not satisfactory. A complaint can be made within one year after the insurer had rejected the representation. The subject matter should not be already before any court or consumer forum or arbitration.

(9) The ombudsman is expected to make a recommendation within one month from the date of receipt of complaint. If the complainant accept his recommendation, the insurer has to comply within 15 days and inform the ombudsman accordingly. If the complainant does not accept the Ombudsman's recommendation, the ombudsman shall pass an award in writing, stating the amount awarded which shall not be in excess of what is necessary to cover the loss suffered by the complainant as direct consequence of the insured peril or for an amount not exceeding Rs. 10,00,000, whichever is lower. The award has to be passed within 3 months. The complainant has to intimate his acceptance of the award within one month by a letter of acceptance to the insurer and the insurer has to comply within 15 days and inform the ombudsman. If the complainant does not intimate acceptance, the award cannot be implemented.

## OTHER ACTS

### Income Tax Act

(10) The tax laws in India have always encouraged people to save through life insurance or other instruments, by providing relief from tax liabilities. The details provided herein are, as on a date when the course was being written. These could change at any time, through budget provisions or otherwise. The agent should keep himself up to date with the changes. Offices of the insurance companies would normally communicate the effect of such changes for the benefit of the agents. Knowledge of tax provisions is essential for an agent as it affects the benefits under a policy.

(11) Any sum received under a life insurance policy, including the bonus additions is exempt from income tax. That

means that income tax does not have to be paid on policy claim amounts. There are some exceptions to this rule. One is the amount to be refunded under 'Jeevan Adhaar' a plan of the LIC, meant for the handicapped dependents. The other is a claim under a key man insurance policy.

(12) Deductions (from taxable income) to the extent of Rs. 10,000 are allowed to an individual in respect of amounts paid or deposited in the Jeevan Suraksha annuity plan for receiving pension (from a fund set-up by the LIC). Similarly, an amount not exceeding Rs. 40,000 deposited with LIC under Jeevan Adhaar plan for maintenance of handicapped dependent is eligble for deduction from total income. This position has changed with amendment proposed in the budget for 2003-04, whereby maturity claim payments will be taxable if the premium paid in any one year exceeds 20% of the SA.

(13) The amount of income tax payable on the total taxable income, is reduced by a percentage of the aggregate amount paid towards insurance premiums (on life of self, spouse or children), contribution to Provident Fund or approved Superannuating Fund, National Savings Certificates, etc. The percentage of deduction was a flat 20% of the aggregate subject to limits. Most of the assessees could get the rebate to the extent of Rs. 15,000. Some could get more. This position has changed since 2002. The deduction reduces as the income slab goes up.

(14) The Wealth Tax Act exempts life insurance policies totally provided premiums are payable for a period of 10 years or more. If the policy term is less than 10 years, proportionate value of the right or interest of the assessed in the policy will be exempted. Hence, such policies will have to be included in the net wealth as on the date of valuation.

(15) Insurance premiums paid under partnership or keyman insurance are allowed as expense.

### Married Women's Property Act, 1874

(16) Section 6 of the WWP Act provides that a policy of issuance effected by any married man on his own life and expressed on the face of it for the benefit of his wife and children shall be deemed to be a trust for the benefit of his wife and children and shall not be subject to the control of the life assured or his creditors or form part of his estate. The implications of this

kind of life insurance policies have been discussed in an earlier chapter.

## FINANCIAL PLANNING AND TAXATION

### Savings and Investment Schemes

(17) Life insurance is often equated with saving and investment schemes. They are not the same. Saving schemes are plans whereby you can part your surplus money and are paid interest for the same. These deposits can be small amounts. In an investment scheme, one puts in a lump-sum of money to produce income, perhaps to increase the capital. Income is mostly not guaranteed. The capital may rise or may go down. But before one can invest such a lump-sum, one must possess it. One must first create it by saving systematically in well selected savings schemes. Many savings plans have both the elements of saving as well as investment combined.

(18) A good savings plan should score high when following tests are applied:

(a) It should be safe.
(b) It should be flexible.
(c) It should have incentives to help save continuously without default.
(d) It should help in saving tax.
(e) It should fulfil the financial objectives, even if one dies.

(19) An ideal investment scheme should answer favourably to the following tests:

(a) Safety
(b) Liquidity (easily encashable)
(c) A high rate of interest (yield)
(d) Capital growth
(e) Beneficial to save tax.

(20) If the above tests are applied, one may be tempted to look around for some 'most perfect' investment from which to expect everything. There is not a single investment, which has all

those attributes together. One cannot have the opportunities of windfall gains of the stock market with the safety or the life cover and tax concessions of life insurance, all in one. A sacrifice has to be made for the sake of one or the other attributes. A prudent person should look for those investments, which offer the best solutions to his personal needs, under his own set of circumstances.

(21) The 'highest' returns and the 'best' returns are also not necessarily the same thing. High returns may be offset by risk to capital. The best return should be determined by the advantages an investment offers to achieve one's financial objectives under one's unique circumstances.

(22) Banks offer 3 main types of accounts:

(a) The current account paying no interest.
(b) The savings bank account paying relatively low interest.
(c) The term deposit account paying varying rates of interest, rarely exceeding 12%.

(23) Interest earned is subject to income tax.

**Liquidity**

(24) The amount invested in current account or savings bank account can be withdrawn and the moneys obtained at any time. In case of term deposits, one has to wait till maturity of the term or the amount can be withdrawn earlier but at a loss of some interest. These amounts do not exceed what was put in and therefore there is no question of any capital gains tax on it.

**Unit Trust and Mutual Funds**

(25) Unit trust and Mutual Funds are based on the principle that a large number of individuals pool their moneys collectively in a single fund. These funds through the expertise of professional managers invest the collected amounts in shares and securities of a large number of companies. Thus, they establish a direct link between savings and the capital market. The investments made in these funds are divided into segments called 'units', normally, the units have face value of Rs. 10 each. One can buy or sell any number of units at current market prices, which may be more or less than Rs. 10.

(26) The tax benefits are not the same for all investments in mutual funds. The income distributed is sometimes completely tax-free. Contribution to specified mutual funds are aggregated with insurance premia for tax rebates. The value of the unit is not protected. The net asset value can vary a lot. In several cases, it is less than the face value.

**Shares**

(27) Shares are the most popular kind of investment. But only person with adequate savings can find investment in shares worthwhile. They are bought mostly for appreciation. Earnings are neither guaranteed nor high in the short-term. Dividends may not be declared even if the company is making profits. Dividends declared on face value may not be significant as a return on the purchase price. The share prices fluctuate, being sensitive to trends in the US markets, rumors, company results, political crises, etc. They can be sold at any time, but the price will depend on market value. The chances of making losses are as great as the chances of making gains. There are no tax advantages.

The table below shows safety, liquidity and return on various investments.

**Comparisons between Insurance Plans**

| | *Safety* | *Liquidity* | *Return* |
|---|---|---|---|
| Savings bank account | High | High | Low |
| Fixed deposits with banks | - | Moderate/ High | Moderate |
| Life insurance | High | Low | Moderate |
| Shares | Low | High | Moderate/ low |
| Provident fund/ PPF | High | Low | High |

(28) Comparison are often unfair. Even while comparing two different insurance plans of the same insurer, it would be wrong to compare only the premiums payable under the plans. A whole life plan is not to be chosen just because the premium is lower than that of an endowment plan. The choice of plan must depend firstly on the requirement of the prospects. That which does not meet the needs is costly. If the plan identified according to needs requires a premium larger than what the

prospect is in a position to spare, one might begin to think of lower sum assured within the same plan, rather than a cheaper plan.

(29) While comparing plans of insurance, one must also take into account the manner in which the benefits are payable, the ease with which death claims can be settled, ease of alteration, availability of loans, etc. Some policies have restriction on all of these.

# 21

# *Information Technology*

## INTRODUCTION

(1) The developments in the information technology (IT) are working wonders in all fields of activity. It has become possible to send and receive information almost instantaneously. If circulars do not reach the agents on time or doubts are not cleared quickly, or the agent does not have details of new plans announced in the press, the agent may face awkward situations with the prospects. These problems can be totally avoided with the use of IT. Insurers, traditionally, have been quick to adapt to latest advances in technology. This is happening in the areas of IT as well. The extent of IT application will vary between insurers. The broad possibilities are discussed in this chapter.

### Intranet and Internet

(2) The Internet is a worldwide system, accessible through computers. Information travels through the Internet at incredible speeds. It cuts across national and international boundaries. Information posted on a 'website' is available to anybody from anywhere in the globe, at no cost, unless the access is protected and made available only to specified individuals, such individuals will be identified by a password. Sometimes they may be required to pay a fee for the information. The availability of the required information will become known to all.

(3) While the Internet allows access for anybody from anywhere, the intranet is an in-house network, working on the same principle. The difference is similar to the difference between a national newspaper and in-house newsmagazine, which is for private circulation. If an insurer has an intranet system, the information in the intranet will be available only to its offices and personnel. The policyholder will not be able to access the data in the intranet. Circulars meant for internal circulation can be posted on the intranet, and everybody will have immediate access to it, however far away he may be located. In the internet also, it is possible to restrict some information to certain categories of persons, who will be identified through passwords.

(4) Both internet and intranet enable users to do the following at any time (24 hours, 365 days):

- Send and receive letters, which are called e-mail. Every person will have an 'e-mail id', which is his address in the net.
- Search, read and retrieve (download) data, files, pictures.
- Exchange letters and discuss with individuals.
- Join discussion groups, including video conferences.
- Communicate in real time (without any delay whatever) across long distances.
- Display information for whoever is interested.
- Buy and sell (e-commerce).

**Benefit to Agents**

(5) If the insurer has an intranet, the agent can, sitting at his place of work, be attending the insurer's office, making enquiries about status of proposals or claims or discussing with any officers or other agent, for clarification or advice, whenever he wants to do it. The physical distance between the agent and the office will not be of any consequences at all. The benefits to the agents will be:

- He can receive all circulars and instructions issued by any office. All delays on account of postal transmission, being forwarded from one level to another, dispatch department, absence of peons, wrong addresses, misplaced through oversight, lost in transit, etc. are avoided.

- Any doubts with regard to proposal, benefits, premium, taxation, medical examination, insurability, etc. can be discussed and got clarified directly from the person concerned.
- Communications to and from the office will be immediate through e-mail and at low cost.

**Benfits to Policy-holders/Prospects**

(6) Prospects can benefit through the internet in the following ways:

- They can get details of the various policies, the benefits thereunder, the premiums payable, etc.
- Prospects can get advice on the suitable insurance plan for themselves.
- Policyholders can get information with regard to the status of the policy, the premiums due, the bonuses attached, the surrender values or loans available, revival possibilities, nearest office for any further transaction.
- Details can also be had about housing loans or other benefits available to policyholders.
- Premiums can be paid without having to go to the office of the issuers, by direct debit to the policyholder's credit card or bank account.

The LIC has included in its websites, for the benefit of the prospects and the policyholders, information relating to health issues.

**Kiosks**

(7) Kiosks are unmanned information centres, placed strategically at public places. They are called interactive touch screen kiosks. A kiosk is a self-contained unit that combines hardware and software to blend all current media including graphics, video, text and quality sound. It consist of a touch sensor and a monitor on which the sensor can be fitted. The user is expected to touch the relevant sensors, according to the choices

offered by the kiosk visually on the monitor. The kiosk then takes him through various interactive screens to provide him the required information or to transact the required business.

(8) The railways have kiosks located at various stations to help passengers find out about the reservation status of their tickets. The kiosk responds to the touch of the passenger. The passenger makes an enquiry by touching the number that constitute the PNR No. on the ticket. The reservation status will be shown on the display panel. He does not have to go to the reservation office, which in big cities, could be miles away.

(9) The LIC has installed kiosks in more than 100 locations covering its Divisional headquarters. The kiosks provide information on policy status, product information about all products including group insurance products. These can be used by persons, who do not have their own computers and cannot access the internet. They can be operated 24 hours a day and do not require any supervision like the ATMs of banks.

**IT in the Rural Areas**

(10) According to experts, the growth of the economy in the future will be faster in the rural areas than in the urban areas. The income levels and lifestyles are changing. As and when the business houses move into the rural areas, they will also bring in the necessary infrastructure. The normal channels of communication are slow, because of the distances involved, the lack of good roads and infrequent transport services. The telephone which has penetrated deep into the rural areas, is not good enough to transmit detailed reports on consumptions, stocks, etc, with retailers, which help the companies plan their logistics better.

(11) But the telephone system is a good base for building the internet. ITC, the cigarette company, with interest in the agricultural economy of the rural areas, has taken a lead in this matter. Called 'choupals' the system had covered nearly a thousand villages by the end of the year 2001. It will expand to many more villages in the years to come. If insures find it possible to work with the ITC or others who may also build such systems in the villages, it will also become easier to extend the services to the policyholders in the rural areas.

# 22

# *IRDA (Licensing of Corporate Agents) Regulations, 2002*

## IMPORTANT PROVISIONS

These Regulations are on similar lines as the IRDA (Licensing of Insurance Agents) Regulations, 2002. The important provisions are as follows:

(1) A corporate agent can be a firm, a company under the Companies Act, a banking company, a corresponding new bank, a regional rural bank, a cooperative society, a panchayat, a local authority, a non-government organization, a micro-lending finance organization, a non-banking finance company, or any other organization that may be approved by the IRDA.

(2) The partnership deed or the Memorandum of Association or any other document that states the objectives of the person wanting to be the corporate agent, must state clearly that soliciting and procuring insurance business is one of its objectives.

(3) The corporate agent has to nominate its partner (in the case of a firm), director (in the case of a company), or one or more of its officers or employees, as a

'corporate insurance executive'. The issue of licence to the corporate agent is subject to the insurance executive's satisfying the requisite educational an other qualifications, as in the case of an individual agent. He is also required to undergo the minimum training requirements and pass the examination conducted by the Insurance Institute of India, as in the case of individual agents.

(4) The corporate agent also has to nominate one or more of its partners, directors or employees as 'specified persons', who will be responsible for soliciting insurance business on behalf of the corporate agent. The specified person must have a minimum educational qualification on the same lines as individual agents, and must also not suffer from any of the disqualifications like being insane, being convicted for a criminal offense, etc. He must obtain a certification, which will be given to him after he undergoes the prescribed training and passes an examination. The fees for the certification is Rs. 500. The certification will be valid for 3 years and can be renewed.

(5) Both corporate insurance executives and specified persons, are bound by the code of conduct for agents, as applicable to individual agents. A violation of the code can result in the cancellation of the licence of the corporate agent, the corporate insurance executives or certification of the specified persons.

# Bancassurance

## INTRODUCTION

(1) In terms of the Regulations issued by the Insurance Regulatory and Development Authority (IRDA), agents for insurance companies have to obtain licenses, such licenses may be issued to individuals or to corporate bodies, like banks, firms, cooperative societies, etc. in the case of corporate agents, the licences will be issued to person who are designated by the corporate bodies as 'Corporate Insurance Executives'. In addition, the corporate agent may avail of the services of 'Specified persons' who will have to obtain certificates. This supplement is written for the benefit of those who are working in banks and seek to qualify for the licences and certificates.

(2) This supplement is to be studied along with the main course, which is the basis of the training and examination for individual agents. So far, there is no such supplement for other corporate agents. It is not expected that there may be any issues affecting all such corporate agents in a uniform manner. In the case of banks, however, there is likely to be such common issues. That is the justification for this special supplement.

### What is Bancassurance?

(3) Bancassurance is a word coined in the western world, when banks began to get involved in the marketing of insurance

business. The involvement took different forms in different countries. In some countries, the same institution would offer both banking and insurance products, separately or together as the customers may need, managing both the businesses themselves. This was possible when the institution was allowed to transact both insurance and banking businesses. This was permitted in certain countries. The product or service offered to the customer was the product of the bank and had in it some elements of insurance. This strictly is bancassurance. In practice, however, there are variations.

(4) One variation was that the bank may offer both services combined, but having done the business, pass on the insurance part of the funds to an insurance company, with whom it had an alliance or business arrangements. Both of them may be under the same industrial group. For example, when the Unit Trust of India offered Unit linked life insurance policies, it had an arrangement with the Life Insurance Corporation to the extent of the term insurance component. The 'Peerless' used to offer its account-holders' insurance cover on accidental death. This was done by arrangement with a general insurance company. Although marketed as one product, the business remained separate. The funds were accounted for and managed separately by separate institutions.

(5) The third method, which is the pattern developing in India, is that the bank markets the insurance product for a fee. None of the bank's services is modified or enhanced by the insurance services. Also, the benefits offered are not in any manner modified or enhanced by the association with the bank. The product is in no way different from what any other agent of the insurer may offer. The bank is only an agent of the insurer.

### Bancassurance Abroad

(6) For years together the world over, insurance and banking businesses were considered to be separate and regulated a such. The principles of managing the funds were different in the two businesses. The risk profiles and the capital needs are different. They have different time horizons, while making investment decision. Even within the banking business, development banking was different from merchant banking, which was again different from commercial retail banking.

(7) The 1970s and 1980s saw these barriers crumbling. The financial sector was becoming one. There was need for a one stop delivery for all financial services. Financial institutions transacting different businesses began to work together in strategic alliances or merged into one entity. Banks could offer insurance policies and insurers could offer banking services.

(8) In 1997, the Credit Suisse bought over the Winterthur, the second largest insurer in Switzerland. Such mergers happened in the Netherlands, Belgium, Germany, France and Spain. This was not permitted in the USA because of the Glass Steagall Act (passed in 1933). This Act was recently repealed and some insurance companies and banks have merged.

(9) In Europe, bancassurance seems to have made the greatest impact in France. It is claimed that 55% to 60% of the life insurance business in France had come through banks. In the U.K., the figure is about 15%. In Portugal and Spain, it was over 70%. In Argentina, Brazil, Chile, Colombia and Mexico, bancassurance is popular. Big international banks have got into the business of insurance and pension funds. In Brazil, the online banking systems are used. Everywhere, the contribution for non-life insurance is low, less than 10%.

(10) The potential impact of bancassurance is much more than what these figures of shares represent. If the Royal Bank of Canada and the London Insurance Co. were to merge or the Chase Manhattan Bank in the US were to merge with the AIG, (the third largest insurer in the US), the impact would be as huge as the State Bank of India and the LIC merging in India. These are not hypothetical, but real possibilities in Canada and in the US. these also raise issues relevant to anti-trust laws. In Canada, the Competition Bureau as well as the Superintendent of Financial Institutions have expressed concern about mega mergers between banks having reduced competition. They also see possibilities of conflict on interests.

**Vale Proposition**

(11) The services offered by banks as well as insurance companies, are related to assets and risks. They have to be managed. These institutions manage risks and assets for the customers, reducing and taking over the risks and transforming the assets. The core of the businesses are similar, though not

same. The basic distinctions in the values offered by banks' insurance companies and other financial institutions are indicated below.

(12) Banks offer to their customers liquidity (while at the same time making long-term loans), safety, trust (managing estates on behalf of beneficiaries), collections of interest or dividends, payment of commitments (rentals and insurance premiums, for example) and annuities. Insurers primarily protect clients from risks (political, financial, commercial, business, and human). In life insurance, there is a major component of management of an asset which is created by the policy. The benefits of the insurer's expertise in asset management, passes on to the clients by way of premium levels and bonuses the liquidity concerns of insurers are different from the liquidity concerns of banks.

(13) Securities firms primarily provide information and advice. They also act as brokers or agents for the customers, but do not take responsibility for risk and assets. Pension funds manage the savings directly or through employers and help the pensioners manage the risk of loss of income in the old age. Mutual Funds are asset transformers, providing small savers easy access to complex portfolios of capital markets and protecting them from the vagaries of the capital market, without sacrificing the needs of liquidity.

(14) Most customers, big and small, individuals and companies, are all interested in all these services. That is the justification for the concept of a single window for all financial services. Bancassurance is a step in this evolution.

### The Indian Context

(15) In India, no company is allowed to transact both insurance and banking business. They are kept separate. In fact, even a company, registered as an insurer has to choose between life and non-life business. It cannot do both. Therefore, the banks in India cannot have the advantages, which are available in the European context.

(16) There are joint ventures in India between banks and foreign insurers. State Bank of India, HDFC, ICICI and Vysya Banks are example. But apart from a greater willingness to help each other, the joint venture will not give either party a greater

advantage in the other's business. The joint venture is an entirely independent unit of operation, with separate personnel and funds and subject to different regulations.

(17) The only way in which banks can be associated with the insurance business in India is by becoming a corporate agent. For a remuneration. The bank can do so for a particular life insurer and/or particular non-life insurer. The bank cannot develop any insurance products. It can of course, make suggestions on the basis of its intimate contacts with the customers. Since 2000, many banks and insurers have agreed to arrangements for mutual benefit. The LIC has tied with more than one bank. So also have other insurers.

(18) For more than a hundred years, insurance business had been sold through insurance agents and their supervisors. This system had not been very satisfactory. The LIC inherited this system. The efforts to make the agents more professional had not yielded very satisfactory results, despite incentives and training programmes. Many of them continued to treat the agency business casually, as just a source of additional income. The turnover had been high and the efforts of replenishing the strength, costly. The banks have skilled staff, to whom the procurement of insurance, can be assigned as a duty. This was an opportunity made available after the regulations of the IRDA.

**Benefits to the Insurer**

(19) The main benefits to the insurer are as follows:

- The market for insurance is very heterogeneous, with customers of widely varying profiles and needs. Therefore, they have to use multiple channels for distribution, to match the different segments. As an additional channel, the banks have a good match with certain segments of the market.
- It gets the advantage of the existing infrastructure of the bank. In India, the public sector banks have 66,000 branches, of which more than 33,000 are in the rural areas and 14,000 in the semi-urban areas. The LIC, the biggest life insurer in the country, had, after nearly 46 years of existence, less than 2500 branches all over the country including the metro cities. The

four general insurance companies also had a similar number of branches.

- Access is easily available to a huge client base. The customers of the banks are similar to the customers for insurance, whether the life or general. Banks have 19 crore accounts, a large reservoir of potential customers for insurers.
- There is a relationship of loyalty and trust between the bank and its customers which can become a valuable base for selling insurance. Bank have much more intimate contacts with their customers than insurers, because (i) the frequency of contact is more, and (ii) they meet under more pleasant circumstances.
- Customers tend to have more trust in the banks than in insurers, with whom their contacts are comparatively much less.
- There is a complimentary relationship between insurance and banking. Loans are given by banks on security and credit of persons and of assets. Insurance ensures that the security is not lost.
- Banks constitute a readily available, competent, trusted, educated distribution channel for the insurer.
- Particularly for new insurers, the association with the banks helps them penetrate the markets much faster and also to give themselves some credibility. They can get some leverage from the bank's branch image.
- Banks can leverage their contact with commercial clients, for developing personal lines of insurance, which is relatively neglected, particularly in non-life business.
- Premium can be paid by debit to the account with the bank.
- Employees bound by the discipline of the banks are easier to monitor and to control than independent agents.

### Benefits to the Bank

(20) Banks are under pressure because of falling interest rates and increasing costs of administration. Competition from global players is making it easy. All banks are looking for fee-based incomes. Insurance commission provide an excellent avenue for such income, it is expected that banks would be looking for fee-based (non-interest) incomes of the order of Rs. 15,000 to Rs. 20,000 crores over the next five years. In India, the fee is only through the commission received on the business placed with the insurer.

(21) Banks can help to develop insurance products, which are relevant to its business, particularly in the areas of international trade, with risks on account of political upheavals, exchange fluctuations, etc.

(22) There is no risk in the business. The bank cannot lose. The only risk is if the chosen insurer gets into trouble or is poor in service. The customer is likely to blame the bank for the problem. This is however, a remote risk.

(23) The other benefits include:

- Better customer retention and stronger relationship.
- Clear competitive advantage in the rural areas.
- Possibility that the insurer's accounts as well as the accounts from the claimants will remain with the bank.
- Insurance products can augment the value of the banking products and services.
- Banks are in a better position to offer complete integrated financial solutions.

### The Legal Requirements

(24) Any scheduled commercial bank or its subsidiary can become a corporate agent.

(25) To float a joint venture, the bank must have to proceed according to RBI regulations:

- Net worth of at least Rs. 500 crores.
- Reasonably low Non-Performing Assets.
- Net profit for the last three years.

- Record of satisfactory performance by its subsidiaries, if any.
- Capital to Risk Weighted Ratio of not less than 10%.
- A share in the insurance company's capital not exceeding 50%. Exceptions may be considered by the RBI.
- Limited share of capital of foreign partner, if any, to 49%.

(26) Unlike in foreign countries, the banks in India are required to maintain separate staff for doing insurance business. These persons will be exclusively dealing with insurance business. The overhead expense will, therefore, remain high until the business increases adequately.

(27) The banks will be entitled to receive commission on the insurance business only if it is licensed to act as an agent and the specified person, who procured the business is an employee of the bank. It will not be entitled to receive any commission, if the business is procured by a person who is employed by the insurers, but is allowed to occupy space or other facilities of the bank.

**The Problems**

(28) Any bank getting into the business of selling insurance cannot afford to have a casual approach to it. The staff, if deputed from within the existing bank staff, will have to be specially trained in the intricacies of insurance and the art of salesmanship. These skills will be required at levels different from the requirements in banking operations. They will have to be persons who have an external orientation.

(29) The amount of business acquired through the bank depends entirely on the personal skills of the specified persons and the corporate insurance executives. An effective and successful specified person might perhaps find it more remunerative to branch off as an insurance agent on his own, instead of being tied to the bank. The options available to the bank to prevent this may lie in developing attractive compensation packages. The relevant issues will be the restrictions imposed by the Insurance Act as well as the relative pressures within the unions of the bank employees.

(30) The commitment of the senior management is crucial to the success of the person deputed for the insurance work. The priorities for the managers may depend on the criteria by which they will be appraised at the end of the year. If the progress in insurance is not an important criterion, the support to the insurance activities may be reduced. They would see mainstream banking activities as more important for their own future growth. The appraisal and reward systems of the bank have to be appropriately aligned.

**Concept of Universal Banking**

(31) Traditionally, development banking was separate from commercial or retail banking. A development bank would evaluate the proposed projects of a company and help it to acquire long-term finance, either as equity or as loans. It may provide these funds by itself, or in conjunction with other financial institutions or give confidence to investing public that the project was sound, by declaring its support. The industrial Development Bank of India (IDBI), the Industrial Finance Corporation of India (IFCI), the Industrial Credit and Investment Corporation of India (ICICI) were such organizations specializing in development banking. There were many other institutions in the States as well.

(32) Current thinking is that there is no need for such division of activities and that commercial banks can take upon themselves the responsibility of all kinds of banking activities. The ICICI has merged with ICICI bank. The IDBI and the IFGCI are also looking at similar options, the Narasimham Committee has recommended that the banking system should move towards universal banking.

(33) Universal banking means that there is full integration of the financial businesses, including securities, insurance, mortgages, etc. Banks in India are already into the business of long-term financing of companies, mortgages, individual loans. Hire-purchase, investments, etc. banks are also involved in performing tasks on behalf of government, like collecting taxes and paying pensions. Insurance is still kept out but may not remain so for too long.

(34) Studies abroad show that banks prefer to have their own insurance companies, instead of working for another as an

agent. The reasons given are of the following kind:

- Efficient operations and good products come only when they are built themselves, not through buying from some other producer.
- There could be differences in the cultures of the two institutions, particularly with regard to customer orientation.
- They do not want to compete with the insurer's distribution channel, which may include other banks.

## Rider—Descriptions and Premium Rates

- Accidental Death Benefits (ADB) Rider
- Accidental Death and Dismemberment (ADD) Rider
- Waiver of Premium (WP) Rider
- Waiver of Premium for MAHALIFE GOLD
- Payer Benefit (PB) Rider
- Five Years Renewable Term Rider
- 10 Years Term Rider
- 15 Years Term Rider
- 20 Years Term Rider
- 25 Years Term Rider
- Term to Age 60 Rider
- Critical Illness Lump-sum Benefit
- Critical Illness Accelerated Benefit

## Accidental Death Benefits

(1) It is non-participating supplementary contract.

(2) Premiums are payable until the insured reaches age 70, the maturity of the basic policy or death of the insured whichever is earlier.

(3) Sum assured is payable upon accidental death of the insured before the insured reaches 70 or before the expiry of the basic policy whichever is earlier.

| | *ADB* |
|---|---|
| Plan Code | ADBN1 |
| Sum Assured – Minimum | 25,000 (per 1,000 increment) |
| Sum Assured – Maximum | 1x Basic FA |
| Sum Assured – Size Discount | No |
| Age Issue | 18-55 |
| Age – Maximum Renewal | 69 |
| Age – Maturity | 70 |
| Premium Unisex | Yes |
| Premium structure | Level according to class 1, 2, 3 or 4 and will change if the insured's occupation is changed during the term of the policy. |
| Payment – Method | Cash / Cheque / Autopay |
| Payment Mode | Subject to basic plan |
| Renewal & Conversion | Renewal only |
| Back Dating | Subject to basic plan |
| Occupation Rating | According to occupation manual |
| RCC | Subject to Occupation |
| Medical Rating | Standard – 3 classes up, Decline if 2 class 5 |
| Medical Requirements | No |
| Financial Underwriting | Yes |
| Attached to basic life | Yes |
| Remarks | Maximum sum of all accident death benefits under all riders is 5 x basic face amount per policy. Maximum capping on accidental riders is Rs. 50,00,000 |

| ADB Annual Premium Rates | |
|---|---|
| *Class* | *Rate per 1,000 Sum Assured* |
| 1 | 1.00 |
| 2 | 1.25 |
| 3 | 2.00 |
| 4 | 2.50 |

Classifications are based on job activities and not on job titles, for detail classifications, refer to Occupational Rating Guide.

**Accidental Death and Dismemberment**

(1) It is non-participating supplementary contract.
(2) Premiums are payable until the insured reaches age 70, the maturity of the basic policy or death of the insured whichever is earlier.
(3) Sum assured is payable upon accidental death of the insured before expiry of the basic policy. Provides additional benefits in case of dismemberment, loss of sight, speech and hearing resulting from accident either in short scale or in long scale.

| | *ADD (Short Scale)* | *ADD (Long Scale)* |
|---|---|---|
| Plan Code | ADDSN1 | |
| Sum Assured – Minimum | 25,000 (per 1,000 increment) | |
| Sum Assured – Maximum | 1x Basic FA | |
| Sum Assured – Size Discount | No | |
| Age Issue | 18-55 | |
| Age – Maximum Renewal | 69 | |
| Age – Maturity | 70 | |
| Premium Unisex | Yes | |
| Premium structure | Level according to class 1, 2, 3 or 4 and will change if the insured's occupation is changed during the term of the policy. | |
| Payment – Method | Cash / Cheque / Autopay | |
| Payment Mode | Subject to basic plan | |
| Renewal & Conversion | Renewal only | |
| Back Dating | Subject to basic plan | |
| Occupation Rating | According to occupation manual | |
| RCC | Subject to Occupation | |
| Medical Rating | Standard – 3 classes up, Decline if greater than and equal to class 5 | |
| Medical Requirements | No | |
| Financial Underwriting | Yes | |
| Attached to basic life | Yes | |
| Remarks | Maximum sum of all accident death benefits under all riders is 5 x basic face amount per policy. | |

There are two types of ADD coverage, short scale and long scale. The respective benefits payable on these two types of coverage are shown in the benefits section below.

**Benefits**

(1) The benefit of both the short scale and long scale is payable if the accident occurs before the insured reaches age 70 or before the policy becomes paid-up whichever is earlier.

(2) Add (Short Scale) benefit:

| *Accident Death and Dismemberment* | *Amount of Benefit* |
|---|---|
| Loss of Life | 100% |
| Loss of all limbs | 100% |
| Loss of sight of both eyes | 100% |
| Loss of sight of one eye | 50% |
| Loss of or loss of use of two limbs | 100% |
| Loss of or loss of use of one limb | 50% |
| Loss of speech and loss of hearing | 100% |
| Loss of hearing in both ears | 75% |
| Loss of hearing in one ear | 15% |
| Loss of speech | 50% |

The insured will be entitled only to the loss which pays the largest benefit, if more than one loss results from the same accident. This supplementary contract will terminate on the date of the accident resulting in any of the losses above.

(3) Add (Long Scale) benefit:

| *Accident Death and Dismemberment* | *Amount of Benefit* |
|---|---|
| Loss of Life | 100% |
| Loss of sight of both eyes | 100% |
| Loss of sight of one eye | 50% |
| Loss of or loss of use of two limbs | 100% |
| Loss of or loss of use of one limb | 50% |
| Loss of speech and loss of hearing | 100% |
| Loss of hearing in both ears | 75% |
| Loss of hearing in one ear | 25% |
| Loss of speech | 50% |

| | |
|---|---|
| Permanent total and irreversible loss of the lens of one eye | 50% |
| Loss of or loss of use of four fingers and thumbs of Right hand | 70% |
| - Left hand | 50% |
| Loss of or loss of use of one thumb | |
| - Both right joints | 30% |
| - One right joint | 15% |
| - Both left joints | 20% |
| - One left Joint | 10% |
| Loss of or loss of use of fingers | |
| - Three right joints | 10% |
| - Two right joints | 7.5% |
| - One right joint | 5% |
| - Three left joints | 7.5% |
| - Two left joints | 5% |
| - One left joint | 2% |
| Loss of or loss of use of Toes | |
| - All one foot | 15% |
| - Great both joints | 5% |
| - Great one joint | 3% |
| Fractured leg or patella with established non-union | 10% |
| Shortening of leg by at least 5cms | 7.5% |

If insured is left-handed, the percentage for the various accidental injuries listed in the above schedule of right hand and left hand will be transposed.

**Accidental Burns**

If the insured suffers third degree burns due to accident, the following amount of benefit will be payable if the burnt area occurs and involves:

| *Area* | *Damage as percentage of total body surface area* | *Amount of Benefit* |
|---|---|---|
| (a) Head | Equal to greater than 2% but less than 5% | 50% |
| | Equal to greater than 5% but less than 8% | 75% |
| | Equal to greater than 8% | 100% |
| (b) Body | Equal to greater than 10% but less than 15% | 50% |
| | Equal to greater than 15% but less than 20% | 75% |
| | Equal to greater than 20% | 100% |

The insured will be entitled only to the loss which pays the largest benefit if more than one loss under items 1 and 2 above results from the same accident. This supplementary contract will terminate on the date of accident resulting in any of the losses under items 1 and 2 above.

### Double Indemnity

The amount of benefit provided in the schedule of benefits under items 1 and 2 above will be doubled if the accidental injury for which the benefit is payable occurs under any of the following circumstances:

(1) While the insured is riding as a fare paying passenger on commercially licensed public land transportation over an established route such as bus, tram or train. A taxi or any form of transport chartered for private travel is excluded.

(2) While the insured is in an elevator car (elevators in mines and on construction sites excluded) duly certified to carry passengers, or

(3) As a direct result of the burning of the following public buildings—only theatre, cinema, public auditorium, hotel, school and hospital.

(4) When the insured is on a commercial passenger airline on a regular scheduled passenger trip over its established passenger route.

| ADD Annual Premium Rates | | |
|---|---|---|
| *Class* | *Short Scale* | *Long Scale* |
| | *Rate per 1,000 Sum Assured* | *Rate per 1,000 Sum Assured* |
| 1 | 1.60 | 2.00 |
| 2 | 2.00 | 2.50 |
| 3 | 3.20 | 4.00 |
| 4 | 4.00 | 5.00 |

Classifications are based on job activities and not on job titles. For details of classifications, refer to Occupational Rating Guide

**Waiver of Premiom**

(1) It is non-participating supplementary contract.
(2) Premiums are payable during the premium-paying period of the basis policy or until the insured reaches age 60, whichever is earlier.
(3) It provides for the waiver of all future premiums of the basic policy and this supplementary contract which falls due while the insured is disabled (provided that the disability commerces before the insured reaches 60 and has continued for at least 12 months).

| | *Waiver of Premium* |
|---|---|
| Plan Code | Subject to basic plan |
| Sum Assured – Minimum | 1 x basic FA subject to financial underwriting |
| Sum Assured – Maximum | 1x Basic FA subject to financial underwriting |
| Sum Assured – Size Discount | No |
| Age Issue | 18-55 |
| Age – Maximum Renewal | 59 |
| Age – Maturity | 60 |
| Premium Unisex | Yes |
| Premium Structure | Yes |
| Payment – Method | Cash / Cheque / Autopay |
| Payment Mode | Subject to basic plan |
| Renewal & Conversion | Renewal only |
| Back Dating | Subject to basic plan |
| Occupation Rating | According to occupation manual |
| Medical Rating | Standard up to + 100% em |
| Medical Requirements | No |
| Financial Underwriting | Yes, subject to 5 x annual income per life |
| Attached to basic life | Yes |

**Waiver of Premium**

1. It is non-participating supplementary contract.
2. Premiums are payable during the premium-paying period of the basic policy or until the insured reaches age 60, whichever is earlier.

3. It provides for the waiver of all future premiums of the basic policy and this supplementary contract which falls due while the insured is disabled (provided that the disability commerces before the insured reaches 60 and has continued for at least 12 months).

| | *Waiver of Premium* |
|---|---|
| Plan Code | 15PWLP1WP |
| Distribution Channel | Agency |
| Sum Assured – Minimum | 1 x basic FA subject to financial underwriting |
| Sum Assured – Maximum | 1x Basic FA subject to financial underwriting |
| Sum Assured – Size Discount | No |
| Age Issue | 18-55 |
| Age – Maximum Renewal | 59 |
| Age – Maturity | 60 |
| Premium Unisex | Yes |
| Premium Structure | Level |
| Payment – Method | Cash / Cheque / Autopay |
| Payment Mode | Subject to basic plan |
| Renewal & Conversion | Renewal only |
| Back Dating | Subject to basic plan |
| Occupation Rating | According to occupation manual |
| Medical Rating | Standard to MR 'D' (+100% em) |
| Medical Requirements | No |
| Financial Underwriting | Yes, subject to 5 x annual income per life |
| Attached to basic life | 15LPWLP1, 15BKLPWLP1 |

**Payer Benefit**

(1) It is non-participating supplementary contract.

(2) Premiums are payable during the premium-paying period of the basic policy or until the insured reaches age 21, or the payer reaches age 60, whichever is earlier.

(3) When the payer dies or becomes disabled before the

reaches age 60, and before the juvenile reaches age 21, all the future premiums of the basic policy and this rider will be waived up to maturity of the basic policy or the child reaches age 21 or the payer reaches age 60, whichever is earlier. The basic policy will be kept in force as though premiums waived were paid in cash

(4) This rider will terminate when the juvenile reaches age 21 or the payer reaches age 60 whichever is earlier.

| | *Payer Benefit* |
|---|---|
| Plan Code | PB |
| Sum Assured – Minimum | 1 x basic FA subject to financial underwriting |
| Sum Assured – Maximum | 1x Basic FA subject to financial underwriting |
| Sum Assured – Size Discount | No |
| Age Issue | Juvenile : 0 (30 days) – 17<br>Payer 18-55 |
| Age – Maximum Renewal | Juvenile reaches 20 or payer reaches 59 whichever is earlier |
| Age – Maturity | Juvenile reaches 21 or payer reaches 60 whichever is earlier |
| Premium Unisex | Yes |
| Premium Structure | Yes |
| Payment – Method | Cash / Cheque / Autopay |
| Payment Mode | Subject to basic plan |
| Renewal & Conversion | Renewal only |
| Back Dating | Subject to basic plan |
| Occupation Rating | According to occupation manual |
| Medical Rating | Standard up to + 100% em |
| Medical Requirements | Juvenile : nil<br>Payer: According to medical evidence table. ½ of the juvenile basic. FA will be used in calculating the Payer's non-med limit. |
| Financial Underwriting | Yes, subject to 5 x annual income per life |
| Attached to basic life | Yes |

## Term Riders

(1) Term periods are for 5, 10, 15, 20 and 25 years or until age 60.

(2) Face amount is payable upon death of the insured before the expiry of the term.

| | *5 years renewal term rider* | *10 years renewal term rider* | *15 years renewal term rider* | *20 years renewal term rider* | *25 years renewal term rider* | *Term to Age 60 Rider* |
|---|---|---|---|---|---|---|
| Plan Code | STRN1 | 10STRN1 | 15STRN1 | 20STRN1 | 25STRN1 | TR60NI |
| Sum Assured Minimum | 100,000 (per 1,000 increment) | | | | | |
| Sum Assured Maximum | Less than and = to 1 x basic FA or less than = 5 x Annual incom e, whichever is lower | | | | | |
| Sum Assured Size Discount | No | | | | | |
| Age Issue | 18-55, 18-50, 18-45, 18-40, 18-35, 18-50 | | | | | |
| Age– Maximum Renewal | 59 | | | | | |
| Age – Expiry | 60 | | | | | |
| Premium Unisex | Yes | | | | | |
| Premium Structure | Renewal premium will be based on attained age level | | | | | |
| Payment– Method | Cash / Cheque / Autopay | | | | | |
| Payment Mode | Annual, semi-annual, quarterly or monthly (autopay) | | | | | |
| Renewal & Conversion | Can renewal only Conversion and renewal not allowed | | | | | |
| Back Dating | No | | | | | |
| Occupation Rating | According to occupation manual | | | | | |
| Medical Rating | Standard to MR 'D' (+ 100% em) | | | | | |
| Medical Requirements | According to medical evidence table | | | | | |
| Financial Underwriting | Yes | | | | | |
| Additional underwriting requirements | (1) Illiterates are not allowed to buy term riders. (2) Juveniles, students and housewives are not allowed to buy termiders. | | | | | |

## Critical Illness Rider (Accelerated Benefit)

(1) It is non-participating supplementary contract.

(2) Premium are payable until insured reaches age 65, the maturity of the basic policy diagnosis of any of the critical illnesses or performances of any of the covered surgeries or death of the insured whichever is earlier.

(3) Sum assured of the rider is payable upon the insured's survival for a period of at least thirty days following diagnosis of any of the critical illnesses or performance

| | *Critical illness Accelerated Benefit* |
|---|---|
| Plan Code | CIABN1 |
| Distribution Channel | Agency |
| Sum Assured – Minimum | Follow Basic |
| Sum Assured – Maximum | 1x Basic FA or 10,00,000 per life, whichever is lower subject to financial underwriting and additional underwriting requirements, |
| Sum Assured – Size Discount | No |
| Age Issue | 18-50 |
| Age – Maximum Renewal | 64 |
| Age – Maturity | 65 |
| Premium Unisex | No (separate rate for males and females) |
| Premium Structure | Renewal premium will be based on attained age |
| Payment – Method | Cash / Cheque |
| Payment Mode | Subject to basic plan |
| Renewal & Conversion | Renewal only |
| Back Dating | Subject to basic plan |
| Occupation Rating | According to occupation manual |
| Medical Rating | Standard to MR 'D' (+ 100% em) : no additional exclusions other than those specified in the policy contrast. |
| Medical Requirements | According to medical evidence table. C1, sum assured to be aggregate with basic and any term covered. |
| Financial Underwriting | Yes, less than = x 5 annual income |
| Attached to basic life | 10 ENDPI / 20ENDPI / 30 ENDPI / END60PI / 21TMAEP1 / 15LPWLP1 / INPNAGP1 |
| Additional Underwriting Requirements | Maximum SA of critical illness rider:<br>•Critical illness SA + Term Rider SA : Basic FA less than = 3:1<br>•Housewives: 250,000 per life, not allowed to be attached to policies with basic FA greater than 250,000. |

of any of the covered surgeries. Policy will be terminated if the CI claim has been paid out as the sum assured is the same as that of the basic policy. The attached RB of the basic policy will be payable.

(4) This rider covers that following Critical illness and surgeries (a) Cancer, (b) Stroke, (c) Heart Attack, (d) Coronary bypass Graft Surgery, (e) Kidney Failure, (f) Recipient of major organ transplant like heart, lung, liver, kidney or pancreas or bone marrow transplant.

**Critical Illness Rider (Accelerated Benefit)**

(1) It is non-participating supplementary contract.

(2) Premiums are payable until insured reaches age 65, the maturity of the basic policy diagnosis of any of the critical illnesses or performance of any of the covered surgeries or death of the insured whichever is earlier.

(3) Sum assured of the rider is payable upon the insured's survival for a period of at least thirty days following diagnosis of any of the critical illnesses or performance of any of the covered surgeries. The basic policy remains in force, unaffected after such a claim payment.

(4) This rider covers that following Critical illness and surgeries: (a) Cancer, (b) Stroke, (c) Heart Attack, (d) Coronary bypass Graft Surgery, (e) Kidney Failure, (f) Recipient of major organ transplant like heart, lung, liver, kidney or pancreas or bone marrow transplant.

| | *Critical illness Lump-sum Benefit* |
|---|---|
| Plan Code | CILBN1 |
| Distribution Channel | Agency |
| Sum Assured – Minimum | Rs. 25,000 |
| Sum Assured – Maximum | Less than = 1 x Basic FA or 1,000,000 per life, whichever is lower subject to financial underwriting and additional underwriting requirements, |
| Sum Assured – Size Discount | No |
| Age Issue | 18-50 |

| | *Critical illness Lump-sum Benefit* |
|---|---|
| Age – Maximum Renewal | 64 |
| Age – Maturity | 65 |
| Premium Unisex | No (separate rate for males and females) |
| Premium Structure | Renewal premium will be based on attained age |
| Payment – Method | Cash / Cheque |
| Payment Mode | Subject to basic plan |
| Renewal & Conversion | Renewal only |
| Back Dating | Subject to basic plan |
| Occupation Rating | According to occupation manual |
| Medical Rating | Standard to MR 'D' (+ 100% em) : no additional exclusions other than those specified in the policy contrast. |
| Medical Requirements | According to medical evidence table, C1 sum assured to be aggregate with basic and any term covered. |
| Financial Underwriting | Yes, less than = x 5 annual income |
| Attached to basic life | 10 ENDPI / 20ENDPI / 30 ENDPI / END60PI / 21TMAEP1 / 15LPWLP1 / INPNAGP1 |
| Additional Underwriting Requirements | Maximum SA of critical illness rider:<br>•Critical illness SA + Term Rider SA : Basic FA less than = 3:1<br>•Housewives: 250,000 per life. |

ANNEXURE I

# PREMIUM COLLECTION PROCESS AND BANK DETAILS

## Premium Collection

### *1. Submission at cashier's officer (New Business)*

1.1. The application form along with the cheque, demand draft or cash will be submitted to the cashier after initial scrutiny by the customer service officer (CSO).

1.2. The cashier will verify the cheque details, i.e. payee name, date, amount, signature and any alternations.

1.3. Agent code, policy number and agent's contact number should be written on the back of the cheque. Agent's personal cheques will not be entertained. In case of return/dishonoured cheque, the management has the right to reject future cheques from the same agent. The amount levied by the banks for the return cheque will be debited to agents.

1.4. The agent should deposit the premium amount within 1 working day from the date of issue of TR to the policyholder.

1.5. For all collections, official receipts will not be issued until the policy is underwritten. Upon issuing the policy, the receipts will be printed and forwarded to underwriting department for onward delivery to policyholders.

1.6. The cashier will provide the temporary receipt after making the necessary system entries.

1.7. The cashier will attach the application copy of the temporary receipt to application form and hand over the same to branch administration.

1.8. Once the payment is made, the cashier will not entertain any request from the agents to refer to the application form again.

***2. Renewal Payments***

2.1. Renewal payments on policies are to be made at the cashier counter.

2.2. Agent code, policy number and agent's contact number should be written on the back of the cheque.

2.3. The agent should deposit the premium amount within 2 working days from the date of issue of TR to the policyholder.

2.4. The cashier will provide the temporary receipt after making the necessary system entries.

2.5. A health certificate should be submitted along with the renewal payment cheque in cases where the policy has lapsed and needs to be reinstated.

***3. Third Party Cheques***

3.1. No third party cheques will be entertained.

3.2. If the payment has been made by any other person other than the insured or policyholder, payment would be accepted only if paid by a close relative (father/mother/brother/sister/spouse of the insured. In all such cases, a duly filled confidential agent repot (CAR has to be attached to the application. The information relating to the payment made should be clearly mentioned in the CAR.

3.3. Demand draft would be deemed to be payments made by insured/policyholder.

**Resignation or Termination of an Agent**

Upon resignation or termination of an agent, the agent has to return to the company, his identity card, all application forms, broachers and booklets that he has with him.

Any business that is introduced by the agent after the date of agency contract termination and even if it is accepted by the company, for any reason whatsoever, such acceptance of the business by the company will not constitute a waiver of the termination of the contract as an agent and no commission shall be due to the agent for such business.

Annexure II

## FORM IRDA/RI–REQUEST FOR REGISTRATION APPLICATION

1. Name of the applicant
2. Address
3. Date of incorporation as a company
4. Registration No. (issued by the Registrar of the Companies)
5. Classes of insurance business for which registration is sought.
6. Amount of authorized capital and face value of shares and their numbers.
7. Amount of paid-up capital and number of equity shares.
8. Classification of shares
9. Voting rights of each class of shareholders
10. Details of shareholders
11. Background information on the applicant
12. Key aspects of the applicant company
13. Capital structure
14. Details of directors and key persons
15. Details of external auditors (Proposed).
16. Details of business to be transacted.
17. Details of proposed locations of insurance business
18. Distribution channels
19. Financial projections
20. Sensitivity analysis
21. Rural business
22. Obligations in unorganized sector and backward classes
23. Particulars of previous application
24. Conclusions viability of the operations
25. Certification and signature of the authorized person (with seal).

The form for applying for registration prescribed under

IRDA Regulations, 2000 is Form IRDA/R2–"Application for Registration". The composition of the form is as follows:

**FORM IRDA/R2–APPLICATION FOR REGISTRATION**

1. Existing or proposed geographic spread
2. Details of market research and analysis on market potential, etc.
3. Description of products to be sold
4. Proposed distribution network
5. Proposed sales promotion
6. Underwriting approach proposed
7. Investment plan
8. Information technology plan
9. Proposed customer service standards
10. Retention limits and reinsurance
11. Approach towards recruitment and training
12. Internal control proposed
13. Expenses of administration
14. New product pricing
15. Information policy
16. Premium rates
17. Certification with signature of the authorized person (with seal)

IRDA has prescribed form IRDA/R3 for issuance of the Certificate of Registration to the Company. The specimen is given below:

**FOR IRDA/R3–CERTIFICATE OF REGISTRATION**

FORM IRDA/R3
Insurance Regulatory and Development Authority
(Seal of The Authority)
Certificate of Registration

Registration Number ____________

This is to certify that (Name of Insurer and his address) has this day been registered in accordance with the provision of sub-section (2A) of section 3 of the Insurance Act, 1938 (IV of 1938) to transact the classes of business specified in the Schedule below:

Given under the seal of the Authority at New Delhi this ________ day of ____________ two thousand and ________________________

INSURANCE REGULATORY AND DEVELOPMENT AUTHORITY

Schedule

Classes of business which may be transacted:

1. ____________________________

2. ____________________________

3. ____________________________

4. ____________________________

For the purpose of issuing a duplicate copy of the certificate of Registration, IRDA has prescribed form IRDA/R4. The specimen is given below:

## FORM IRDA/R4 ISSUE OF DUPLICATE CERTIFICATE OF REGISTRATION

To
Insurance Regulatory and Development Authority,
New Delhi.

*Sub: Application for issue of duplicate certificate of registration.*

We request you to issue a duplicate certificate of registration for which we give below the following details:

1. Name of insurer

2. Registration number
3. Date of Certificate of Registration
4. How original certificate has been lost, destroyed or mutilated?
5. Particulars of remittance of fee

Place: Yours truly

Date: Signature of the Principal Officer
(Name of the Principal Officer)
(Seal)

For applying for renewal of the Certificate of Registration, IRDA has prescribed Form IRDA/R5. The specimen is given below.

**FORM IRDA/R5–APPLICATION FOR RENEWAL**

Date:

From: (Name of insurer)

To Insurance Regulatory and Development Authority

Dear Sir,

As required by Regulations 20.... of Insurance Regulatory and Development Authority (Registration of Indian Insurance Companies) Regulations 2000, we hereby apply for renewal of registration for the year ________ to __________.

Our total gross premium written direct in India during the financial year __________ to ______________ was Rs. _____________________

Accordingly, we enclose a bank draft no. __________ dated ___________ drawn on ____________________ Hyderabad, for Rs. __________________
Kindly issue the renewal of registration certificate.

Yours faithfully,

(Name of Signatory)
(Designation)

IRDA has prescribed Form IRDA/R6 for renewal of the Certificate of Registration of the company. The specimen is given below.

**FORM IRDA/R6 CERTIFICATE OF RENEWAL OF REGISTRATION**

Registration Number
Date of Renewal of Registration

The certificate of registration of (Name of Insurer) hereby renewed under setion 3A of the Insurance Act, 1938 for the year _________ to ________

Issued at New Delhi on ________ day of __________ 2011.....

(Seal of the Authority)

(Authorized Signatory)

Forms relating to the intermediaries' licensing

As per various regulations of the IRDA relating to different intermediaries, all intermediaries in the insurance market have to file the necessary applications with IRDA.

**Agent's Licensing:** There are different forms prescribed for agents, which are listed below:

1. Form IRDA – Agents – VA has been prescribed for

individuals applying for renewing a licence to work as an insurance agent.

2. Form IRDA – Agents VC has been prescribed for firms or companies applying for/renewing a license to work as an insurance agent.
3. The IRDA grants the license vide form IRDA – VB.
4. The IRDA grants identity cards to individual agents vide form IRDA – VZ.
5. The IRDA grants identity cards to corporate agents vide Form IRDA – VY.

**Broker's Licensing:** There are different forms prescribed for brokers, which are listed below:

1. Form A under the IRDA (Insurance Brokers) Regulations, 2002 has been prescribed for applying for renewing a licence to work as an insurance broker.
2. The IRDA grants the license vide Form B under the IRDA (Insurance Brokers) Regulations, 2002.

**Third Party Administrators' Licensing**: There are different forms prescribed for TPAs, which are listed below:

1. From TPA–I under the IRDA (TPA Health Services) Regulations, 2001 has been prescribed for applying for licence to work as a Third Party Administrator.
2. The IRDA grants the licence vide Form TPA –2 under the IRDA (TPA Health Services) Regulations, 2001.
3. Form TPA-3 under the IRDA (TPA Health Services) Regulations, 2001 has been prescribed for renewing a licence to work as third Party Administrator.
4. TPAs have to present their annual report as per Form TPA-4.

# Bibliography

C. Arthur Williams (Jr.) and Richard M. Heins, Risk Management.

D.G. Hart, R.A. Buchanan and B.A. Howe, The Actuarial Practice of General Insurance, Institute of Actuaries of Australia.

Fire Insurance in India by P.A.S. Mani, Hindustan Advertisers, Bombay (1952).

Insurance (1950). Henery Kete and L. Gurney, Guide to Marine Insurance Sir Isaac Pitman and Sons, London (1948).

Organization of Indian Insurance by Prof. S.P. Sharma, Allied Publishers Pvt. Ltd., 1967.

P.A.S. Mani, Fire Insurance in India, Hindustan Advertisers, Bombay (1952-62).

Standing Committee on International Financial Standards and Codes Report of the Advisory Group on Insurance Regulation by R. Ramakrishnan, T.G. Menon and others, DEAP, Reserve Bank of India (2000).

The Royal Exchange Assurance—A History of British Insurance (1720-1970) by Barry Supple, Cambridge University Press (1970).

# Index


Accidental Burns, 343
Accidental Death and Dismemberment, 341
Accidental Death Benefits, 339
Actuarial Valuation, 259
Agent's Role, 277
Agreed Value, 94
Analytical Ability, 313
Assessing the Risk, 266
Asset-Liability Management (ALM), 238
Assignment and Nomination, 149

Balance Sheet Structure, 240
  Liabilities Side, 240
  Assets Side, 241
Balance Sheet Structure: Implications for Asset-Liability Management (ALM), 240
Bancassurance Abroad, 331
Bancassurance, 330
Behaviour with Others, 313
Benefit to Agents, 325
Benefits to the Bank, 336
Benefits to the Insurer, 334
Benfits to Policyholders/Prospects, 326
Business Premises' Burglary Insurance, 63
Business Target, 304

Calculation of Age, 256
Cash Insurance, 62
Causes of Risks, 17
  Natural Causes, 18
  Unnatural Causes, 18
  Other Causes, 19
Characteristics of Fire Insurance, 51
Characteristics of Insurable Risks, 14
  Insurable Interest, 15
  Pure and Major Risk, 15
  Quantifiable Risks, 15
  Risks in Money Terms, 16
  Risks that are Common, 16
  Risk must be Causal, 16
  Risks with Legal Objective, 16
  Risk must be Real, 16
  Catastrophic Risks, 17
  Risk having Reasonable Insurance Cost, 17
Characteristics of Insurance, 31
  Contract, 31
  Consideration, 31
  Sharing of Financial Risk, 33
  Co-operative Device, 33
  Risk Evaluation in Advance, 33
  Good Faith, 33
  Contract of Indemnity, 33
  Amount of Payment, 34
  Insurance is not a Gambling, 34
  Large Number of Insured Persons, 34
  Insurance is not Charity, 34
  Insurable Interest, 34
  Compensation at the Occurrence of Contingency, 34
Characteristics of Life Insurance, 47, 127
Characteristics of Marine Insurance, 56
Classification of Insurance from the Business Point of View, 64
Classification of Insurance, 45
  Classification on the Basis of Nature of Insurance, 45
Co-insurance or Co-pay, 101
Communication Skills, 311
Comparisons between Insurance Plans, 322
Concept of Universal Banking, 338
Condition of Average, 96
Conditions for Indemnity, 80

Consumer Protection Act, 1986 (COPRA), 316
Contents of the Act, 210
Contractor's All Risk Insurance (CAR), 62
Control of Pure Risk, 22
Control of Speculative Risks, 22
Creating a Level Playing Ground, 174
Critical Illness Rider (Accelerated Benefit), 349-50
Customer Orientation, 304

Data for Underwriting, 266
Data Repository and Risk Evaluation, 177
Defects in the Acts, 186
Definition of Contribution, 89
Definition of Fire Insurance, 50
Definition of Insurance, 28
  Functional Definitions, 28
  Legal/Contractual Definition, 29
Definition of Life Insurance, 47
Definition of Marine Insurance, 55
Definition of Risk, 14
Definition of Subrogation, 83
Demand for Another Act, 188
Departments of a Divisional Office of LIC, 161
Distinction between Life Insurance, Fire Insurance and Marine Insurance, 67
Double Indemnity, 344

Ensuring Long-term Financial Solvency, 173
Erection All Risks Insurance (EAR), 62
Essential Features of Group Insurance Schemes, 273
Essentials of Subrogation, 84
Ethical Behaviour, 301
Evolution if Insurance, 3
Evolution of Indian Insurance Market, 10
Excess and Deductibles, 100
Export/Import Duty Insurance, 62
Extra Premiums, 255

Features of Subrogation, 85
Female Lives, 269
Financial Planning and Taxation, 320
Financial Underwriting, 265
Forms of Social Insurance, 60
Functions of a Branch Office, 162
Functions of a Zonal Office, 160
Functions of an Agent, 289
Functions of Central Office, 154
Functions of Insurance, 35
  Primary Function, 35
  Secondary Functions, 36
  Other Functions, 38

General Average, 97
General Insurance, 50
General Rule Relating to Insurable interest Applicable in Life Insurance, 145
Group Insurance, 271
Group Leave Encashment Scheme (GLES), 276

Health Insurance, 277
Householder's Insurance Policy (HHI), 64
How is Insurance Regulated?, 172
How Right of Subrogation Arises?, 86

IAIS Core Principles, 112
Impact of Privatization and Liberalization on Insurance Industry, 226
Important Provisions of Insurance Act, 1938, 189
  Wide Scope, 189
  Requirement as to Capital, 191
  Deposits, 192
  Registration, 192
  Submission of Returns, 195
  Restriction of Commission and Prohibition of Rebating, 196
  Limitations of Expenditure on Commission, 197
  Licensing of Insurance Agents (Section 42) of the Insurance Act, 198
  Investments, 200
  Prohibition of Loan [(U/S 29(1)] of the Insurance Act, 202
  Investigation (Under Section 33) of the Insurance Act, 202
  Duties and Power of Controller of Insurance, 202
Important Provisions, 328
Important Terms Used in Insurance, 30

Insured, 30
Insurer, 30
Premium, 30
Compensation, 30
Insurance Policy, 31
Insured Amount, 31
Risk, 31
Contingency, 31
Peril, 31
Income Tax Act, 318
Indian Insurance Act, 1938, 11
Indian Insurance Scenario, 7
Information Technology, 324
Insurable Interest, 142
Insurable Interest in Policyholder's Own Life, 142
Insurable Interest in the Life of Others, 143
Insurance Act of 1938, 188
Insurance Core Principles and Methodology, 112
Insurance for Rural and Social Sectors, 278
Insurance Legislation in India, 164
Insurance Regulatory and Development Authority (IRDA), 206
Insurance:
Meaning, Definition and its Nature, 27
Interest Rate Risk (IRR), 245
Measurement of Interest Rate Risk, 246
Intranet and Internet, 324
IRDA (Licencing of Corporate Agents) Regulations, 2002, 328
IT in the Rural Areas, 327

Keeping Customers Happy, 292
Kinds of Risk and Risk Management, 13

Legal Provisions, 278
Level Premiums, 254
Liability of Insurer to Pay Compensation, 80
Life Fund, 259
Life Insurance and Non-life Insurance (General Insurance), 46
Life Insurance, 46
Life Insurance Corporation of India: Organisational Set-up, 152
Life Insurance in India, 125
Life Insurance is Based on Utmost Good Faith, 146
Which are the Material Facts?, 146
Life Insurance Marketing, 285
Life Insurance:
Nature and Uses of Life Insurance, 125
Liquidity Risk, 241
Measurement of Liquidity Risk, 242
Long-term Relationships, 308

Machinery Breakdown Insurance, 62
Machinery of the Insurance System, 169
Main Features of Indemnity, 79
Malhotra Committee's Recommendations, 225
Marine Insurance, 55
Market Risk, 248
What is Premium?, 252
Married Women's Property Act, 1874, 319
Material Fact, 95
Meaning and Definition of the Doctrine of Causa Proxima, 87
Meaning of ALM, 239
Meaning of Insurance, 27
Meaning of Life Insurance, 126
Meaning of Risk, 13
Methods of Indemnifying, 82
Milch Cattle and/or Draught Animal Insurance, 63
Miscellaneous Insurance Schemes, 61
Miscellaneous Principles, 90
Mobilizing the Savings for Development, 153
Monitoring Re-insurance, 175
Motor Insurance, 61

Nature of General Contract, 138
There must be an Agreement, 138
Competency of the Parties to Contract, 139
Free Consent of the Parties Essential for a Valid Contract, 141
Lawful Consideration is Necessary Element in Contract, 141

Legal Object is the Foundation of a Valid Contract, 141
Nature of Life Insurance Contract, 137
Nature of Life Insurance, 131
Economic Nature of Life Insurance, 132
Legal nature of Life Insurance, 133
Need of Subrogation, 85
Net Earned Premium, 109
New for Old Part(s) Principle, 92
Non-Medical Underwriting, 268

Objectives of Asset-Liability Management (ALM), 239
Objectives of Life Insurance Corporation of India, 152
Office Premium, 255
Organizational Set-up of LIC, 153
Organizational Structure of the Life Insurance Corporation of India, 159
Other Features of Life Insurance, 150
Alcatory Contract, 150
Unilateral Contract, 150
Conditional Contract, 151
Contract of Adhesion, 151
Indemnity Contract is not Applied, 151

Particular Average, 98
Payer Benefit, 346
Performance Ratios, 103
Personal Development through Insurance Business 303
Personal Growth, 305
Persuassive Skills, 312
Plantation/Horticulture Insurance, 64
Practical Aspects of Doctrine of Causa Proxima, 87
Preamble of IRDA Act, 206
Pre-Approach, 296
Premium Calculation, 256
Premiums and Bonuses, 252
Prerequisties for Success, 295
Present Day Trends in Insurance, 179
Preventing Fraud and Speculation by Insurers, 174
Pricing of Insurance Products, 176
Priciples of Insurance, 70
General Principles (or Essentials of Insurance Contract), 70
Specific or Fundamental Principles of Insurance Contracts, 74
Principle of Causa Proxima (Immediate and the Nearest Cause), 86
Principle of Contribution, 88
Principle of Mitigation of Loss, 88
Principle of Subrogation, 83
Principles of Insurance, 69
Privatization of Insurance Industry in India:
Steps Taken by the Government to Privatize the Insurance Sector, 224
Privatization of Insurance Sector, 227
Procedure for Taking a Fire Insurance Policy, 53
Procedure for Taking a Life Insurance Policy, 48, 129
Procedure for Taking Marine Insurance Policy, 57
Marine Insurance from an Insurance Company, 58
Marine insurance by Lloyd's Association, 59
Product Knowledge, 303
Product Liability Insurance, 62
Proximate Cause, 148
Purposes of Malhotra Committee, 224

Rajeswari Mahilla Kalyan Bima Yojna, 64
Reasons for Replacement of Act of 1912, 187
Reasons for Rise of Risk Management Practices, 26
Recent Trends, 269
Reciprocal Duty, 95
Records and Review, 305
Reinstatement, 93
Reserving, 178
Retrenchment Schemes, 276
Return of Premium, 150
Rider:
Descriptions and Premium Rates, 339
Risk Handling Techniques, 24
Avoiding Risk, 24

Risk Reduction, 24
Assumption of Risk, 24
Transfer of Risks, 24
Insurance, 25
Risk Management or Control over Risk, 21
Risk, Net and Pure Premium, 252
Role of an Insurance Agent, 294
Rural Insurance (Agricultural/Allied Activities), 63
Rural Sector, 281

Savings and Investment Schemes, 320
Scenario of Insurance Industry in India as it obtains today, 235
Scope and Dimensions of Insurance, 45
Scope of Asset-Liability Management, 241
Scope of Fire Insurance, 52
Scope or Subject Matter of Marine Insurance, 57
Selling Insurance, 296
Sheep and Goat Insurance, 63
Shopkeepers' Insurance Policy, 63
Social Insurance, 59
Social Sector, 282
Sold Not Bought, 287
Solvency Margin, 111
Special Schemes, 276
Sports Insurance, 64
Standardizing Insurance Products, 173
Strengthening Relationships, 288
Sue and Labour/Particular Charges, 99
Summary of the Above Discussion, 179

Target Market, 307
Term Riders, 348
The Customer, 288
The Distribution Channel, 286
The General Insurance Business (Nationalization) Act, 1972 (GIBNA), 167
The Indian Context, 333
The Insurance Act, 1938, 164
The Insurance Amendment Act, 1950, 165
The Insurance Amendment Act, 1968, 166
The Legal Requirements, 336
The Problems, 337
The Set-up of LIC Involves, 153
Theory of Large Numbers, 178
Time Management, 306
To Act as Trustees, 153
To Meet Insurance Needs, 153
To Provide Protection, 153
To Provide Services to the Public, 153
To Widen the Scope of Insurance, 152
Trustworthiness, 308
Type of Risks, 19
Financial and Non-financial Risks, 19
Pure and Speculative Risks, 19
Dynamic and Static Risks, 20
Fundamental and Particular Risks, 20

Underwriting by Agents, 269
Underwriting, 263
Unit Trust and Mutual Funds, 321
Uses/Role and Importance of Insurance or Relevance of Insurance in Developing Country like India, 39
Relevance of Insurance to an Individual, 41
Relevance to Business, 43
Relevance to Society, 44

Vale Proposition, 332

Waiver of Premium, 345
Warranties, 147
Watch on Funds, 172
What is Bancassurance?, 330